Educational Policy in an International Context

Education Policy

Series Editors

Lance Fusarelli, North Carolina State University
Frederick M. Hess, American Enterprise Institute
Martin West, Harvard University

This series addresses a variety of topics in the area of education policy. Volumes are solicited primarily from social scientists with expertise on education, in addition to policymakers or practitioners with hands-on experience in the field. Topics of particular focus include state and national policy, teacher recruitment, retention, and compensation, urban school reform, test-based accountability, choice-based reform, school finance, higher education costs and access, the quality instruction in higher education, leadership and administration in K-12 and higher education, teacher colleges, the role of the courts in education policymaking, and the relationship between education research and practice. The series serves as a venue for presenting stimulating new research findings, serious contributions to ongoing policy debates, and accessible volumes that illuminate important questions or synthesize existing research.

Series Editors

LANCE FUSARELLI is a Professor and Director of Graduate Programs in the Department of Leadership, Policy and Adult and Higher Education at North Carolina State University. He is co-author of *Better Policies, Better Schools* and co-editor of the *Handbook of Education Politics and Policy*.

FREDERICK M. HESS is Resident Scholar and Director of Education Policy Studies at the American Enterprise Institute. An author, teacher, and political scientist, his books include *The Same Thing Over and Over: How School Reformers Get Stuck in Yesterday's Ideas* and *Common Sense School Reform*.

MARTIN WEST is an Assistant Professor of Education in the Graduate School of Education at Harvard University. He is an Executive Editor of *Education Next* and Deputy Director of Harvard's Program on Education Policy and Governance.

Ohio's Education Reform Challenges: Lessons from the Frontlines
  Chester E. Finn, Jr., Terry Ryan, and Michael B. Lafferty

Accountability in American Higher Education
  Edited by Kevin Carey and Mark Schneider

Freedom and School Choice in American Education
  Edited by Greg Forster and C. Bradley Thompson

President Obama and Education Reform: The Personal and the Political
  Robert Maranto and Michael Q. McShane

Educational Policy in an International Context: Political Culture and Its Effects
  Edited by Karen Seashore Louis and Boudewijn van Velzen

Educational Policy in an International Context

Political Culture and Its Effects

Edited by

Karen Seashore Louis
and
Boudewijn van Velzen

EDUCATIONAL POLICY IN AN INTERNATIONAL CONTEXT
Copyright © Karen Seashore Louis and Boudewijn van Velzen, 2012.
Softcover reprint of the hardcover 1st edition 2012 978-0-230-34041-1
All rights reserved.

First published in 2012 by
PALGRAVE MACMILLAN®
in the United States—a division of St. Martin's Press LLC,
175 Fifth Avenue, New York, NY 10010.

Where this book is distributed in the UK, Europe and the rest of the world, this is by Palgrave Macmillan, a division of Macmillan Publishers Limited, registered in England, company number 785998, of Houndmills, Basingstoke, Hampshire RG21 6XS.

Palgrave Macmillan is the global academic imprint of the above companies and has companies and representatives throughout the world.

Palgrave® and Macmillan® are registered trademarks in the United States, the United Kingdom, Europe and other countries.

ISBN 978-1-349-34300-3   ISBN 978-1-137-04675-8 (eBook)
DOI 10.1057/9781137046758

Library of Congress Cataloging-in-Publication Data

    Educational policy in an international context : political culture and its effects / edited by Karen Seashore Louis, Boudewijn van Velzen.
      p. cm.—(Education policy)

    1. Educational and state—Cross-cultural studies.
    2. Education—Political aspects—Cross-cultural studies.
    3. Political culture—Cross-cultural studies. 4. Educational change—Cross-cultural studies. I. Louis, Karen Seashore. II. Velzen, Boudewijn van.

LC71.E3465 2012
379—dc23   2012011018

A catalogue record of the book is available from the British Library.

Design by Newgen Imaging Systems (P) Ltd., Chennai, India.

First edition: October 2012

10 9 8 7 6 5 4 3 2 1

Transferred to Digital Printing in 2013

This book is dedicated to:
Dan,
Who consistently provides the simple message that
everything will be all right

And to
Principals and teachers all over the world who sincerely try to make education policies work in their work with students, day after day

Contents

List of Figures and Tables   ix

Acknowledgments   xi

Part I   Political Cultures, Education, and History—An Introduction   1
Karen Seashore Louis and Boudewijn van Velzen

1   Political Culture and Educational Reform   5
Geert Devos, Mats Ekholm, Kaspar Kofod, Karen Seashore Louis, Lejf Moos, Michael Schratz, and Boudewijn van Velzen

2   Historical Perspectives on Educational Policy and Political Cultures   29
Kasper Kofod, Karen Seashore Louis, Lejf Moos, and Boudewijn van Velzen

Part II   Introduction   49

3   Many Cooks Will *Not* Spoil the Broth: Educational Policy in Sweden   53
Mats Ekholm

4   Denmark: Bildung in a Competitive State?   63
Lejf Moos and Klaus Kasper Kofod

5   The Netherlands: The Clergyman and the Merchant Revisited   73
Boudewijn van Velzen

6   Flanders (Belgium): Regulated Anarchy in Catholic and Public Education   85
Geert Devos

7   Austria's Balancing Act: Walking the Tightrope between Federalism and Centralization   95
Michael Schratz

8 The More Things Change, the More They Stay the Same:
The English Case   105
Karen Seashore Louis and John MacBeath

9 E Pluribus Unum? Dissonance in US Educational
Political Culture   115
Karen Seashore Louis

Part III The Cross-Country Studies   125

10 Reform in Stable Systems (Austria and Belgium
[Flanders]): The Impossible Dream?   127
Geert Devos and Michael Schratz

11 Political Cultures in England and the Netherlands:
Similar Discourse, Different Results   139
Karen Seashore Louis and Boudewijn van Velzen

12 Examining the Myth of Nordic Uniformity:
The Production of Educational Policy in Denmark
and Sweden   155
Mats Ekholm and Lejf Moos

13 North Carolina and Nebraska: Two States, Two Policy
Cultures, Two Outcomes   171
Molly F. Gordon and Karen Seashore Louis

Part IV Reflections   189

14 "Wer Vorwärts Kommen Will, Muss Auch Mal
Rückwarts Denken": Reflections on the Case Studies   193
*Boudewijn van Velzen, Karen Seashore Louis, Geert Devos,
Mats Ekholm, Kasper Kofod, Lejf Moos, and Michael Schratz*

15 Policy Cultures and Education Policy: A Central
and Eastern European Perspective   213
Gábor Halász

16 Reflections from Practice on Political Culture
and Education Reform   223
Ben Levin

Appendix   233
Bibliography   237
Index   251

Figures and Tables

Figures

2.1	Swedish timeline	36
2.2	Danish timeline	37
2.3	Dutch timeline	38
2.4	Belgium/Flanders timeline	39
2.5	Austrian timeline	40
2.6	English timeline	41
2.7	US timeline	42
5.1	Relationship between partners in the education arena	77
7.1	Overview of the Austrian school administration	98
14.1	Types of change in political culture	205

Tables

3.1	Framework for analyzing state political culture: Sweden	61
4.1	Framework for analyzing state political culture: Denmark	70
5.1	Framework for analyzing state political cultures: The Netherlands	82
6.1	Framework for analyzing state political culture: Flanders	93
7.1	Framework for analyzing state political culture: Austria	103
8.1	Framework for analyzing state political culture: England	111
9.1	Framework for analyzing state political culture: The United States	122
11.1	English and Dutch political cultures compared	152
11.2	English and Dutch policy levers compared	152

Acknowledgments

The genesis of this book emerged from a study that was funded by the Wallace Foundation, which allowed Karen Seashore Louis to examine the tricky question of how state political cultures affect school leaders and teachers in the United States. These questions became even more interesting when similar conversations were raised as part of a project, funded by the Dutch government and headed by Boudewijn van Velzen, to examine the governance of schools in The Netherlands. The unexpected intersection of two entirely separate ongoing projects provided an interesting space that was gradually expanded to include the other authors in this book.

The larger project would not have been possible without the support of each of our work institutions, who generously allowed us to meet in various countries and freed each of us up to carry out interviews with public policy figures in our respective countries. In particular, we want to mention the College of Education and Human Development at the University of Minnesota, which provided financial support for the portion of the project that was completed in England and The Netherlands during Karen's sabbatical. The Institute of Education in London provided a home base for Karen in England, and Professor Kathryn Riley was instrumental in gaining access to some of the people who were interviewed. APS, National Centre for School Improvement in Utrecht, and Gerard van de Hoven, then director of APS, helped with access to a number of key figures in The Netherlands, and he participated with Karen and Boudewijn in some of the interviews and early analysis. We have all also benefitted from discussions with many of our colleagues, both at home and from other countries, who invariably asked difficult questions that sent us back to our analysis.

This book would never have been completed without the extensive editorial contributions of Dan Bratton, who provided constant assistance with the stimulating but tough job of making Danish, Swedish, Belgian, Austrian, and Dutch writers sound as if they were born speaking American English. No ordinary editor, he immersed himself in the content of the book and its ideas so that he could point out inconsistent ideas as well as make suggestions about how best to communicate essential meaning.

Finally, we should mention the wonderful artwork on the cover, which was produced in the studio of Jacqueline Wils.

KAREN SEASHORE LOUIS
University of Minnesota
BOUDEWIJN VAN VELZEN
APS

Part I

Political Cultures, Education, and History—An Introduction

Karen Seashore Louis and Boudewijn van Velzen

This book is the unexpected outcome of a casual conversation between two colleagues who were working on a project investigating the consequences of school autonomy in the Netherlands. They decided to write about what was happening in that realm in both of their countries and to present the results in an international conference. Among the participants were scholars from three other countries who decided to join in. A year later, a second presentation inspired two others to jump aboard. Our conversation had grown into a real project.

Our collaborative work examines how national political culture has shaped educational policy in a world characterized by the rapid dissemination of research findings and policy prescriptions across national boundaries. The project summarized in this book grew out of the sustained personal interactions of a community of researchers and practitioners brought together by a series of sometimes small, sometimes large international conferences over the last four years. The chapters are drawn from participants in Denmark, the Netherlands, Sweden, Austria, England, Flanders (Belgium), and the United States. They are based on original data collection from respondents in each country who tell "the story" of how policy is made in their country, as well as from analysis of key events, described by stakeholders in the educational policymaking process.

Over time we had all observed a global shift to the use of a common language to describe elements of the "New Public Management" model that focuses on efficiency and effectiveness in formal schooling, and the collateral "standards movement" that seeks to measure a relatively narrow array of agreed-upon outcomes. From our initial perspective, we observed that the nineteenth-century educational factory analogy was entering the twenty-first century.

Three common questions emerged as we each reflected on our own national experiences:

1. Is the meaning of common linguistic elements translated into practice in the same way across countries? In other words, is the apparent emergence of global trends real or illusory?
2. Do people who effect government and system policies reflect on the historical events and underlying cultural assumptions as they carry out their work? How does this cultural understanding affect the character of the policies that are proposed and carried out?
3. Does the accumulation of policies that are motivated by different strands of global "policy borrowing" result in policy contradictions as they are grafted on to existing systems?

We began with three assumptions: (a) New educational initiatives filter through a political culture that is long-standing and unique to each country; (b) policy initiatives shift over time and currently those initiatives call for local accountability to stakeholders; and (c) local accountability demands are concurrent with the development of international standards for cognitive student achievement outcomes.

All participants in this project developed a common framework and language to investigate the politics of education in their own setting. This approach uses a number of categories to analyze the underlying factors that affect policymaking. These include:

1. The basic value dimensions for analyzing a political culture, which include *openness* (broad availability of participation); *decentralism* (distributed power sources); *rationalism* (emphasis on logical/comprehensive solutions); *egalitarianism* (redistribution of resources to minimize disparities); *efficiency* (economic cost-benefits and emphasis on returns for public investment); *quality* (focus on excellence and improvement and the major goal); *choice* (opportunity to make policy decisions at multiple levels).
2. The history of critical policy events that occurred in the past and continue to influence current choices. These vary between countries, but are deeply embedded in both lay and policymakers' assumptions about the possibilities and limits of new actions.
3. We know, however, that political culture is mutable over time and is influenced by dominant ideologies that cross national boundaries.

While underlying policy cultures may change slowly, they may shift to accommodate to changes in public policy discourse.

To accomplish the objective of both examining differences in political culture and policymaking, and comparing across countries, we propose a volume that will be divided into four main sections:

1. Part one (chapters one and two) will set out both the framework, a brief overview of each country's unique national events (as identified in our interviews) and the key provocative questions that readers will need to keep in mind as they read the book.
2. A set of short country cases in part two will provide the historical background of critical events, key actors, and embedded decision processes that represent how educational policy ideas are translated into actual legislative/parliamentary decisions or government mandates. This section will focus on what is permanent and what is shifting over time in the educational political culture.
3. Part three applies the same framework and the background from the country cases to present four comparisons that illustrate the differences and similarities between two nations or states in responding to the same global policy influences.
4. A final section, part four, will present some of the critical conclusions of the participants in this research project, along with the reflections of two additional policy scholars (one from North America and one from Central Europe) on the meaning of the chapters for the development of educational reforms.

We are, as a group of colleagues, thrilled to participate in creating the first book to consider the intersection of educational political cultures and their response to international discourse around standards and accountability. We recognize that, because our project was sustained by a group of volunteers who represent Northern Europe and the United States, we have missed many interesting nuances—and possibly major questions—that might have arisen if we had been able to engage scholars from other parts of the world. Although international in scope, the work is hardly global. However, we hope that the organization of this book will engage the reader in reflective questioning of current assumptions about the inevitability of a global policy environment, even if they are located in other continents and cultures.

1

Political Culture and Educational Reform

Geert Devos, Mats Ekholm, Kaspar Kofod, Karen Seashore Louis, Lejf Moos, Michael Schratz, and Boudewijn van Velzen

Introduction

A puzzling feature of contemporary education emerges from two widely shared assumptions that are contradictory and incompatible. The first is that modern educational institutions have the same degree of rich diversity as modern airports—in other words, the educational world is becoming flat. The second is that in the educational sphere, global meets local in the way that a wave meets a rocky outcropping. Visible disturbance occurs, but (barring a tsunami) little is changed.

The first assumption is backed up by decades of research on international trends. Popular and more systematic reports indicate that educational systems are becoming increasingly alike (Clemens & Cook, 1999; Fielden, 2001; Ramirez & Boli, 1987; Ramirez & Meyer, 1980). The adaptation of former Soviet Union countries to achieved or aspiring membership in the European Union have resulted in rapid changes in educational structures, while the Bologna process is creating alignment of higher education policies and practices. These trends are reinforced by the waves of international achievement results, which foster policy borrowing on a grand scale, as countries try to figure out how they can adapt Finnish and Singaporean initiatives and practices to their own countries.

The second perspective, in which wave meets rock, emphasizes the equally well-documented finding that no matter what initiatives, programs, or policies are provided by international agencies and national governments, local adaptation continues to sustain meaningful differences at the national and local levels, and results in little fundamental change in schools and classrooms (Berman & McLaughlin, 1978; Clemens & Cook, 1999; Wassmer & Fisher, 2002; Weatherly & Lipsky, 1977). Adaptations within the "old Europe" to make national systems more alike have proven difficult to achieve, in spite of the rhetorical similarities in policy language. Germans and Dutch continue to prefer a system that separates children at a young age to enter educational streams that have different curricula and narrow occupational options later. Swedes are as deeply attached to a comprehensive system that requires the same curriculum and schools for all students until the age of 16, when some choices are introduced. Other countries may trumpet the findings of international studies, but cling to federated systems that limit national policies that might create a more coherent national response.

On the one hand, there are several explanations for the coexistence of global trends, and, on the other, local adaptations and preferences. One is that educational differences between countries and states are largely "leftovers" that are eroding in the face of the compelling need to minimize variation in order to meet the economic challenges of borderless work environments and technological demands. At the beginning of the twenty-first century, the views of those who saw globalization as inevitable differed profoundly in predicting how this trend would play out at the local, regional, and national levels. The European Commission, for example, viewed educational globalization as contributing to knowledge-based "learning societies," a perspective that was echoed in publications from other international development organizations (Spring, 2008). Others were less sanguine, providing evidence that globalization in education has potentially harmful effects on the quality and outcomes of education that might contribute to lessened opportunities for some citizens and countries (Barbules & Torres, 2000).[1] Some authors accepted the globalization hypothesis, but argued that resistance movements to create more locally responsive educational systems should occur at the local level (Gandin & Apple, 2002; Olssen, 2005). Still others pointed out that emergent regional tensions (e.g., between the developed countries and the Middle East) might create particularly challenges for education and all areas that are deeply tied to cultural values (Lieber & Weisberg, 2002).

A group of economic voices, largely absent from the educational literature, have taken another perspective. Globalization language is viewed as a form of neoliberal rhetoric that is not necessarily consistent with the behaviors of either nations or individuals (Heron, 2008). Yasher (2007) suggests that resistance movements are not a reaction to globalization, but rather a response to strong national identities and states. Moreover, the assumption that globalizing trends result in cookie-cutter models of social and economic institutions lacks an evidentiary base. Historically, these institutions have been molded and shaped by national and regional cultures and the evidence does not yet suggest that this will change:

> [T]he specific inheritance that each society bears from its history under prior forms of social order shapes even the most apparently radical exercise in reengineering. Thus, at the level of individual nation-states, the path of development along which the embedding institutions of capitalism evolve take on a distinct national flavour, and it is highly probable that these national *differentia specifica* continue to be reproduced. (Radice, 2000, p. 723)[2]

Radice's statement represents our point of departure for this study. We accept the notion that there is increasing convergence in the way in which people in various countries generally think about specific social phenomena and change, but argue that we need to understand more about how the local context and traditions shape the specific policies and practices that emerge from those conversations. As Radice points out, the global conversations expose the public and policymakers to ways of thinking that challenge current practices. This is, in fact, the point that is most emphasized by those who argue for globalization. And we also want to avoid the flaw of a purely comparative approach, which often articulates differences but ignores similarities (Strange, 1997). However, distinctive political cultures have deep roots that should not be ignored as we examine the impacts of educational policies on schools and citizens.

Defining Political Culture

As nations and states endeavor to attend to the information that they receive from globalized conversations about education, political culture will play a role in determining how they balance conflicting expectations. This book assumes that most countries have had, traditionally, a relatively unified political culture with respect to education and a national role in educational policy. Others have, for historical reasons, given great latitude to maintaining distinctive state/regional cultures, including the development of autonomous educational systems (Canada, Belgium, and the United States are clear examples). In these cases, the educational system has full or nearly full autonomy, with the exception of laws or regulations that may conflict with the national constitution. In this book we treat autonomous states/regions as similar to nations and, for the sake of parsimony, we sometimes use the term "nations" to encompass the governance units that we have determined are genuinely autonomous except when regional or state policies conflict with the national constitution.

Radice (2002) points to the continuing differences between nations in terms of economic structures and institutions, in spite of the continuing press toward congruence. In the United States, variations among the states are so large as to challenge the very idea of "national educational policies" (Lee, 1997; Mazzoni, 1993; Sacken & Medina, 1990). Similar variations within some European countries are confirmed by other studies (Marquart-Pyatt & Paxton, 2007). A nation's or state's political decisions are visibly affected by power (Gritsch, 2005), but decision outcomes, particularly in the case of complex policies, are only modestly predicted by the preferences of those with the deepest pockets and legislative or parliamentary majorities. Rather, "culture affects political transformation by determining the context in which social actors make collective and individual political decisions" (Berezin, 1997).

Political culture is more than the aggregation of individual preferences and values, but emerges from individual and group efforts "to make those preferences publicly common" (Chilton, 1988), and is identified by repeated patterns of behavior during the policymaking process. The accumulated history of public discourse, repeated actions, and expressed preferences of groups are critical elements of the context within which power holders can affect decisions. The key to political culture, furthermore, is embedded in relationships and shared values among groups, which become the backdrop of how public preferences play out in the political arena (Wirt, Mitchell, & Marshall, 1988).

We rely on the traditional definition of "political culture" as enduring political attitudes and behaviors associated with groups that live in a defined geographical context (Elazar, 1970; Lieske, 1993). Thus, one may compare distinct government entities (states, nations) or regions that share similar characteristics (Marquart-Pyatt & Paxton, 2007). In other words, political culture persists over time and affects how the polity addresses new issues such as environmental concerns or educational policy as well as the more traditional governmental function of taxation, foreign policy, and labor laws.

Elazar (1970) identified three basic types of political cultures based on his analysis of differences among the US states:

1. *Traditional:* Policy is made by elites, with an emphasis on continuity and control; limited interparty competition.
2. *Individualistic:* Political arena is a marketplace; policy determined by public demands; high competition.
3. *Moralistic:* Emphasis on the broadest good for the public; the common citizen is viewed as the primary actor.

While this typology may have some potential for examining differences among nation-states, we felt that the categories were too broad to capture the interaction between historical events and cultural preferences that Radice (2002) advocates. We therefore turned to the general political literature, and looked specifically for educational applications of the idea of political culture.

Four components of political culture that are revealed by looking at patterns of policy development in the United States (Herzik, 1985) were determined, in our analytic sessions, to be applicable to studies of other countries:

1. *Openness:* Broad availability of political participation as contrasted with constrained or elite dominance.
2. *Decentralism:* Distributed power sources; no one center versus concentration of power in the legislature or governor's office.
3. *Rationalism:* Policies based on comprehensive and/or coherent solutions to social problems as contrasted with either multiple, unrelated initiatives or limited government activity.
4. *Egalitarianism:* Persistent policies to redistribute resources to minimize disparities versus limited efforts in redistribution.

Each component has a corresponding pattern of political behavior. For example, in open political cultures the general public influences the operation of government structures and political processes; closed political cultures have more stringent requirements for participation that may lessen public influence. In the United States, states exhibiting a tendency toward rationalism in their political cultures enact comprehensive school reform programs to solve specific identified problems, while decentralist political cultures place more emphasis on local control and choice (Timar & Kirp, 1988). As we shall see in the chapters to follow, these differences are equally apparent within Europe. The long-term effects of culture may not be visible in every legislative session, because no government is entirely consistent. They do, however, become apparent when viewed in the context of a wider time frame.

Educational research reinforces the significance of Herzik's components, and suggests their relevance in understanding educational policy (Amrein & Berliner, 2002; Wirt, Mitchell, & Marshall, 1988; Wong, 1989). Some analyses also point out emerging norms and values that may be important for understanding how and why various issues dominate the educational policy process (Marshall, Mitchell, & Wirt, 1986; Wirt, Mitchell, & Marshall, 1988). For example, enduring interstate and between-country differences are based on divergent assumptions about the importance of efficiency in public services (Kwok & Solomon, 2006;

Wood & Theobald, 2003). This leads us to add a fifth characteristic to the four cited by Herzik:

1. *Efficiency:* An emphasis on cost-benefits and optimization of policy performance versus limited discussion of input-output considerations.

An emphasis on efficiency is often visible in public discussions about the importance of applying business-like models to social policy initiatives, whether in education (O'Toole & Meier, 2004) or in other sectors (Bailey, 2007; Ferner, Almond, & Colling, 2005). A reference to efficiency is frequently used to support policies in public discussions of budgets. In formal settings, this has increasingly led to the use of cost-benefit models to evaluate social policy initiatives in arenas as diverse as public safety, housing, and health.

The current tendency to link the word "quality" with standardized testing may distract us from underlying differences in what is meant by the word. The emphasis on the significant of public quality indicators has deep roots in education (Bryk & Hermanson, 1993), and we therefore propose adding it to our list:

2. *Quality:* An emphasis on an elaborated state role in providing oversight and monitoring the quality of public services, versus a less systematic, laissez-faire approach to determine quality.

Examining differences in the way in which quality is understood and assessed provides critical insights into a nation's cultural values. In England, for example, the national inspectorate includes a measure of how well schools engage their communities in their definition of quality schools, while this feature is not an element of the equally active Dutch inspectorate.

Finally, we decided to include attention to a basic question that is particularly relevant to the educational sector, namely, "whose schools are these?"

3. *Choice:* An emphasis on increasing the range of options available to citizens (in the case of education, families) and opportunities to influence policy at multiple levels.

Choice is connected with different value systems in different settings. In some cases, it may reflect a society's guarantee of the collective freedom of people with varying beliefs to choose a school that meets their religious, philosophical, or linguistic values and norms. In other settings choice is inextricably tied to a strict liberal strand of political culture that emphasizes the importance of markets and privatization (Whitty & Edwards, 1998; Whitty & Power, 2000).³ On the other hand, in different settings, particularly during the early desegregation period in the northern United States, choice was largely viewed as a social engineering tool to create equality of opportunity, with an emphasis on magnet schools, voluntary interdistrict transfer, and special-focus charter schools (Mazzoni, 1993).

Explicating the Elements of Political Culture

In the remainder of this chapter, we will explain in greater detail why each of the seven elements that we have identified earlier is critical to understanding political cultures. Our focus is on demonstrating their centrality to examining differences among parliamentary systems in Europe, where basic democratic governance structures are shared, but where national histories and values are still deeply embedded.

Openness

Governments that construct political processes and structures so that citizens' access is facilitated are called "moralistic." They *"embrace the notion that politics is ideally a matter of concern for every citizen"* (Elazar, 1972: 91 in Herzik 1985, p. 414; emphasis added). Those governments are characterized by an "open" political culture that has multiple routes for citizens and stakeholders to exercise influence on the policymaking process. Herzik defines four categories of political openness that are US centric.[4] In our work, we build on one category that transcends any particular set of national practices and laws: citizen access to legislative proceedings.

Legislation is, however, not an event, but a process, which occurs in three phases: development of premises and definition of frameworks, decision-making, and connection to existing administrative and legal practices. The second phase, decision-making, occurs when an act is written up or approved by a parliament or other legislative body. The third phase, connection, occurs as politicians and civil service administrators follow up in implementing the decision, which typically affects multiple aspects of a civil society, including the legal system, law enforcement, educational and public communication that promotes or assesses the impact of the law. However, the most interesting phase, in contemporary polycentric, complex, or networked democracies, is the first one: construction of premises and frameworks.

There are numerous ways of constructing the background, the basis, or the premises for decision-making, both formally and informally, which affect the degree of openness. The generic, formal form of citizen participation is indirect, through the participation of elected parties in the parliaments' legislative procedures. In some situations—often when there is a minority government—this work is based on open negotiations between all or most political parties. In other situations we see that a political majority finalizes bills without inviting the minority parties into the negotiations. The "winner takes all" approach to defining policy initiatives reduces the indirect openness of a system, because those who voted for minority parties are effectively disenfranchised.

Another formalized way in which citizen participation is secured is through their inclusion in the discussions and framing of ideas that are eventually included in legislation. This may be regulated by legislation or developed as a common administrative routine, in which the representation of citizen groups (like professionals, stakeholders, interest groups) are included as part of the formal proceedings before a final initiative is presented for a debate and vote (Gramberger, 2001). Where this is part of routinized practice, when relevant stakeholder groups oppose a bill it may be altered before it is finalized. If a permanent or ad hoc political majority in parliament is unconvinced by their voices, the influence of citizens is small at this stage. Virtually all democracies have some processes that require formal input at this stage, but the duration and importance attached to the consultative process may vary.

But what happens before the parliamentary or legislative discussions begin is where openness varies most. No parliament can consider every idea that emerges from within the political parties or other groups. Prior to any formal consideration by a parliamentary committee, there is a period in which decisions are made about what ideas will appear on the agenda, which typically involve informal discussions (Kingdon, 2003). The informal period in which decisions are made about what will become part of a parliamentary agenda may encourage wide participation or may be confined to a smaller number (e.g., key party members and advisors).

The importance of informal agenda setting is expanding in many contemporary democracies (Gramberger, 2001). Ideas are increasingly discussed in formal and informal networks before the ministries take over and finalize the writing of the bill. Informal networks may establish themselves as semipermanent coalitions, and create the expectation that they are part of the formal proceedings. In education, for example, there are often networks of politicians, ministry officials, and municipality servants and representatives of unions and professional associations, labor market, stakeholders (like parent associations and student associations). If a member of the government (minister or secretary) excludes network representatives that have previously been consulted, it is regarded as a closing of the policy process.

A major source for construction of premises occurs in the public debate and exchanges that form a dominant discourse, where the media play a role in screening whose voices and what ideas will be prominent. University and private sector researchers are a particular segment of the citizenry whose voices have become prominent because of the demand for "evidence-based" policies (Moos, 2006a). There is a tendency to see the relations between research and politics as linear: research produces the evidence that policymakers use as the basis for legislation. This is a questionable assumption, as politicians are not bound by evidence alone, but are subject to other realities related to the nature of power and coalition building. In some cases research is contested because it is inconsistent with a politician's preferences or those of other key stakeholders whose participation in the parliamentary process is required.

In this book we focus on the degree to which the agenda-setting and issue formulation processes in educational policymaking are more-or-less open. This perspective must also be examined in the context of the openness that characterizes a society as a whole. At least one study suggests that there is a tendency for national institutions to protect themselves from what is thought to be "outside influence" even when they have strong internal traditions of open access to influence in the parliamentary process (Koster, 2007). The relevance of overall openness to policy options that are developed elsewhere is worthy of increased attention as the influence of transnational agencies like the OECD and the EU is growing.

Decentralism

Decentralization may best be most easily understood as the opposite of centralization. In decentralized systems the power to make decisions is situated closer to the setting where the decision will have an impact. Organizational theory suggests three distinctive advantages to decentralizing management decisions:

1. In larger and more complex settings, a person in the center will not be able to see or appreciate all of the nuances on the ground, and may never become aware of the unintended consequences of a decision.
2. A more decentralized mode of decision-making will enable the group to respond better and faster to new developments and challenges.
3. A certain amount of autonomy can motivate members. (Mintzberg, 1990)

These organizational conditions are often thought to apply to decentralized political systems as well. At least one cynical observer of a country that was considering a significant decentralization policy observed that the primary motivation was that the central government had run out of ideas, and wanted to give the improvement problems to someone else. Others argue more positively that decentralization leads to greater educational innovation (Clune, 1993).

Decentralization can also create its own problems, however. The radical decentralization of New Zealand's educational system in the late 1980s appears to have resulted in increased between-school inequity in educational outcomes (Duru-Bellat & Suchaut, 2005) in spite of significant efforts by the government to target equity and diversity in its voluntary programming. Decentralization also creates problems for governments that are expected to retain responsibility for promoting the quality of educational systems, as it reduces the levers available for stimulating more comprehensive system improvements—even when there is broad agreement about their necessity.

Not all center-to-periphery relationships are alike, however, and we need to distinguish among some key terms. In political settings, *territorial decentralization* refers to a situation where specific tasks that could be executed by a central agency in a given region are deliberately given to agencies in subregions. Each subregion more or less mirrors the region. To give a specific example, in Canada, the provinces have full responsibility for managing the funding and oversight of schools; the national government has no role, although the constitution calls for providing schools that meet the diverse preferences of Catholic and French-speaking citizens. All Canadian provinces have the same responsibilities (defining the curriculum, taxing to raise resources for education, etc.) but they are autonomous in executing them. This means, for example, that provinces have different approaches to many issues including minority schools, accountability systems, curriculum, and funding arrangements.

Where previously centralized functions are given to a newly established region, we often refer to devolution. Green (2002) notes that "[a] number of countries have substantially devolved power to geographical regions (Spain) or lingual communities (Belgium)." *Functional decentralization* occurs when specific tasks that earlier were executed at central levels are delegated to organizations that focus on one specific task. In the Netherlands, for example, day-to-day management responsibilities are delegated to school boards, but the national government retains most responsibility for funding, determining quality, and basic professional qualifications for teaching staff.

Deconcentration should not be confused with *decentralization*. We define deconcentration as semipermanent delegation of tasks and responsibilities to internal units that are "wholly owned" by the larger unit. The French educational system is an example of deconcentration, in which regional agencies are arms of the national agency, but bear an increasing responsibility for administration. Decentralization implies that power is distributed among different legal entities, each of which has the same standing as the others, while deconcentration maintains organized units within a web of hierarchical responsibility and control.

Deregulation involves the reduction of legal rules and obligations, which does not automatically accompany decentralization. McKevitt (1998) argues, for example, that decentralization of publicly funded services like health care and education often precede a process of reregulation unless problems of quality control and client advocacy are dealt with. The Dutch National Education Council recently suggested that a successful decentralization process requires a careful analysis of what can be done locally and what should be done nationally. It also demands patience from the central authorities since it will take time for the system to adjust to a more decentralized mode of operating. A crucial component of this successful transition will be a stronger role for school staff, parents, students, and the industry as they deal with more autonomous school boards and principals (Onderwijsraad, 2002). A recent Dutch report also revealed a major issue that affects any decentralization effort: the central authority, when giving up control, must come to trust the capacities of semiautonomous agencies to "get the job done" (Commissie Parlementair Onderzoek Onderwijsvernieuwingen, 2008; Parliament, 2008).

Decentralization, deregulation, and deconcentration do not guarantee more professional autonomy. Kuzmanic (2007) defined autonomy as the capacity to design and live within laws that are designed by oneself. Examinations of policy efforts to create more autonomy for schools and professionals suggest that this ideal is difficult to achieve, because even within countries variation in autonomy is high, and often higher than between countries with different policies (Whitty, 1997). From the perspective of those who work in agencies that are not at the center, making use of decentralization will require some courage and a mindset that desires and accepts the responsibility that autonomy implies. It is by no means clear that this aspiration is high on the list of priorities for schools.

Egalitarianism

Egalité is one of the three concepts that were used as the basis for the French revolution. It is often closely linked to the concept of justice and is used as one of the cornerstones of modern democracies. In politics there are divergent ways to understand the intersection of justice and equality (Dryzek & List, 2003; Gregg, 2002). One has to do with the right of a citizen to keep what is earned through his or her efforts, which is subject, of course, to the democratically agreed upon taxes to support the common good. This can, however, inherently lead to an unequal accumulation of wealth, which, in turn, often conflicts with equal access to other social goods, such as health and education. From a practical perspective, it therefore conflicts with another principle of egalitarianism, in which all citizens should be treated equally and have equal opportunities. Finally, a third perspective on equality emphasizes the need for social policies that actively remove barriers to the success of individuals and groups, rather than simply ensuring equal access to social good. Discussions of egalitarianism inevitably create tensions between these interpretations of social justice and equality and have been deeply woven into the way in which educational policies are developed in different countries.

Virtually everyone agrees that all members of their society should have equal access to economic opportunity and to justice under the law. We recoil when access to high-priced legal talent allows clients to avoid justice while the less fortunate or innocent fare poorly in the legal system. Our reaction is, however, more nuanced when someone who has played by the rules to accumulate wealth chooses to spend that wealth to provide his or her children with more educational and developmental opportunities. Education has become, in modern society, both a tool to create equality and a perpetuator of economic inequality (Collins, 1971).

In an egalitarian society we all have the same right to fulfill our life projects: to grow up and become educated, to find peers and friends, to participate in work and to earn our own living, to find a place to live and make it a home, to form a family and bring up children, to share the responsibility with others for the common good, to keep our health throughout life and to be able to meet illness and injury, to shape a comfortable standard of life and preserve our human dignity facing the unavoidable weaknesses we meet as we age. Society and its institutions shall serve human beings here and now so that they can realize their life projects. When doing so they do not threaten the future of anyone else (Palme, 1984).

The task of modern politicians is to guarantee that citizens can fulfill their most different life projects, without imposing a particular morality. In most countries, the ability to have a fulfilling life has been linked with the ability to access and take advantage of education for several hundred years. It is not surprising that the cornerstone educational policies in all democratic countries involve establishing a free or low-cost educational system that is open to all without compromising their own values. In modern societies, this minimal definition of equality of educational opportunity quickly rubs up against a different social justice agenda. When equality is on the agenda, politicians look for evidence that their laws and regulations do not directly disadvantage citizens identified by gender, race, social class, or immigration status. To one degree or another, all democratic countries pay some attention to this at the level of accessing educational opportunities. This task has, however, been challenged in recent years by the increasing immigration of citizens whose basic religious and ethical beliefs are different from those of their host countries (Gregg, 2002; Lewis, 2007).

If equality is defined as equal outcomes for all citizens things become murkier. The simplest case of equality is when something is identical, for instance, when the attendance to higher education is 50 percent for both gender. Most things that are scrutinized with egalitarian eyes are not that simple. For example, if 50 percent of men and women attend higher education, but women are entering studies in the humanities and men are entering studies in the sciences, does higher education reflect genuine equality? If women's university attendance outstrips men, but men still hold most high-paying and influential positions after completing their studies, can we argue that society has failed to promote equality for males (Field, Kuczera, & Pont, 2007)?

Political design decisions may lead to equality within a society. In educational policy, the most common way to embed ideas of equality into a policy is to compensate those who start with disadvantages with special support. This approach is often called *vertical equity* policy. This political strategy contrasts with one that emphasizes providing everyone with the same resources to engage in their life project, an approach that is often called *horizontal equity*. Different countries typically have an approach that is more consistent with one of these strategies. For example, in some countries (the United States) special grants for higher education are given to students from less wealthy homes and little or no support is given to students from wealthier homes. In other countries, such as Sweden, all students are given an allowance to use for studies and/or access to a loan with a low interest rate. Free education does not, however, mean equal access if there are too few places in the best schools and institutions are allowed to choose on the basis of "merit."

In most countries, the political culture reflects an inconsistent approach to egalitarianism, often because of the historical piling on of policies that are designed with egalitarian goals, but are not comprehensive in their approach, in part because of competing values. England, for example, is increasingly enacting policies that are consistent with vertical equity in education (increasing fees coupled with additional support for schools in poor areas), mixed with horizontal equity in health care (maintaining a single payer comprehensive national health system). To create a consistent focus on egalitarianism, governments need to discuss to the state's redistributive role and the priority placed on social inclusion and equality. When a country emphasizes egalitarian solutions, it usually leads to high levels of taxation and public spending that challenge the principle that the citizens can keep what they earn. An emphasis on inclusion on the other hand may undermine the rights of individuals to enact their life projects in their own way. An example of this tension is France's policy prohibiting certain religious clothing for public service employees. Comprehensive discussions about how to define and address equality quickly fragment into multiple definitions and priorities of equity, which blunt the ability to reach a social consensus.

When political actions focus on equalizing the outcomes of the educational system instead of focusing on equalizing inputs, the tension between core political values becomes very evident. In the United States, debates about the national importance of "closing the gap" in academic performance between brown/black and white students, while at the same time preserving local autonomy of school districts (decentralism), is suggestive of a common issue affecting many countries (Borman & Kimball, 2005). Several political systems that have enacted comprehensive reforms of their primary and secondary schools have treated their students with equality of outcomes in mind; others avoid mandated comprehensive programs because they conflict with other values, such as local choice.

Comprehensive school systems have been adopted in many countries with the explicit goal of decreasing the differences in access to higher studies between social classes. Other countries, like Germany, are willing to live with substantial inequality in outcomes, as measured by international tests, because they also value a system that they believe sorts students into the educational streams that will best serve their life projects. The results of recent analyses of international test data suggest that equality and achievement are not highly associated, but have also provided a mirror for countries that have prided themselves on their achievement. In many countries, like the Netherlands, New Zealand, and Germany, overall performance is high, but the gap between the performance of students from poorer and wealthier backgrounds is also very high (Schleicher, 2009).

Quality

Quality has become a key word in recent policy development, since it serves as a benchmark for the "effectiveness" of an education system. Etymologically, the word goes back to the Latin word *qualitas* (character, nature, essential), which is derived from the Latin word *qualis* (what kind, sort, condition). The quality question therefore asks for the character or nature of a matter, in our case of an education system: What is the nature of education in Nebraska? Of what character is the education system in Austria? How is evaluated quality closely linked to the educational policy culture in a country.

For a long time (in Europe, well into the second half of the last century), the educational quality question was answered by general descriptors (goodness criteria) that reflected what was understood as quality. Schools were not publicly labeled as "good" or "bad," but rather were characterized by certain attributes according to which they were similar to each other or different from each other (e.g., traditional curriculum and pedagogy vs. comprehensive vs. Montessori). Globalization in education has brought in a comparative moment, which turned the quality question into a quantitative one that makes direct comparisons possible through large-scale international assessments such as PISA. Etymologically, quantity goes back to the Latin word *quantitas* (magnitude, quantity, multitude) derived from the Latin word *quantus* (how great; how much, many). This shift from a qualitative, descriptive perspective to a measurement and quantitative one has brought about a major change in how policymakers think about how to assure the public that the schools in their country are "good."

Public demands for a high-quality education are reinforced by persistent arguments that suggest that without the best schools, economic decline lies in the foreseeable future (Brown & Lauder, 1996; Miller, n.d.). This has led to a more differentiated view of alternative ways of thinking about quality, which reflect different philosophical underpinnings (Garvin, 1984; Hämäläinen & Jakku-Sihvonen, 1999; Ingenkamp, 1995; Van den Berghe, 1995; Winch, 1996). Five of these are summarized here:

1. *Quality as innate excellence.* This implies that something or somebody is simply the best. This approach can only be understood through comparison with other people or objects that display the same characteristics. It is called the transcendent or philosophical approach, which also underlies the Olympic ideal of *citius, altius, fortius* (faster, higher, stronger). Innate excellence implies a holistic judgment rather than a ranking or rating on a few criteria.

This quality approach has a long tradition in education systems of many countries, where students, teachers, or schools are awarded a prize for their excellence (e.g., student of the year, math Olympics, spelling bee, the yearly school award by the Bosch Foundation in Germany, the most innovative school system in the world by the Bertelsmann Foundation).

2. *Quality based on measurable attributes.* This approach implies that quality can be defined and measured as a product. In many countries this is the traditional form of measuring student achievement through grading and attributing marks. The transfer of a measurable norm system into the sphere of education suggests that the quality of student achievement can be objectively and reliably assessed. While intuitively obvious and an assumption that permeates the international testing movement, this concept has been criticized on empirical grounds (Baker, 2007; Ingenkamp, 1995; Linn, Baker, & Dunbar, 1991) as well as by those who argue that a few criteria cannot capture the quality of a school.

3. *Quality as conformity to requirements.* This is a manufacturing-based approach (Crosby, 1979), which obeys specific standardized norm systems (e.g., DIN, ISO). In many countries, teaching was expected to conform to national curriculum and syllabi, and today it often has to meet national or state standards, both for teaching performance and the achievement of the school's students. Conformance to the requirements is assessed in a variety of ways in different countries, ranging from student self-assessment of students, measures of intersubjectivity (more than one teacher marking students' work in final exams) to national performance examinations (using the quality measures suggested in approach 2). Recent large-scale assessments (like PISA) have introduced a system that ranks countries according to standardized expectations in literacy, math, and science. The development of standards for teaching practice and more standardized approaches to the assessment of teachers is an increasing topic of research and policy discussion.

4. *Quality as what the customer asks for.* In economics this is called the user/customer-based approach, which follows the philosophy that market mechanisms give distinction to quality by the choice of the users, customers, or clients. A focus on customer-driven systems is associated with some proponents of a more "business-like" approach to public services, and is often defined by a "fitness for use" criteria (Juran, 1992), which emphasizes people's right to choose among social services that meet a minimal standard. In several countries this approach is deeply connected to choice,

for example, by allowing parents to choose their child's school or by introducing vouchers that allows less-affluent parents to "buy" the best education. An alternative perspective on the customer-parent is to co-opt them by involving them as participants in decision-making on different levels of the school system, which allows them to ask for what they want rather than simply buy from another source if they are dissatisfied.

5. *Quality as value for money.* This is also termed the value-based approach. This concept is borrowed from business and industry and follows a performance/price ratio. Educators are often asked by politicians to justify spending on programs by balancing the results gained from the money spent. It is very difficult, however, to judge value for money in education since sustained success is often associated with a wide array of "soft" variables, such as developing creativity or becoming a self-motivated learner, which are highly valued but difficult to measure. However, the language of value-for-money is also associated in contemporary political culture with an emphasis on efficiency, which will be discussed later. It is important to note that value for money is always in the eye of the beholder: People pay a lot for objects that might not meet higher standards (e.g., private religious schools in countries where they are not fully publically funded) because they are of high value for them.

The five definitions of quality do not contradict each other, but simply present different approaches or perspectives. As Hämäläinen & Jakku-Sihvonen (1999) point out:

> In the 90s, for example, a customer-based, market-based approach has been central, whereas the first of these definitions represents the traditional vision of education. Characteristic for these trends is the fact that they also reveal clearly different trends in management cultures, which in turn are strongly connected to the orientation of education policy which has taken place within the administration. Regardless of the point of view, attention may focus on different parts of education, such as learning, teaching, effectiveness in promoting cohesion or preventing exclusion, the economic efficiency of education, or management. (p. 6)

One recent overview argues that these five interpretations of quality often reflect differences in the perspectives of groups of stakeholders in a political system. Parents have a different understanding of quality than teachers; teachers have an interpretation that differs from the inspectorate; politicians focus on system quality in terms of productivity while students are looking for relevance (Scheerens, Luyten, & Ravens, 2011).

Efficiency

The consideration of efficiency in political discussions is new to the modern era. In agrarian cultures, the term made limited sense, because the basis for political and social life was driven largely by controllable inputs (human energy) and uncontrollable external factors (weather, war, disease). With the rise of classical economic liberalism and Smith's notion of the "invisible hand," there emerged a new emphasis on looking at wasteful allocation of resources. In early and mid-twentieth century, efficiency as a political concept was largely confined to discussions about the role of government in stimulating or regulating the private sector. In the latter part of the twentieth century, issues of efficiency in the public sector were raised as part of the emergence of what is often referred to as a "neoliberal movement" (Ong, 2006). In this context, the emphasis is on scrutinizing public expenditures with an eye to improving the use of resources. The value placed on efficiency is clearly present in virtually all developed countries. How this is reflected in the deeper political culture still varies, however. In some countries, the focus has been on shifting public services into the (presumably) more efficient private market. In other countries there is only a public recognition that government services can be delivered with less waste, but less emphasis on privatization. In most cases, an emphasis on efficiency requires accepting a degree of inequality in income.[5]

Some have viewed the argument for increasing government efficiency as part of a right-wing effort to dismantle or reduce social services (Fox-Piven & Cloward, 1997). However, the neoliberal emphasis on efficiency has characterized both centrist and center-right educational politics in most Western countries. In particular, the notion that social services can be assessed on the degree to which public resources produce a reasonable amount of valued public outcomes is unassailable in most countries— the alternative perspective implying that graft, corruption, and weak services for the less fortunate are tolerable. As noted earlier, at its core the emphasis on government efficiency is focused on determining quality by whether there is "value for money."

Carnoy (2000) argues that the emphasis on efficiency is increasing around the world as a consequence of three interrelated pressures:

- pressure to reduce expenditures;
- pressure to increase highly skilled labor pools to attract investment; and
- increased opportunity and pressure to compare the national educational system to others due to increased international testing and indicators.

The introduction of an efficiency emphasis in public policy discussions is due to the global diffusion and acceptance of logically compelling paradigms from business and economics (Carnoy, 2000).

This acceptance of efficiency as a goal inevitably leads to a search for measurable and objective units of comparison. In many countries, there is a tendency to equate (as noted previously) quality and efficiency, with less attention to the alternative ways of defining quality that might require deeper discussions about innate excellence. Critics argue, for example, that policies that promote efficiency do so with little attention to softer social goals, such as liberty and social justice. Their arguments are usually framed in the context of efforts to link efficiency to free and unregulated markets, where codifying the potential negative effects of increased inequality in the distribution of social resources. In many countries, there is a tendency to equate (as noted previously) quality and efficiency, with less attention to the alternative ways of defining quality that might require deeper discussions about innate excellence.

These arguments are often abstract because the political language of efficiency is not the same as the economists' language. When educational efficiency is promoted in parliaments and legislatures, the conversation is often about the management of perceived waste. For example, in one state in the United States the governor argued that resources that do not go directly into classrooms are evidence of bloated and inefficient educational systems. In reality, local education authorities were allocating significant nonclassroom resources for teacher professional development to enhance effectiveness—at the request of teacher unions. In a 1998 study, McKevitt compares the outcomes of New Public Management inspired initiatives in public services in five countries, and defines schools (which, like health institutions, social services, and police, provide services to inelastic markets) as Street Level Public Organizations. He observes that:

> If the SLPO is measured solely on criteria of efficiency and resource management, the original mission of the SLPO (social cohesion and interdependence) may be lost sight of (. . .). An emphasis on citizen voice will also help redress one of the existing weaknesses of the SLPO—its provider orientation. (pp. 171–172)

Choice

As we have hinted in previous sections, discussions about social values often begin with a question of how to resolve the tension between a focus on individual rights (and obligations) and social responsibilities. Nowhere is this more evident than in the discussions around choice of public services. Educational choice can be the result of different intentions. Historically, educational choice was legitimized by religious, linguistic, and philosophical considerations in countries like Canada, Denmark, the Netherlands, and Belgium. In these countries the right to choose a school according to one's own preferences was and remains a fundamental pillar of the educational system, reflecting the value of pluralism. In many countries, freedom of education is a constitutional right, which includes government funding for all schools that satisfy parliamentary conditions. Private schools are run by independent governing bodies that include stakeholder and parent representatives. Public schools are governed by municipalities or the national government. Public and private schools in countries like the Netherlands and Belgium form networks that are part of the vertical structure in society that differentiates social groups according to their religious or philosophical values. In this vertical structure each "pillar" has its own church, union, schools, hospitals, health care insurance, newspaper, and political party (Huyse, 1970).

In the Netherlands, earlier research suggests that parents' school choice depends primarily on whether parents felt comfortable with the school's philosophical values. The position of the school in annual rankings based on test results played a secondary role (Louis & van Velzen, 1991). However, many parents choose a school because of its reputation and its image, which includes visible socioeconomic and racial mix of students (Andersen, 2008; Kristen, 2008; Saporito, 2003). Choice is, thus, in a state of tension with the value placed on equity, particularly racial and social segregation.

In countries like the United States, choice has recently been associated with increasing competition between schools and marketization (Baily, 2010). A critical tenet of capitalism is that when products compete in a free marketplace, they are forced to improve. It is a simple extension of this observation that the product of the educational system would likewise show improvement when subjected to the same dynamic forces. It is also claimed by advocates of market theories that such an environment would encourage schools to be more responsive, resulting in educational practice that better meets parental needs and preferences (Chubb & Moe, 1990; Tooley, 1993). The premise that the introduction of choice will increase educational quality is, however, empirically unproven (Carnoy, 1998).

The concept of choice as an instrument of competition has been introduced to public school systems primarily in three ways:

- In *magnet schools*, students are offered specialized curricula within the core curriculum of the local school district. This approach has

been used most often in urban school districts to attract middle-class families and to encourage social integration (Checkley, 1997). Magnet schools also typically receive extra monetary resources compared to traditional public schools (Davenport & Moore, 1988).
- *Charter schools* are public schools governed by a charter (contract) with the local or state school board. In exchange for reduced bureaucratic regulations and increased program freedom, the charter school is responsible for proving increased academic achievement in a specified area within a three- to five-year time frame (Nathan, 1996).
- *Voucher programs* are the most controversial of the choice options. In a voucher system, parents receive public funding for their children to attend fully (fee-paying) private schools. The school may or may not accept them, and the school may also charge additional tuition or fees. Although voucher programs offer schools choice, there is often limited accountability for increased student achievement or benefit (Nathan, 1996).

Additional forms of choice are springing up as well, including dual credit programs, which allow students to attend a postsecondary institution while still in secondary school (Schefers, 2012) and voluntary transfer programs that allow students who reside in one local education authority to attend a school in another authority.

While the discussions in some countries have emphasized the importance of markets as a driver of quality, this is not the only language that underlies policy discussions. Sweden enacted a policy that subsidizes "charter-like" schools (most with religious affiliations) based on the value of pluralism. In the Netherlands and Belgium, the entire educational systems are based on choice as a value of educational pluralism while Denmark's long-standing policy regarding "free schools" reflects a strong populist value system. Charter schools in the United States remain part of the public school system (although they are not always financed equally) and are supported both by those who advocate a market approach, and those who strongly support pluralism, while the role of academies (charter-like schools in England) have support from people with widely divergent political perspectives on most other issues. However, the underlying focus on competition is an issue that cannot be ignored, even when pluralism is the espoused value underlying choice systems.

Choice policies may also be intertwined with other aspects of educational policies. In the United States, for example, states exhibiting a tendency toward rationalism in their political cultures enact comprehensive school reform programs to solve specific identified problems, while decentralist political cultures tend to place more emphasis on local control and choice (Louis et al., 2006; Timar & Kirp, 1988). In the Western countries, there is a relationship between choice and equity: countries that permit more parental choice typically exhibit a stronger association between the student's socioeconomic status and achievement. A recent OECD (2008) report concludes that "school choice requires careful management from an equity perspective."

Conclusion

The framework that we have outlined in this chapter has been developed from a preliminary perspective based largely on North American scholarship. The broader overview presented in this chapter reflects the lived experience and reflective writings of scholars from seven countries, six of which share a form of government (parliamentary) that is very different from that of the United States. Our conclusion is that the main categories that emerged in the United States have meaning in other very different settings, and we present them as a framework that illuminates similarities and differences among the large and small nation-states represented in this book. We invite the reader to keep them in mind as we present an overview of our collective views about the importance of two lenses—globalization and localism—in the next chapter, and consider specific examples as we explore each of the seven countries in more detail in part two, and make specific comparisons between pairs of countries in part three.

Notes

Authors of this chapter are listed in alphabetical order since all contributed equally to the development of our framework. We would like to acknowledge the contributions of Dan Bratton, who heavily edited our drafts for conceptual clarity.

1. In a later publication, Torres (2002) provides a more mixed picture of globalization, pointing to its potential through educational systems reform as a mechanism for improving human rights and opportunities.
2. A more radical interpretation (Gritsch, 2005) argues that nation-states vary in the degree to which the owning classes are able to impose the neoliberal language to foster their own interests, or are contested by other powerful groups within the state that seek a "nonglobal" response.
3. Throughout this book we use the term "liberal" in its European sense, referring to a political perspective that emphasizes individual freedom and limited government, rather than to the typical meaning in the United States,

where it refers to political perspectives that are more aligned with social democratic theories.
4. Voter registration, general election laws, campaigning finances and party registration, and citizen access to legislative proceedings.
5. The concept of efficiency is often associated with Vilfred Pareto (1991), an Italian economist who argued that efficiency occurs when resource allocations are adjusted to improve the lot of some individuals without harming others. Pareto's law, which suggests that all societies will have a significantly skewed distribution of wealth, signaled a distinct challenge to utilitarianism and the egalitarian political values that emphasized the "greatest good for the greatest number."

2

Historical Perspectives on Educational Policy and Political Cultures

Kasper Kofod, Karen Seashore Louis, Lejf Moos, and Boudewijn van Velzen

Introduction

This chapter explicates a core assumption of our collaborative project: *This history of educational development and policies within a country will affect the way new ideas are received from outside and are incorporated into national and local discussions within that country.* We look at history as a critical component of culture because it creates collective memories and "mental models" (Senge, 1990) that frame the opportunities for new ideas to enter political discussions. We do not examine events as historians, who are committed to teasing out the details of what actually happened, and how they affected participants. Our more sociological view is that "[h]istory reveals not only change but continuity. Social structures and cultures possess a resilience that fosters ideologies of stability and preservation" (Warwick & Williams, 1980, p. 333). History and events in the past have been formed not only by broad social or economic trends, but also by the preferences of often powerful groups and individuals who then determine how others react. Culture is the crucial variable that shapes how the powerful view their own interests, and how those possessed of fewer resources respond to leaders and events over which they individually have less control.

Two Lenses: Global and Local

As suggested by this perspective, a sociological-historical approach to understanding policy discussions must incorporate two distinct lenses. A global perspective acknowledges that there are historical trends affecting large, minimally connected groups of people that do not fit the definition of a political culture as offered in the previous chapter, and which they may not be aware of until the trend is almost past. Nobody, for example, predicted that Spinoza and Locke would, in the mid-seventeenth century, help to create the Enlightenment that changed the shape of Western thought, any more than an "Arab Spring" was accurately predicted for 2011. Historians and sociologists can, retrospectively, "see" the origins and develop explanations for why broad and sweeping changes emerge in what seems to be an almost spontaneous way.

Conversely, a local perspective views global events and paradigms as a force that becomes distorted and dulled when filtered through the meaning and perspectives that a more tightly knit group develops to interpret them. This view emphasizes the role of localized cultural interpretations that can cause disruptions and shape future decisions. These local interpretations can create significant barriers to the simple flow of new ideas in "epistemic communities" of policy conversations. As we put it in chapter one, it is the view that the international tide of ideas meets the rocky shore of local realities. Eventually the rocks will change their shape, but the process can be quite gradual.

Globalization and "New Public Management"

Globalization can be understood as an intricate pattern of connections in economics and the labor market, where local events can have global repercussions and supranational forces in turn can relentlessly pressure local political and economic structures. Globalization has led to the emergence of more than fifty thousand transnational companies that are only loyal to their shareholders and therefore able to impel governments to shape their financial policies according to the logic of the market, as well as the emergence of a global financial market with its complex web through and across national economies that allows problems in one country to rapidly affect a region—which rapidly affects the world.

Globalization is more than an economic phenomenon; it is culturally infectious in ways that manifest its presence in all but the most remote regions in the world. The revolution in communication allows ideas and trends that once took years or even decades to disseminate from one region to another to become available almost instantaneously. The global-local nexus can occur on any computer screen, in any airport, or any time a child comes home with a new idea gleaned from using Google in the classroom.[1] The force of these ideas has left standing only one political system with global credibility—a liberal democracy—while the diffusion of "Hollywood culture" competes with and often overwhelms local interpretations to tell us who we are (Martin & Schumann, 1997; Moos, 2006b).

Global trends, whether in popular culture, economic decisions, or political theory, affect national politics in a variety of ways. Global economic forces can create problems that must be addressed politically. Inflation, deflation, unemployment, smuggling, and the perceived loss of traditional values all have international connections that demand political solutions. Large transnational agencies like the WTO (World Trade Organization), IMF (International Monetary Fund), the World Bank, the GATS (the General Agreement on Trade in Services), the OECD (The Organization for Economic Co-operation and Development), and the EU (European Union) have been established in order to coordinate financial and labor market collaboration between countries. All of these agencies accept the fundamental assumptions of liberal and neoliberal market logics, in large measure because the governments that fund them assume that globalization is a permanent condition of the postmodern world.

This exchange of ideas has led to neoliberal trends in more localized political discussions in different nation-states, where the perceived international forces of globalization are reflected in efforts to change internal structures, which, in line with today's global cultural thinking, results in increased emphasis on decentralization, privatization, output, and competition and on new politics in the public spheres. These trends have been captured and reflected in the idea of New Public Management (NPM) (Hood, 1991). While the notion that public agencies should operate under these principals originated in Europe and the English-speaking world, these overarching tendencies to harness and exploit the logic of markets is influencing thinking and acting in most developing countries as well (Cerny, 1994).[2]

National policies are influenced by the supranational communication systems and agencies "that create, filter and convey the globalization process" (Antunes, 2006, p. 38). In several of the cases presented later in this book, agencies such as the OECD and the EU have formally extended their influence to educational policies within the member states. Although not in the original vision of these organizations, as labor has come to present a greater capital investment, it is natural that educational policies join with tariffs, trade laws, and banking regulations in attracting international guidance. This sets up a conflict between a macroeconomic view of education versus education as an institution to transmit cultural identity and values.

The OECD has become one of the most influential transnational organizations in education. The agency within the OECD that deals with education and educational research is CERI (Centre for Educational Research and Innovation). The OECD does not see itself as, nor was it established to be, a superstate with regulatory authority over its 30 sovereign member countries, and it has no formal power. However, OECD/CERI was established as a powerful player in the globalization of economies (Henry et al., 2001) in order to influence the policies and practices of member countries without overt regulation. CERI grew out of the OECD with the realization, rightly or wrongly, that education belongs in the arena of economics (Moos, 2006b).

The influences are not linear and straightforward. According to Lindgard (2000, p. 83), they interact as "mutually constitutive relations" between distinctive fields or spaces. Lawn and Lindgard (2002, p. 302) claim that transnational organizations like the OECD act as shapers of emerging discourses of educational policy, expressed in reports, key committees, funding streams, and programs. The OECD sets an agenda, as in the case of international comparisons like PISA (Program for International Student Assessment) and TIMMS (Trends in International Mathematics and Science Study), and helps individual member nations to do so as well (Schuller, 2006). If a government wants to put an issue on its national agenda, but has difficulty in gaining attention internally, it may call on the OECD for help. The OECD then forms an external team of experts that reviews the state of affairs in the member state. The report then often comes back to form the basis for political action; discussion of the new agenda then starts with the following observation: "The OECD review says that..."

This strategy is clearly laid out in the OECD publication "Education Catalogue" (OECD, 1998, p. 2) where it says: "This 'peer pressure' system encourages countries to be transparent, to accept explanations and justification, and to become self-critical. This encouragement for self-criticism among representatives of member countries is the most original characteristic of the OECD." The "peers" are the political, research, and educational systems in the member countries. The understanding is that by assessing or reviewing aspects of member country policies and practices and making the review public, OECD/CERI enables countries to be self-critical. This approach has been taken by PISA in the areas of literacy and other proficiencies in the primary and secondary schools, and is also being taken in the area of educational research. A similar concept has been introduced in the EU. Here it is called "the open method of coordination" (Lange & Alexiadou, 2007; Pollack, 1997).

A sociological perspective applied to the study of these trends is typically associated with what has come to be known as the "new institutionalism," a perspective that focuses on the importance of environmental forces that explain the behavior and decisions of key social institutions such as education systems or legislatures. Broad cultural assumptions within an organization or a political entity may constrain the application of rational choice (March & Olsen, 1984). Political perspectives often examine the interactions among the preferences of individual leaders, the distribution of "political resources" to other groups and institutions, and the "rules of the game" in a particular context. Studies in education that have used a new institutional perspective have often taken a different tack, and have focused on the way in which policies and perspectives travel across countries even when there is limited contact among politicians and other influential actors. Examples of this type of influence is the speed with which mass schooling spread across Europe and other countries (Ramirez & Boli, 1987) and the rise and decline of vocational education across multiple countries following broader international education theories and trends (Benavot, 1983).

This new institutionalism is not a "theory" but a loose collection of perspectives that are held together by the assumption that policy and the programs that it creates cannot be understood by looking only at individual countries or specific policies in isolation. A historical perspective in the new institutionalism emphasizes the importance of "path dependence"—which recognizes that past events and understandings can shape the way in which later decision opportunities are interpreted.

The interviews we conducted in all seven countries reinforced the importance of path dependency. In each country there is easy consensus about historical experiences that are deeply embedded, and determine "the (local) rules of the game." Once a tumultuous event has occurred, and has resulted in some kind of resolution, it may shut off alternative opportunities that were present at one time while creating a new path that has implications for further decisions:

> The "path not taken" or the political alternatives that were once quite plausible may become irretrievably lost. "Path dependence analysis" highlights the role of what Arthur Stinchcombe has termed "historical causation" in which dynamics triggered by an event or process at one point in time reproduce themselves, even in the absence of the recurrence of the original event or process. (Pierson & Skocpol, 2002, p. 695)

In some spheres these events or resolutions may become transnational, as in the triumph of neoliberal economic structures and practices through

New Public Management ideas. In others, the influence is less clear. For example, one quantitative study found that the OECD has had very limited effects on policies related to economic redistribution and support within the member nation-states (Crepaz, 2002). Education has historically resisted this homogenizing influence, with a more localized cultural transmission of concepts that reinforce national values and identity.

Global and Local: Significant Changes in Educational Policies in the Different Countries

Some New Institutionalism scholars argue that the nation-state itself is a product of worldwide forces that press toward common structures and behaviors (Meyer et al., 1997), and that regional differences are becoming less important. Some policy analysts in education agree, and point to the spread of the language of New Policy Management from its origins in New Zealand to the "New Europe" countries of the former Soviet Union as they emerge from a socialist past (Tolofari, 2005).

We believe that the use of common language, and even common theoretical perspectives, masks local adaptation and perseverance, and that the tensions between global and local are critical to understanding the evolution of educational policies in the countries included in this book. When we interviewed policy actors in each of our countries, we were told clearly that in order to understand educational policies of today, we needed to look at critical events that had shaped the way in which new decisions were interpreted. Our respondents built their stories about how and why the policy process works the way it does in their countries by referring to important events in the history of their country. We therefore decided to develop a short chronology of events that most or all respondents in each country mentioned as critical—events that have become part of a national "mental model" through which international words and policy language are filtered. In part two we will present cases that elaborate on the details of what our respondents told us about critical events; later in this chapter we refer to a selection of them in each country in order to illustrate the unique stories that will emerge.

We all appreciate the broad perspectives that have dominated academic and popular history from Fernand Braudel to Jared Dimond. We also subscribe, however, to a competing perspective suggesting that highly localized events can cause disruptions and shape future decisions *in that context* in ways that create barriers to the flow of new ideas of "epistemic communities" that result from big discoveries or global policy conversations. Social history is not comprised only of the inevitable roll-out of international trends, but it also owes to enduring local effects of what has happened in the past that are passed down in the collective memory of "how we got to be this way." To give just one simple example, the response to a wide variety of perceived crises in the United States is dominated by the collective understanding of "the greatest generation" of World War II Yanks who went to war and bravely liberated the world. As a model for how to solve problems, this poses a very different context than that found in the Netherlands, where the human suffering of civilians during and after the war is a far more powerful legacy. The assertive US approach to engagement in global conflicts, which contrasts with a more cautious approach of the Dutch, is partially guided by these deeply embedded collective memories. A focus on the importance of local history—often at the level of communities and smaller groups of people—has been a growing trend as anthropological perspectives and oral history have become a more prominent focus of historical inquiry. The increasing importance of local history reinforces people's belief in the "specialness" of their experiences over time.[3]

Globalizing forces, which are increasingly fed by the development of epistemic communities of both intellectuals and policymakers who meet regularly to exchange ideas, are, nevertheless, influencing the political cultures and the ways educational reforms are formulated. It is nonetheless difficult to compare policy development across the board when each country has its own unique historical memory and political culture. Sweden and Denmark are relatively homogenous with respect to their populations and political systems and also exhibit a high degree of continuity in educational policy development, whereas Belgium, the United States, and Austria are federal states with high autonomy in states or provinces that creates a less coherent picture of educational policy. England and The Netherlands are both characterized by a high degree of autonomy for individual schools, but the relationship between schools and the national government is organized very differently. But in all these countries there has been considerable evolution in the policy development during the last 30 years that can be traced back to global influences.

Significant Events to Keep in Mind

First we briefly lay out the events that each country's respondents pointed to as critical to understanding the policymaking process in each country.[4] We then summarize similarities and differences regarding significant changes in educational policies across countries, and reflect on the way in which these events have conditioned contemporary national reactions to global trends.

Sweden

The goal of comprehensive education emerged slowly in Sweden until the middle of the twentieth century. In the nineteenth century, few students had the opportunity to advance beyond a basic education that was heavily skewed toward religious instruction. In 1905, vocational and practical middle schools were established, and in 1919, a more modern curriculum, which limited religious education and introduced science and civics, was introduced for basic education. Little change occurred in the system, which was highly selective and provided few opportunities for children from lower-income families, until after World War II. In 1949, a national consensus emerged with a new vision of a comprehensive school system that would educate every child through lower secondary school. This vision took a decade to work out through experiments made by local school authorities until in 1962 all children between 7 and 16 years of age attended a grundskola. The upper secondary schools that follow the grundskola were also gradually reformed during the 1970s and 1980s. Not surprisingly, this overhaul required a persistent national vision as well as adjustments to structures and curriculum that could only be

1905	Passages between different school forms are established. Real schools and practical middle schools are introduced.
1919	The first modern curriculum is introduced for the Folkskola. Christianity as a subject is limited to 10% of the time. Science and civics growth.
1949	A decision is taken by the parliament that a unified school system will be introduced. The decade that follows is used for experiments with different designs of the new school system. The kommuns make the experiments and the state agency collects and evaluates the results.
1962	A grundskola system is introduced where every young person goes to school between 7 to 16 years of age. No streaming allowed.
1986	The upper secondary school becomes a school for everyone. Vocational as well as academic preparation program becomes three year long.
1991	The school system becomes decentralized. The kommuns become responsible for the use of money and for the results. The national school inspection agency is closed down. Central knowledge tests were introduced in the 1960s and continue to be used as a calibration basis for the marking that teachers do.
1994	The option of "free standing" schools, independent of the kommun, is introduced.
1998	Preschools become a part of the educational system instead of being a part of the social welfare system.
2003	School inspections return within the National Agency for Education and become a separate agency in 2008.

Figure 2.1 Swedish timeline.

carried out by strong parliamentary action. Then, in 1991, with the basic system fully functional, a critical decision was made to decentralize system operations, including funding, to the local kommuns.[5] Current policy initiatives represent the final working out of the appropriate balance between national and local responsibilities. The key events that have shaped Swedish perspectives on educational matters are summarized in figure 2.1

Denmark

Danish respondents emphasized a long-term commitment to both a comprehensive education, which was introduced very early in the nineteenth century, and to the freedom of parents to choose a school, which was formalized at the end of the nineteenth century. The comprehensive model was elaborated, in 1937, with the development of a lower secondary school that built on a vision of "Bildung," which emphasized a broad vision of educating the whole person. In 1975, the system was transformed into a nonstreamed middle school with a common curriculum for all students, and in 1993, streaming was abolished until grade 10 (17 years). While the emphasis on Bildung has been augmented in recent years with the idea that education was also a preparation for future studies and work, the comprehensive ideal, and local control over schools, has remained consistent. The 2006 parliamentary act allowed, however, for schools to develop a "special profile" in curriculum, which is regarded by some as a step away from the comprehensive Folkeskole model. The most commonly articulated events shaping modern Danish education are summarized in figure 2.2.

1899	The parliament requires that freestanding schools receive public funding, which supports parental choice of schools
1903	The comprehensive schooling model (Folkskole) with passages between all levels was initiated.
1937	The next step was formed with the 'Middle-school', a comprehensive school build on the 'Bildung' vision
1958	The next step towards the comprehensive school was formed with the streaming postponed to year 7
1975	Streaming was made softer
1993	Streaming was abolished in the 'Folkeskole' and the 'Bildung' vision reiterated
2006	The school was seen as a 'preparation for further studies' and the 'Bildung' vision was softened. Introduction of national testing

Figure 2.2 Danish timeline.

The Netherlands

Freedom of education (parental choice) is part of the deep history of Dutch educational policy. In 1917, this was supplement by constitutional guarantees of funding for all private (largely Catholic) schools. Government funding allocations ensured that both private and public schools were organized in a selective system in which children were assigned to educational tracks at the age of 12. The consequence was that 70 percent of Dutch schools are private and minimally accountable to the government, although sharing key structural features. Discussions about increased equity began under a Social Democratic government in 1968, where the focus was on increasing participation in secondary education. This was followed by an influential white paper that set out a vision for a more comprehensive school system. This vision has been the subject of debate (and minimal implementation) since then. Instead of structural reform, the government has introduced a wide variety of curricular changes designed to "soften" the tracking system, and developed a support system that provided an attractive alternative to more traditional curriculum and pedagogy. In addition, successive governments, both left and right, have focused on decentralizing the system to autonomous school boards to promote innovation from below, and to minimize the role of national and local governments. Events that continue to shape policymakers' reactions to educational proposals are listed in figure 2.3.

1917	"Freedom of Education" for non-public schools in the constitution was supplemented with equal funding for private and public schools.
1968	"Mammoatt Law" restructured secondary education to make it more accessible to more students by reducing the number of tracks, eliminating entry examinations and increasing the number of schools.
1975	The Contourenota – a white paper – outlined a new educational vision intended to promote higher quality and equity.
1985	"Basisschool" Law: integrated early childhood (kindergarten) and primary education.
1986	Wov (Wet op de Onderwijsverzorging): Articulated a formal support system with quasi autonomous non-governmental institutions that deliver curricula, leader training, tests, consultancy to schools and school boards.
1990s	A wide variety of non-mandatory curriculum reforms are introduced; national "attainment targets" are introduced.
2010	Public school boards, like those of private schools, become autonomous and responsible for the quality of education and governance of participating schools.

Figure 2.3 Dutch timeline.

Flanders—Belgium

Education has been hotly contested in Flanders since 1830, which ushered in a period that is referred to as the "school wars" between Catholic and non-Catholic educational systems. This was not resolved until 1959, when the government recognized both "freedom of education" and its responsibility to fund all schools. The outcome is two coequal systems: a Catholic network and a public network. In 1989, constitutional devolution of the educational system resulted in a separation of the Flemish-speaking and French-speaking school systems: there is no unified Belgian educational system. The Flemish system continues to operate within the framework of the School Pact, which limits the authority of the Flemish parliament. Changes in Flemish schools result from negotiated agreements between the minister and the Catholic and public school networks. Agreement was reached in 1991 on a limited number of attainment targets that would apply to both Catholic and public Flemish-speaking schools systems. A 2007 act reaffirmed the autonomy of schools within their networks, further limiting ministerial control. Figure 2.4 presents the most critical events that continue to influence modern Belgian/Flemish education.

Austria

Austria's history of public education started as early as the eighteenth century, but the twentieth century ushered in a period of turmoil that has had lasting effects. The Austro-Hungarian Empire was managed by a vast bureaucracy that could only be effective if the population was able to read and write. After World War I, the monarchy was abandoned and transformed into what is known as the First Republic—a republic that was no longer overseeing a vast empire but a small country of nine provinces. During this period a first attempt was made to decentralize education by giving the provinces more authority in education matters. However,

1959	The School Pact: Guarantees the right for everyone to organize education and establish schools that have to be recognized on government; all schools are publicly funded, and School boards are granted autonomy over curriculum and staffing.
1989	Constitutional reform gives almost complete autonomy in education to the Flemish and French communities.
1991	Attainment targets established for primary and secondary education
2007	Funding of the operating costs equalized for all schools, public and private; schools responsible for governance and management.

Figure 2.4 Belgium/Flanders timeline.

1918	After WW1: The First Republic: transition of school laws
1938	Third Reich rules and regulations implemented in Austrian education
1945	Reintroduction of school laws of the First Republic
1955	The Second Republic: Federal state of 9 provinces with distinct identities and strong culture of centralized thinking in national policy making
1962	Federal school laws require a two-thirds majority to take effect
1974	The School Education Act defines core curriculum framework and gives teachers, parents, and students power on decision making at classroom and school levels
2010	Federal government assumes more responsibility for employment and working conditions for staff, and upper secondary schools.

Figure 2.5 Austrian timeline.

in 1938 Austria became part of the German Third Reich and the education structures and laws were synchronized with those in Germany. After 1945 Austria was occupied for almost a decade by the allied forces. The country became a fully independent federal republic with nine provinces only in 1955. Since then it gradually adopted a more democratic way of governing the public sectors, including education. A legacy of its concerns about the possibility of any powerful central authority, be it an Emperor or a dictator, led to a 1962 law that made it impossible for governments to change national education laws without a two-third majority. This parliamentary act was intended to safeguard the interests of provinces and political parties. The federal government is responsible for employment and working conditions of teachers and staff in schools, but the provinces administer the processes and procedures involved. The major events and decisions shaping Austrian education are shown in figure 2.5.

England

Until the middle of the twentieth century education was the province of local education authorities (LEAs, typically municipalities), but beginning in mid-century the system began a shift to a more centralized and standardized system. The local system of education was challenged in 1944 (Education) when the then existing national Board of Education was transformed into a Ministry of Education, and a clear distinction between primary and secondary schools was articulated. Conservative governments continued, in the 1980s, to diminish the power of the LEAs, initiate school-level governing bodies, and give parents more choice of schools. An emphasis on improved quality led to the development of an independent national inspectorate (OFSTED) in 1992, and a variety of nationally funded but semiautonomous units began to work on school improvement

1944	Comprehensive act defines the shape of the post-war educational system, distinguishing between primary and secondary education, providing support for secondary schools for all students and establishment of the Ministry of Education
1988	"The Thatcher Revolution": National curriculum, key stages, testing at 7, 11 and 14 with published results, power to let head teachers take control over their budgets
1992	School Standard and Framework Act: attainment targets and accountability through inspections as a means to induce improvement.1998 Omnibus bill revising elements of 1988 Act: Improvement/attainment targets and accountability through inspections ; Regulating the admissions process to secondary schools and eliminating the "grant maintained schools";
2004--	Targeted initiatives: Focused on literacy and numeracy teaching, extensive curriculum mandates, professional development, and required teaching strategies; Target resources for educational improvement to "Education Action Zones"

Figure 2.6 English timeline.

issues. The landslide victory of the Labour Party in 1997 was followed by national literacy and numeracy strategies, additional attainment targets, and a variety of other initiatives focused on improving schools serving poorer students. An Every Child Matters policy made local governments responsible for creating integrated service delivery programs to children and their families. English respondents point to a number of key decisions that were made in the latter half of the last century that continue to affect policies and policy discourse. These are summarized in figure 2.6.

United States

The US Constitution, passed in 1790, does not mention education and explicitly indicates that functions not mentioned under the constitution are delegated to the states. This arrangement meant that, until the middle of the twentieth century, federal support for schools was almost nonexistent.[6] In the mid-1950s, both the federal courts and the national legislature began to intervene in state educational affairs to a greater degree. On the one hand, the federal legislature responded to Sputnik by providing incentive grants to states to improve science and foreign languages. At the same time, a Supreme Court decision forbade the "separate but equal" school policy that characterized many of the states, and a decade later this was accompanied by funding to support both desegregation and supplementary funding for schools serving poor students. A decade later, the rights of special needs students received similar attention, and the federal legislature provided ongoing funding to support their integration. Most federal programs are incentives (temporary grants) for schools or districts

1954	"Brown vs. Board of Education" forbids segregating schools according to race
1964	Civil Rights Act enforces desegregation in schools and higher education
1965	Elementary and Secondary Education Act (Title I) provided federal funding for low income and minority students (reauthorized continuously since then)
1975	Court decisions supporting the rights of special needs children was followed by legislative allocation of funding to support their integration into regular schools and classrooms (PL 94-142).
1980	Congress establishes the Department of Education as a cabinet-level position. Federal support for K-12 education amount to 5% of the total primary/secondary education budget.
2001	No Child Left Behind Act requires states that accept federal funding to conduct tests of student achievement and to provide information about the performance of specific student groups (minority, special education, English language learners, etc.).
2008	Federal support of K-12 education amount to 9 % of the total – on average state provided 46% of the funding for schools, local communities provided for 45%.

Figure 2.7 US timeline.

to pursue federally stated objectives, or provide supplementary funding to state departments of education to support statutory obligations; federal funding is administered through the states. In 2001, the federal role was expanded to require states to develop a standardized measure of student achievement and the equity of the outcomes of students (the No Child Left Behind Act), but these tests are designed by states and are not comparable. Coherence is achieved only when one or more states agree to develop similar curricula and/or tests, but when this has happened it has been voluntary. Federal support and requirements remain limited (typically about 9 percent of the national educational budget) to areas that do not infringe on state's rights. Figure 2.7 summarizes some of the key events that continue to guide current educational policy.

Integrating the Global and Local Perspectives

The traits that Ramirez and Boli (1987) point to as characterizing "modern" school systems are all present in these countries, and have been refined in all of them during the last part of the twentieth century. In that sense they are fully globalized and a visitor from one country would clearly recognize the common traits in the schools of another. Similarities are easily visible, although they also vary when one probes below the surface. A visitor from the United States to the Netherlands or Belgium would be surprised at the large number of "private" religious schools; an Englishman (or woman) going to Austria or the United States would be astonished at the relative autonomy of the provinces/states. All the countries have an educational ministry or department, but they are of different institutional forms; all have some sort of state authority over schools, even if a country, such as Belgium, has several autonomous school systems (Flemish and French).

Transnational Tendencies

All of the countries participating in this book are members of the OECD and participate in the major international testing activities; all except the United States are part of the EU and are influenced by the "open coordination" initiatives. "Open coordination" is very much alive within the United States through the National Governor's Association and other similar bodies, all of which are linked with partners in the EU and promote the adoption of "international standards" (CommonCore, 2011). International developments have influenced the educational development in all the countries. Agencies like the OECD and in the European countries the OECD and the EU have since the 1980s become prominent players that influence the formulation of national educational policies, which has had repercussions on the formulation of educational policies and changes in educational political culture.

Educational policies were originally not part of the EU's prerogatives, but in the Lisbon Agreement of 2000 education became defined as an aspect of social services, and therefore part of the EU Commission's regulation.[7] The limited role of the EU suggests that member states and institutions should inspire each other through "peer review" and policy learning such as best practice. Organizations such as the OECD act as shapers of discourses of educational policies through reports, key commissions, and programs. The OECD is the most prominent in setting this agenda, although they are filtered through a local lens (Moos, 2009).

During the 1980s, all the countries covered in this volume adopted international comparisons such as PISA and TIMMS tests. These measurements have consistently influenced the discourse about educational policies. Testing has been introduced in various forms in the countries be it by the national government (Denmark and Sweden), by states/autonomous regions (United States and Belgium), or by extragovernmental inspection agencies (the Netherlands).

In the last 30 years, all of the European countries in this study have either maintained or increased some form of decentralization in the governance of the schools to make them more responsive to local conditions and concerns: in the Scandinavian countries it has been decentralization from the state to the municipalities (the kommunes); in Belgium the system increasingly functions as two more or less autonomous systems within the same country; in the Netherlands, as increasing constraints on the role of state authorities; in England, with the growth of semiautonomous schools; and in Austria with a reaffirmation of provincial responsibility for administering decisions in primary and secondary schools. The United States is an exception, since the early twenty-first century saw the first effort on the part of the national legislature to create a system for monitoring the quality of schools; this legislation did not, however, require states to use a common test. The centralization of monitoring and comparing results also represents a trend in Europe, where we see national governments increasingly defining attainment targets.

In Europe, we observe both a *loosening* of the ties between the national government and provinces or municipalities, and a *tightening* of oversight through more elaborated curriculum, testing, and inspection systems. Organizational theory suggests that this should be expected: the more the system is characterized by loose coupling the more there is a need for tightening the couplings in other parts of the system (Weick, 1976, 2001). If the administrative requirements that bind the units of a system are only loosened, the system may fall apart and be unable to renew itself. If system requirements are too detailed, there is little room for innovation when conditions demand change. The variations in different countries, as they attempt to find a balance between loose and tight, will be explored in more detail in the remainder of this volume.

Persistent National Identities

In all the European countries, education has also been a means to build a national identity, regulating and instilling desired citizen ideas and behavior. Ramirez and Boli (1987) contend that all education reforms of the early twentieth century reflected the desire to reinforce the development of a national identity through education. Although their research covers a period that now seems to be part of the distant past, we see some of the same factors at work in our cases. An example of this can be seen in the Danish case, where the concept of "Bildung" has achieved a prominent place in the objects clause of the Danish law on the folkeskole. The concept of Bildung in the law stresses the school's responsibility to bring up the students to become responsible Danish citizens. In 1975 the objectives of the system clearly states: "The folkeskole prepares the students to be engaged and co-determining individuals in a democratic society and to accept co-responsibility for the solution of joint tasks. The school's instruction and whole daily life must therefore build on spiritual freedom and democracy" (Lov om folkeskolen, June 26, 1975, § 1,3). Bildung is thus understood as more than the desire for individual development, but as a means to create Danish citizens. In Sweden, the new comprehensive school that was introduced after World War II emphasized the need for democratic training and the use of knowledge in an independent and initiative-rich way to vaccinate the nation against the kind of fascism that the neutral state had seen destroy other countries. Even in a country like Belgium, where the educational system has fractured into distinct Flemish-speaking and French-speaking schools, the notion of citizen identity is critical.

A relative weakening of the state, or military defeat, produces educational reforms in order to enhance the country's survival (Ramirez & Boli, 1987). In the United States, the Russian launching of the Sputnik was seen as an embarrassing national humiliation, and it ushered in a new era of federal incentives to stimulate math and science, which is still supported as part of retaining the country's self-image as a nation of technological innovation and new ideas. Austria's intricate post–World War II governance arrangements were designed to make sure that every Austrian student knows that the preservation of the unique cultures of each province coexists with the development of an Austrian state. In Denmark, education was a prominent issue as a nation-building endeavor after the wars with Austria and Prussia in the mid-1880s, and the Danish nation went from being a middle-sized European nation to becoming a weak state with a strong and aggressive neighbor. Schools are viewed as a tool to protect the national identity in order to survive and thrive as an autonomous state (Lidegaard, 2005).

Because national identity formation has been caught up in the modernization and globalization processes of the latter part of the twentieth century, they account for some of the tendencies for these countries to "manage" transnational trends differently. In the United States, educational policies are largely the prerogative of the states but are influenced by national rhetoric promoted by the national secretary of education, who is always well connected to ministers of education in other countries. In England and the Netherlands there is a tradition that changes in educational policies are centralized and influenced by "experts" who are not always part of the parliamentary system, and these experts are often recruited because they are believed to understand international trends. In these countries, the growing influence of international agencies, such as the OECD and PISA, becomes reinterpreted to adapt to the average citizen's image of education.[8] On the other hand, the inability to rhetorically position education as central to national identity is typically viewed with alarm by those who promote the importance of nation-states in a modern economy. Belgium's fragmented educational system is seen as evidence that the country may not survive as a single nation. The Belgian preference for making sure that no one lingual group has too much power is perhaps best exemplified by their inability to form a coalition government for more than a year after the last national election.

There are centralized and decentralized ways to handle educational policies in all countries, and these vary. However, in addition, all of the countries in this study are experiencing some effort to make education an explicit part of a nation-building endeavor in ways that are more prominent than they have been since the period just after World War II. All of the countries we looked at view education as the primary tool to promote their own wellbeing and success in the competitive environment of the global economy.

Summary and Observations about the Global and Local Lenses

The seven countries differ in terms of their culture, history, and political systems. They are all products of their respective histories, and the recent changes in their educational systems and how policy decisions are arrived at vary widely, as the country case studies in part two will show. In spite of this there are also similarities and forces that push in the same direction. We view the adoption of educational reforms in our increasingly interconnected world through a lens that argues that a nation's unique history and culture is critical to understanding how outside ideals and concepts penetrate that society. This adaptation process does not, however, mean that countries will look very different from one another to a casual observer. Research has shown that, over time, all developed countries come to have certain structures in common: early school education becomes integrated into basic school; vocational education is absorbed into the regular education system and becomes less distinct; and now the idea of testing all students to determine whether they meet certain standards that are set by the governing system is widely entrenched. Do these changes mean that we have one global education system, and that the nation-state and the nation-building endeavor will inevitably be swept away? We believe that the practical outcomes that we witness when global crashes into local are best illustrated by examining how local political cultures transform and shape the global message.

Notes

The authors contributed equally to this chapter and are listed in alphabetical order.

1. Sugata Mithra's experiments with childrens' self-teaching in groups using the Internet suggest that the genie of teachers and nations determining what

children will learn is already out of the bottle. See http://www.youtube.com/watch?v=dk60sYrU2RU.
2. The term New Public Management is often traced to New Zealand (Boston et al., 1996), but has been rapidly adopted and refined by other countries.
3. At least one country—Norway—has a government-funded Institute of Local History that has activities in all of the institutions of higher education in the country. http://www.localhistory.no/countries/norway.html#academic
4. We validated respondents' identification of key events by examining other written documents. We discovered a consensus in each country about the core events.
5. Kommuns are a functional equivalent to a municipality, but often include more than one municipality in less populated areas.
6. The timeline is limited to primary-secondary education; federal support for higher education began in the middle of the nineteenth century.
7. http://www.europarl.europa.eu/summits/lis1_en.htm.
8. For example, in the United States, reports of international test results are typically ignored after an initial splash because the focus is on how states compare to each other. Some states pay for additional testing in order to demonstrate that they perform as well as other countries, and much better than the US average.

Part II

Introduction

Discussing a global trend in abstract terms is easy; trying to describe the impact of global trends on specific policy negotiations or concrete initiatives in a particular setting is more difficult. As the group involved in our research project met over the course of several years, we found ourselves struggling to understand both the globalizing forces and the local differences. As we acquired greater knowledge of each other's settings in long meetings, we found it easy to misinterpret what was going on in another setting based on what we experienced in our own country. This was particularly true when contemporary conversations that seemed momentous to insiders suggested little apparent impact on major policies, and we (the outsiders) had to demand concrete evidence of change that might persist beyond a year's election rhetoric. Conversely, as a group, we struggled with the occasional observation that "outsiders" saw major changes afoot when the "insiders" thought that nothing much was happening.

In sum, we concluded quite quickly that understanding the political culture of the country in which one was born and bred, and the consequences of that culture for policymaking in education—the ecosystem for all authors since they were four years old—is not an easy task. Nor was it easy to understand how the structures and processes that were taken for granted in another country affected the range of policy outcomes that were within the realm of possibility. It forced us not only to write country cases, but also to "grill" our colleagues on various occasions in order to be sure that each of us understood what was presented.

The results of this lively and sometimes tendentious process are presented in this section. Each author is fully responsible for the content and "facts" of his or her case; we collectively agree that each author captured the story in ways that we could all understand and found compelling.

The authors of this book are all researchers and research-practitioners: It was important that we arrive at descriptions of our countries that were data-based, rather than reflecting our own predilections and personal views. Therefore, at the beginning of the project, we collectively agreed that we would interview between 8 and 12 policy informants, using a common (but flexible) open-ended interview protocol (see the appendix for the English version). Because the countries had rather different ways of organizing the formal policymaking process, we allowed everyone latitude in choosing respondents, but in every case they included at least one person who had held a position as a minister, deputy minister, or a very high-ranking civil servant, several elected politicians, a representative of professional associations or unions, and representatives of other associations that were either formally consulted during policymaking or who had a consistent informal role. Where possible, we also interviewed someone representing the business sector, and a person who had a long-term influence on educational policy, but who had not necessarily held a visible elected or appointed position. These interviews were critical in challenging our own beliefs about how policy was really made, but also in shaping our perspective on the policy cultures of our own settings. We also, in each case, relied on documentary analysis (which now includes what can be retrieved from electronic search engines) to either challenge or affirm the views represented in the interviews. In order to ensure the candidness of responses, we chose to give most of our well-known interviewees anonymity, which means that we avoid using frequent quotes that would make it easy to identify them.

With the country timelines in mind (see chapter two), as well as the dimensions of political culture that we agreed on (chapter one), this section presents chapters that are intended to inform the reader about "the way we do things" in Sweden, Denmark, the Netherlands, Flanders (Belgium), Austria, England, and the United States. Each of the chapters concludes with a summary that indicates how openness, decentralization, rationalism, egalitarianism, efficiency, quality, and choice play out in that country.

If you have read chapter two, you will already be familiar with the problem that we faced in examining nation-states as the unit of analysis. This was particularly true where nations are organized along federal lines (Austria, Belgium, the United States) with its different constituting entities (*Länder* in Austria, the Communities of Flanders or Wallonia in Belgium, the states in the United States). We gave the authors of these countries the latitude to present their case as they preferred—and in the case of Belgium, to treat the fully autonomous Community of Flanders as a nation-state for the purposes of educational policy. What we see are quite unique patterns of regional and functional decentralization in each country, patterns that have great impact. In all the country cases we will see evidence that there are checks and balances in the educational sector. Even in the most centralized countries, parliaments face serious limits when they try to create change in schools. But the way checks and balances are institutionalized are very different between the counties involved in this study.

We cannot, of course, know the future. What we present in the following chapters is, however, the story of continuity in policymaking processes and policy culture amid the globalizing forces that, based on newspaper headlines, seem to be eroding differences.

3

Many Cooks Will *Not* Spoil the Broth: Educational Policy in Sweden

Mats Ekholm

This chapter uses some critical policymaking periods in Swedish educational history to illustrate some fundamental aspects of the political culture in Sweden. Like the other chapter authors, I have interviewed a number of former and current actors in the system including the secretary of state at the Ministry of Education, the former secretary of state at the Ministry of Education, the chairman of the largest teachers' union in Sweden, and a longtime civil servant responsible for schools in the National Association of Kommuns[1] in Sweden. However, I also draw on my personal experiences in the National Agency for School Improvement and at the Ministry for Education, and as director general of the National Agency for Education. These positions gave me an insider's perspective on the processes of the educational policy system.

Perhaps the most dominant characteristic of the Swedish political culture is the long tradition of openness in policymaking. This open engagement occurs both within and among political parties and involves stakeholders of many kinds. Openness has been formalized within parliamentary practices, including the obligation for extensive hearings/consultations before legislation is passed. Another aspect supporting openness is the wide variety of national standing and ad hoc committees. Researchers are used as experts who contribute to these committees, and policies are now and then created after a period of formal experimenting with different solutions. These key conditions persist, even when the locus of policymaking changes.

All of these consultative processes are fundamental to the Swedish form of democracy, but make the process slow and sometimes cumbersome. The initiation of an educational political issue, the policy preparations or the construction of premises for decision-making, the decision-making itself, and the follow up on decisions are used as a basis for the understanding of the policy process (Moos, 2009)—and each has its own associated consultations and investigations. As a consequence, in Sweden, the actual policies have shifted slowly over time, and many aspects of the process of policymaking are remarkably stable.

Roots of Today's Systems: Consensus-Driven Reform

The modern Swedish educational system was born in a radical restructuring that was initiated after World War II. Prior to that, the system was designed (similar to that of Germany) to focus on selection at an early age, with a relatively rigid course of study designed for students of "different abilities." The educational system was highly centralized: the national government employed the teachers, negotiated pay and duties, and set rules for the work of professional staff and students. The state also formulated curricular frameworks for each grade level and subject, including the number of lessons for each subject and attainment targets. The state controlled examinations directly and conducted inspections through regional advisers. While the reorganization changed some key aspects of the system, the tradition of detailed planning by the national parliament and by the government was deeply embedded, although imbued with the spirit of openness noted earlier.

Stability in educational political cultures benefitted from stable governments. Between 1945 and 2006 the Social Democrats were the dominant party in the government in Sweden for 50 out of the past 61 years. Although there have been shifts in government partners, a tradition of unanimous cooperation in decision-making around educational issues has been the case. The traditional methods of developing new policies in education have consisted of the involvement of people other than politicians in the preparatory work before decisions are taken. In cases of disagreement, they are worked through to a level of minimal agreement of the major actors and parties before a bill is presented in parliament. Because of this consensus most bills are passed without any problem.

The post–World War II educational reforms were motivated by a strong concern among all parties with the advancement of social justice through a comprehensive and untracked school that crossed political party lines. The basic elements of the reform were initiated in 1949, and were supported by the Conservative, Liberal, Social Democratic, Communist, and Farmers' parties. Aspects of the reform were worked out over the next decade and a half and were finalized by 1962. The main characteristics of the modern Swedish system include a common curriculum for all students in all schools from age 7 through 16. After the common school (grundskola), students are allowed to specialize in the three years of upper secondary schools, but they remain under the same "organizational roof."[2] The focus is on providing a common experience for all students in public schools. The basic elements of the grundskola/gymnasieskola system have persisted with few changes since then.

In the beginning of the 1990s, however, a radical reform of the governance system was introduced, and this involved a decentralization of the school finance and oversight responsibilities. Kommuns were put in charge of managing a "lump sum" budget that mixed educational funds with those of other social service sectors. Like the first radical change, this shift too was supported by the major political parties, but the policy process was slow because it was dependent on the previous several decades of consolidation of kommuns, which resulted in larger and more effective local governance units.[3] During this second period of radical governance reform, state control over schools was loosened in yet another way. Private (fee-based) schools have always been permitted in Sweden; in 1992 parents were also given the option of forming kommun-funded "free schools," which are similar to US charter schools or English academies. These schools are also responsible for delivering a common school experience, but report directly to the Ministry and Inspectorate.

The kommuns loosened the firm grip of state control over school finances. Each kommun (depending on size) has one or two boards of education in charge of the local schools. These local boards of education reflect the political preferences in the kommun, and must work with other social service sectors to best reflect the needs and preferences of the local communities. After kommun elections, which are held every fourth year, the boards of education are appointed by people from the local political parties, who continue to shape the work of the boards throughout their tenure.

Today the kommuns are responsible for hiring all professional and nonprofessional personnel that work in the schools. Although unions negotiate with the national association of the kommuns, local agreements determine the salaries of the staff in each school within the broadly agreed upon framework. The kommuns organize the use of time in schools and determine facilities and student transportation, although many of these tasks are delegated to the rektor of the school (the formal manager and leader of the local school) from the kommun educational office. As a guiding principle, educational decisions are made as close as possible to those who must comply with them. The most recent case of decentralization and reform occurred when the kommuns were given responsibility for preschools, following the central guidelines. The smooth and largely uncontroversial way in which this change occurred provides another illustration of the continuity of the process of policymaking, from initiation through implementation.[4]

Is There a Change in Political Culture?

Until the middle of the 1980s, political initiatives in Sweden were usually raised by national politicians. To prepare a decision, the proposal often was given to a committee that was composed either of representatives from the political parties represented in the parliament or of organizational stakeholders (professional associations and others). A committee created to prepare a proposal typically engaged researchers or other specialists to produce "objective knowledge" about the chosen issue (Husén, 1984). Often a committee worked for several years to produce the foundation for a decision before it was taken up in parliament or by the government. It was also common for the committee system to incorporate divergent opinions that different actors held and reach a compromise in the committee so that a consensus proposal could be presented.

In some cases the government organized field-based experiments with new ideas to "test" the viability of proposed solutions and to create a new empirical basis for decision-making. The best known are experiments made by kommuns between 1950 and 1960 that looked at alternative ways of organizing the first nine years of comprehensive schooling. This approach to create a solid basis for system change decisions has been used in Sweden several times since then. In the 1980s, for example, the government invited the kommuns to experiment with different ways of organizing the three upper secondary school years, while at the beginning of the new millennium 79 out of 290 kommuns initiated experiments around different ways of allocating time for the various school subjects during the grundskola years. The local decision-makers have been, thus, faced with a continued pattern of responsibility for contributing to the national dialogue, while also facing the many political initiatives and decisions needed to be dealt with at the local level instead of at the national level.

As we have shown, during the last few decades the pattern of responsibility in Sweden has changed. However, parliament and the government are still in charge of an overarching education policy framework and perspectives that are solidly formalized in acts and guidelines. In addition, in Sweden the national organizations of teachers and school leaders have a good deal of influence on political decisions, and thus carry many of the important policy issues into a national conversation. The kommuns are in charge of articulating the details and carrying them out, but also contribute to the national framing of educational policy issues through their own national association. One reason for this is that the level of participation in the national stakeholder organizations is very high compared to many other countries, but also the long tradition of consultation by national authorities, which continues in spite of the radical decentralization, has kept an interest in educational policy processes (at least at the level of developing a consensus framework) at the national level very much alive

Recently there have been some shifts to accommodate this governance model. The tradition to prepare a political decision by putting a committee to work (even so if it includes a system change) is still in use. However, some processes have changed. For example, the committee consultation process is still very evident, but from the 1990s onward, committees have begun to work much faster (usually reporting in less than a year) and with more limited ambitions. They are less likely to produce broad consensual descriptions and analyses of the problems that the policy attacks, and often do not pay as much attention to the divergent perspectives of all political parties or interest organizations. The appointment of cochairs from different groups is less common, and they are usually headed by a politician or a government official. Thus, the working committee influence on broad political solutions has diminished somewhat.

Insights Into the Recent Political History of Sweden

To understand these shifts in the educational policy field in Sweden, it is important to know something about recent political history. From World War II through the mid-1970s, Sweden was relatively affluent and had a stable government led by Social Democrats. The election of a coalition of liberal and conservative parties initiated a conversation that ultimately led to the decentralization of educational functions as described earlier. This conversation that began during the interregnum of the liberals and conservatives was finalized by the Social Democrats once they were back in power. In other words, following the long-standing tradition of consensus policies, another major change that occurred in the 1990s was supported by all major parties. In the early 1990s, Sweden entered a period of economic crisis and a growing national debt. The Social Democrat government that won the 1994 elections chose a tough austerity course to cure the national economy, with the education sector being among the targeted areas. These dramatic budget cuts occurred during the first years of the new governance system in which kommuns and schools were required to take on many new decisions. The new system showed itself to be robust. Although the schools suffered, the cuts were taken care of and new solutions found that demonstrated kommuns were capable of producing good education with less money. The center-right government that has been in power since the mid 2000s (and that currently does not have a majority in parliament) has never questioned the overall efficiency of the decentralization.[5]

National and Local Responsibilities

Although almost everything that is of importance to the inner life of a school is controlled by the kommun and the local school itself, some few details are still controlled by the state. In Sweden the schools have to follow the same central *Läroplan* in which the overarching aims of the school system are described and they are also obliged to follow the same subject curricula (*kursplan*) that are presented by the government for the "grundskola" (covering students in the age group of 6–16) and by the National Agency for Education for the gymnasieskola (covering students in the age group of 17–19). They must use the same grading system. Today marks are given to students from their sixth school year (when the students are 13 years old). Schools are also obliged to use national tests in some of the school subjects in grades 3, 6, and 9 of the grund school system and in the late years in several subjects in the gymnasieskola. The national testing system has been in use since the 1960s, when it was implemented after a couple of decades of experimental work to be used by teachers for the calibration of student grades. The schools also prepared a quality review each year and presented it to the kommuns. The kommuns used these reports to compile a kommun school quality review during the first decade of the twenty-first century, but at the moment are no longer obligated to do so.

Minor changes in the distribution of responsibilities of the state and the kommuns constitute only one component of an array of recent adaptations regarding how policy work is done. Because most issues are dealt with at the kommun or the school level, there are more opportunities for actors other than the national politicians or the leaders of interest groups to get involved. Local teacher union representatives, school leaders, and local politicians now have the greatest influence over decisions that affect the inner life of the schools. As a consequence, there are fewer questions left for politicians, civil servants, and union people at the national level to discuss. Most of these possible policy issues are rooted in long-term political discussions and old compromises that are rarely challenged, such as the choice of school subjects, time allocated for learning in schools, or the age at which students start at the grundskola.

The few issues that remain for the national actors to debate have become popular topics to win support for party political platforms. One such issue is what perspective should be taken on the quality of the Swedish educational system compared to national educational systems in other countries. At the end of 1990s the largest newspaper in Sweden (*Dagens Nyheter*) began a campaign to show that Swedish school standards were low, both in terms of cognitive mastery of subjects and inculcation of social norms. Some national politicians joined in to accuse the Social Democrats of ignoring both pervasive quality and inequity issues in the national system. During the last decade many national discussions have been held about how to interpret the results of international comparative studies from the OECD and IEA. The media have eagerly grasped opportunities to add to the ongoing debates about educational quality. Some media and politicians have been accused of cherry-picking international test data to present a bleak perspective on the quality of Swedish schools in order to promote their own political purposes.

National politicians seem to be anxious to appear as if they are really doing something in educational policy. However, as a consequence of the processes described earlier, most initiatives at the national level are minor in scope because most authority rests with the kommun. For example, the current coalition has changed the grading system so that students receive their first marks in the sixth grade rather than the eighth as was done until recently, and the previous three-step scale for the grading process was transformed into a six-step system. This issue has been useful for the politicians in their efforts to gain access to the media, but have a minimal impact on the structures and processes of the educational system, especially in the classroom. A similarly touted change was the 2002 decision to divide the National Agency of Education into two agencies, one for quality control in the school system and one to support the kommuns in their improvement efforts. In 2008 the latter of these two agencies was closed and the school inspectorate was reopened as a new national agency. Although dramatic for the employees of these units (and hotly debated at the time), changes in the central bureaucracies have had limited impact on the larger system.

In spite of a sometimes un-Swedish sharp rhetoric, the main principles that drive the system appear to be continuity and consensus decision-making, irrespective of the level at which it occurs. Sweden's decision to join the EU in 1994 had a relatively limited impact on discussions educational policy issues in and insofar issues have emerged within the EU these are largely regarded as in harmony with policies that Sweden has worked for during many years. International policy trends have not provoked significant discussion about the need for Sweden to adjust to new norms.

Although national initiatives are smaller in scale, serve more limited aspirations today, and are driven by a desire for media attention, stable patterns continue to work when real educational policy issues arise. Decisions are prepared by work in committees. The minister of education less often consults the interest organizations during the policy initiation process, but the routines by which a working committee's texts are sent to those who will be impacted by the proposals are still firmly in place. Teacher unions, the kommuns, universities, and other organizations that may be affected by the changes have time to write down their

Table 3.1 Framework for analyzing state political culture: Sweden

Dimensions of political culture

Openness	Highly open—many groups are able to be involved at both the national and the local level
Decentralism	The system is highly decentralized since the 1990s, with some efforts by the national government to gain influence through changes in tests and inspections. However, the decentralized system has proven popular and is unlikely to change
Rationalism	The overall system is highly rational, within the decentralized structure. The national conversations ensure that key aspects of the educational system are similar across schools and regions
Egalitarianism/equity	Strong emphasis on egalitarianism across all parties for more than 50 years; deep commitment to creating opportunities for all students. The presence of independent schools and concentrations of immigrant students have increased conversations about equity, but have not challenged this as a fundamental value
Efficiency	Efficiency is not a key issue in rhetoric, but many decisions over the last 50 years have been motivated by efficiency (e.g., reduction of the number of kommuns and a reduction of the national civil service in education)
Quality	National testing as a means of assessing quality has been in effect since the 1960s. Quality is rhetorically discussed, but the main responsibility for quality lies with kommuns. The national government has made modest changes to tests and inspection systems to promote quality
Choice	Choice is present with the expansion of independent publicly funded schools, but is not a major focus of the political culture

views on the proposal, and the government is obligated to respect these views to a reasonable degree in their final proposals and decisions. The notion still persists that an educational policy enacted by one government should be acceptable to the next one whose political coalition may be quite different.

Summary

In Sweden, two notably radical system changes have occurred during the last 50 years, followed in both cases by years of stability. Stability does not, of course, mean an absence of any perceptible change. For example, there have been shifts in the actors who are involved in the policy process due to decentralization and changes in coalitions. The use of national research experts in educational matters has decreased somewhat, while the involvement of local professional associations has increased. However, the robust routines for consultations with different stakeholders in the final stage of decision preparations keep the openness in the political process intact.

As should be apparent, there has been limited impact of the New Public Management (NPM) calls for greater efficiency and accountability on the Swedish political culture (table 3.1). While the decision to decentralize seems to parallel similar decisions in other countries, it was not couched in terms of NPM management theory and efficiency, but in terms of democratic participation and ownership. The current center-right government uses the language of NPM more frequently than previous governments, but has made only limited efforts to make significant changes in the system. The tone has changed slightly, but not the policy process or major decisions.

Notes

1. "Kommun" will be used instead of the English expression "municipality," mainly to help the reader remember that the text deals with Swedish conditions. Swedish kommuns are geographic areas in which there may be more than one municipality and where taxes are collected and kept within the kommun. The kommun has its own local parliament and government, which reflects the political preferences of the inhabitants, who express themselves in elections directly to the kommun.
2. Upper secondary schools are sometimes housed in several buildings, but they are considered the same school.
3. The number of kommuns decreased from 2,500 in the late 1940s to 290 in 2007.

4. Before 1998 the Ministry of Health and Social Affairs was responsible for day-care and preschool programs. From 1998 the Ministry of Education was made responsible for these issues and a central Läroplan for the preschool activities of one- to five-year-olds was presented; decentralization of responsibility to the kommuns occurred as a consequence.
5. The Social Democrats were in power from 1994 to 2006 and maintained the national discourse in the educational policy arena. Government funding was increased, but included some prescriptions about how it should be used. However, the basic agreement that kommuns are in charge is intact.

4

Denmark: Bildung in a Competitive State?

Lejf Moos and Klaus Kasper Kofod

Introduction

Danish values are deeply influenced by the agrarian cooperative movement, which emphasized the need to establish democratically organized local self-help organizations. In education, this foundation was reflected in the emergence of a free school movement and the embrace of the ideas of an influential mid-nineteenth-century thinker who advocated freedom of choice for parents in educating their children.[1] In 1903, the comprehensive school model—the Folkeskole—was introduced as the locally controlled but nationally based model, with the freestanding school at its center.

The values of individual choice and localism were incorporated into post–World War II efforts to build a welfare system that would protect Denmark's citizens against external threats. The welfare state was built on the tradition of participatory democracy at the individual, local (municipal), and state levels. The Danish system that emerged was less centralized than that of many other countries, with strong local governance. This provided a foundation for the development of a modern, comprehensive educational system, which was also "owned" by municipalities, but that reflected the dominant values of "Bildung" that predominated in German and Scandinavian educational philosophy. The concept of Bildung is difficult to translate into English, but it encompasses an educational approach that promotes the formal and informal development of a person as a whole—mind, heart, selfhood, and identity—rather than focusing primarily on knowledge and skills.[2]

During the twentieth century, as Denmark made a gradual transition from a predominantly agricultural society to an industrial and service economy, the educational system also changed. The emphasis on freestanding schools shifted toward a nationally guided but municipally based system that provided comprehensive and (by the mid-1960s) untracked experiences for all children from seven through sixteen. Freestanding schools became less common than in the early decades of the twentieth century, but still represent an important component of Danish education in both rural and urban areas. Free schools are funded by the government and parents are still able to choose this alternative if they prefer to do so. Approximately 13 percent of children attend free schools (UndervisningMinisteriet, 2008).[3]

As Pedersen (2010) points out, the last few decades have seen the emergence of a new phase, in which Denmark—a very small country that is physically and culturally connected to the economies of Northern Europe—has been adjusting to the increasing presence of the integrative forces. Pederson describes the development in three phases:

1. 1864 until WW2 was a nation-building period. Denmark was defeated by Prussia and Austria in 1864 and quickly declined from a recognized European power to a very small and economically unimportant nation. At the same time the agricultural sector experienced a major economic crisis. The educational focus was on the need to educate next generations to build a new, national community.
2. From WW2 to 1990s was a democracy-building period. Politicians wanted to prevent another war by raising democrats in school. Therefore democratic participation became a pivotal value in schooling.
3. The present era: The state is competing for survival in the global competition and thus schools must make sure that children grow up to be skilled and willing workers.

The current challenge in Denmark is defined by two competing needs. On the one hand, it seeks to be an open and flexible participant in cooperation with transnational agencies like the World Trade Organization (WTO), the Organization for Economic Co-operation and Development (OECD), the International Monetary Fund (IMF), and the European Union (EU), while on the other hand Danes want to maintain their traditional and uniquely Danish values. These competing needs have created a tension between economic policies aimed at survival in the global marketplace and the need for a skilled workforce, and educational traditions and policies that developed over the last century.

The Folkeskole Act of 1993 completed the development of the comprehensive "a school for all" that was based in the combined traditions of local control and social democracy.[4] Shortly thereafter, however, in 2002, national tests and assessments were introduced, which inaugurated the period of adjustments between the traditional and global pressures. The tensions were clearly revealed in the Folkeskole Act of 2006, which had support from most political parties, and articulated the primary purpose of schooling as producing an excellent, talented workforce.[5] Participation in the international comparisons of the outcomes of schooling: PIRLS (Progress in International Reading Literacy Study), TIMMS (Trends in International Mathematics and Science Study), and PISA (Program for International Student Assessment) were important for this development. This act represented a departure from the focus on Bildung, and reduced local control by consolidating municipalities from 274 to 98. External observers noted that this represented a shift toward more centralized control over education, including evaluation and assessment of student learning (Shewbridge et al., 2011).

The values of previous eras are still prominent in a complex political and educational situation, but so are adjustments to changing global pressures. In the remainder of this chapter, we will highlight the emerging contradictions and dilemmas as they are reflected in the debates about values and culture in educational policymaking.

The Year 2001: "A Contract with the Danish People"

Every decade or so Denmark encounters parliamentary power shifts between proponents of a market-driven economy (center-right wing) and proponents of a mixed state-/market-driven economy (center-left wing). The parliamentary election in October of 2001 changed the balance of power in the parliament from a center-left to a center-right majority, and therefore a new government was formed with the liberals and the conservatives. The new government was supported in parliament by an agreement with the Danish People's Party (a conservative populist party that was not a formal member of the coalition.

The basis for the collaboration is the "Government Agreement," as is usual with coalition governments in Denmark. When more than one political party agrees to form a new government, they also agree on the main political issues for the election period, and this agreement was negotiated within the top circles of the government and with the Danish People's Party each time a new government was formed (in 2001, 2005, and 2007).[6] The agreements are detailed and are regarded by civil servants and government ministers as lists of compulsory tasks to be carried out during the election period. The former prime minister named it his "Contract with the Danish People: This is what you can expect to get from this Government." The contract often leaves little room for maneuvering or negotiating with parties outside the coalition parties, and also limited opportunity for influence by other stakeholders, whose input may be included as part of the coalition agreement. The general political discourse on the contract is that the government can only change this "contract with the Danish People" prior to an election, so the voters will know what they vote for and thus what they get after the election.

The government's coalition was solid over the first decade of the twenty-first century, and representatives from the other political parties often complained that there was little room for compromise when new legislation was initiated because the smallest details has been agreed upon earlier as part of the contract. The tradition of discussing and negotiating initiatives with stakeholders like the Teachers' Union has been sustained, but focuses mostly on how to implement legislation, rather than on its content. A former minister of education reported in our interview that rather than inviting consultation with other stakeholders, his priority lay in solidifying broad majorities in parliament when significant policy changes were being considered. As an example, he referred to the 2008 legislation on compulsory student plans for the Folkeskole. He knew that the Teachers' Union would oppose, so he did not invite them to preliminary discussions. He noted, however, that this was a departure from "normal practice."

"Bigger is Beautiful"

The emphasis on efficiency in local government is not new, but began in earnest in the 1980s. The main argument for decreasing the number of municipalities (mentioned earlier) was that local units needed to be bigger in order to be able to shoulder the responsibility for tasks that were decentralized from state to municipalities during the 1970s. In other words, consolidation recognized the significant role of municipalities, but also challenged local ownership by increasing the size of the units. Some tasks were also taken from the counties and given to the municipalities in the course of the restructuring of the municipal landscape (e.g., special needs institutions). This trend can be interpreted as a centralizing process within a fundamentally decentralized system. The effects on education and schools are still emerging.

As part of this shift, municipalities were given more explicit responsibility for the "output" of their schools. When international comparisons of the students' performance were conducted, it was discovered that the Danish students were poor readers and weak in math. These results started a debate on how to rectify that picture, from which a broad agreement among major stakeholders emerged. National testing was introduced with the endorsement from a broad majority in the parliament and among central stakeholders in the schooling system. According to several respondents, the Ministry of Finance became increasingly influential and began to participate in educational discussions, which contributed to a shift from developmental Bildung to a more output-centered policy in the educational area. This shift was framed as a necessary policy response to the weak results of the Danish schooling system on international tests.

The representatives of the "school owners," The National Association of Municipalities (NAM), have lost some of their influence on negotiating national policies over the past few years. Danish schools have traditionally been governed in a mix of national frameworks related to control and quality, and local steering in the municipalities, where decisions about finances, personnel, and the daily work of school are made. But the coalitions in power during the first decade of the twenty-first century concluded that even the larger municipalities (and thus the NAM) had been able to fulfill the expectation that they would ensure a quality of education and student outcomes that was adequate for the "knowledge society" and the competitive state. This argument was, again, based on PISA, TIMMS, PIRLS, and OECD reports. The logical conclusion was that national politicians should assume responsibility for the problem by producing detailed national learning goals, implementing mandatory student plans and local quality reports, and by introducing more indicators of educational performance, as recommended by the OECD (Shewbridge et al., 2011). The previously mentioned former minister of education summarized the results of this development in this way: "We have got a culture of evaluation and with that a culture of knowledge and of leadership." This has meant that the influence of individual schools and the school owners has been reduced, while the influence of the Ministry of Education has increased—another indicator of some centralization inside a still largely decentralized system.

At the outset the Teachers' Union was not fond of these initiatives, and for the first time in Danish history stepped out of a political agreement in 2006. As in many countries, they were opposed to more testing because they regarded it as limiting teachers' professional judgment. Increasing recommendations and scrutiny from international bodies like the OECD have, however, created a sense of urgency in the government that they need to respond more rapidly than has traditionally been the routine in Danish policymaking processes. Urgency has replaced consensus, and the older image of a slow, decentralized, compromise-driven Danish political culture has shifted in ways that have, perhaps temporarily, constrained involvement of actors outside the parliamentary coalition in decisions that are taken at the national level.

An Overview of Political Culture

Overall, however, less has changed than might be expected from a decade of relatively stable government coalitions. Broad participation of all political parties and groups has characterized the Danish policy process for over a century. From parents and practitioners, whose experiences and practice influenced the political thinking, to the stakeholders, who are represented through associations and unions, all expect to have a voice. The balance of power is constantly shifting between parties, and no single party ever holds a majority of seats. Therefore, governments have had to negotiate with a broad range of parties with divergent views about the future of the country. While there have been some changes in the influence of particular groups, depending on the political preferences of the government in power, the basic assumption that conversations about policy will be open to all stakeholders remains unchallenged.

We have already indicated that this tradition may have been modified, with the tendency for the entire policy process, from initial formulation to the preparation of legislation, to occur in smaller and narrower forums. Political negotiations sometimes seem to occur outside of the parliament and public sphere. The tradition of stakeholder representative councils and boards serving in an advisory capacity has also diminished somewhat in favor of advisory committees staffed by civil servants. These represent, however, adjustments rather than fundamental changes in how people expect policy to be developed.

For the entire period of the modern state, the Danish educational system has been highly decentralized within a framework of national aims and frames. Parliament and government are in charge of overarching lines and perspectives in acts and guidelines while the municipalities—city councils and local authorities—are in charge of both second-order rules and regulations and maintenance of schools. School boards (each school had one with a parental majority), school leadership, and staff in collaboration with parents and students create school-based policies, maintaining some of the character of the earlier freestanding school tradition even within the municipal system. The principle of subsidiarity assumes that decisions should be made as to those who must comply with them as possible, and this has changed very little in spite of the modest centralization initiatives of the previous government.

Decentralization of financial and management decisions from the national to the local level has continued, with the main change limited to a somewhat more detailed curriculum standards, testing, and an annual public "quality report." But far from a radical change, the arguments for these shifts in educational policies have been articulated as adjustments to the long-term commitment to comprehensive and socially just

"Democratic Bildung." Reforms are justified on the grounds that they would make the existing system work better to accomplish the agreed-upon social and educational purposes. In recent years, the arguments have shifted to include language that reflects a new value: schools should produce students who are able and willing to enhance the country's position in the global marketplace. This logic is also seen in the demand for more accountability for basic skills outcomes. However, the long tradition of "free schools" has always meant that parents who disagree with the public value system have another option, which provides a brake on effort to introduce far-reaching changes that are not broadly popular. These principles of local and individual responsibility and choice again suggest that the broader saga of Danish education is evolving rather than changing in fundamental ways.

The center-left wing and center-liberal parties reinforce a commitment to minimizing social injustice, which underpins the hundred-year journey toward a comprehensive and nonstreamed Folkeskole; the establishment of kindergarten classes beginning in the second half of the nineteenth century; the support of leisure time institutions connected to schools; the "continuation school"[7] and "Folk High Schools," and the tuition-free university policy that is augmented with the "Danish State Education Grant and Loan Scheme" that funds most of the living expenses for university and other students continuing their education. It is too early to determine whether the emergence of the competitive state or economic exigencies will undermine the demand for equality, although concerns have been expressed by some parties. Public opinion does not, however, support a major debate about this core value.

Until recently, efficiency has not been a major component of educational policy discussions. Although it has been an element of the language used in political debates since 2001, it has not driven many educational decisions, and its influence on actual policies is very limited (other than the cost-cutting exercises that most countries have been faced with). One example is the persistence of public support for free schools, which are often small and "inefficient" in their use of public resources, but which are highly valued as part of the commitment to individual choice. Although they are now justified in using the language of parental choice and privatization arguments, there is no additional demand for oversight of free schools related to efficiency, cost, and outcomes.

Denmark continues to spend more on primary and secondary education than most OECD countries, although a liberal-conservative coalition government was in power for more than a decade. In Denmark, educational debates that are framed using New Public Management (NPM) language focus less on "value for money" than on whether students are staying in school and are prepared for further education. Nor has a tighter coupling of national, local, and school levels through increased testing and public reporting resulted in a rush to a "high stakes" system of evaluating students and schools that prevails in some other countries. In other words, efficiency arguments are in the air, but are less obvious in major policy initiatives.

There are some visible shifts in ongoing debates about quality in education that focus on the meaning of quality in a system whose traditional emphasis is on comprehensive "democratic Bildung" and social justice. Until a few years ago policymakers at the national level left the determination of quality in education to teachers, school leaders, and parents, who were expected to assess the innate quality of educational excellence consistent with the Bildung perspective. NPM-influenced versions of quality as a measureable outcome have now entered the national consciousness, and Bildung persists in a somewhat uncomfortable relationship with an increasing emphasis on preparing a demonstrably able workforce.

Table 4.1 Framework for analyzing state political culture: Denmark

Dimensions of political culture

Openness	Highly open—many groups are able to be involved at both the national and the local level
Decentralism	The system is highly decentralized to municipalities since the early twentieth century, with some efforts by the national government to gain influence through changes in tests and inspections. However, the decentralized system is popular and is unlikely to change
Rationalism	The overall system is rational, within the decentralized structure. The national conversations ensure that key aspects of the educational system are similar across schools and regions
Egalitarianism/ equity	Strong emphasis on minimizing social injustice across all major parties for more than 50 years; deep commitment to creating opportunities for all students. The presence of freestanding schools and concentrations of immigrant students have increased conversations about the meaning of equity, but have not challenged this fundamental value
Efficiency	Efficiency is a key issue in rhetoric, but policies that promote a more efficient educational system are not prominent
Quality	National testing as a means of assessing quality has been in effect since the 1990s. Quality is rhetorically discussed, but the main responsibility for quality lies with municipalities and individual schools
Choice	Choice is prominent, with the well-established freestanding schools and is part of a strongly held value

The language of the center-right coalition includes an emphasis on strengthening the link between educational outcome and financial remuneration, and on parent/consumer satisfaction. It is less clear that these concerns are reflected in the choices made by municipalities (which control most schools) and parents (who already have the option of choosing a school).

The Danish educational political culture has always been quite comfortable with long-standing internal contradictions in its espoused and implicit value system. On the one hand there is the vision of community and shared responsibility that focus on social democratic and egalitarian systems; on the other there is a coexisting vision of individual choice, which is reflected in a century-old commitment to freestanding schools. Where the social values obviously conflict, adjustments are made. For example, municipalities have, in some cases, distributed immigrant students across schools (rather than allow free choice) in order to reduce racial isolation. However, neither the value placed on parental choice nor the principle of a socially just education has been challenged by any major political party in modern times. Table 4.1 summarizes the underlying values using the framework developed in chapter one.

Notes

1. N. F. S. Grundtvig (1783–1872) was a Danish writer, theologian, poet, philosopher, historian, priest, and politician, who "invented" the ideal of the folk high school (folkehøjskole) in Denmark, an exam-free school originally meant for sons and daughters of peasants in order to augment their cultural upbringing. "Grundtvigianism," was a highly influential cultural movement in Denmark.
2. Bildung is often associated with the writings of the German philosopher Wilhelm von Humboldt.
3. Parents can establish a school of their own choice and get almost total state funding for it (85 percent of the expenditure) and they can also freely choose the school for their children, be it private or public.
4. The 1993 Consolidation Act No. 730 of June 21, 2000.
5. The Consolidation Act No. 170 of June 2, 2006.
6. In the most recent election (2011), the coalition returned to center-left. This chapter will not discuss educational policy in the new coalition, as it is just emerging.
7. Continuation schools are alternative comprehensive schools for at-risk students.

5

The Netherlands: The Clergyman and the Merchant Revisited

Boudewijn van Velzen

Introduction

In 1917 the Dutch constitution was amended to contain a clause that guarantees "freedom of education." This means, in practice, that all schools, whether municipal or private, have equal government funding. On a national level the Department of Education and Culture is required to support schools no matter what religious denomination or pedagogic philosophy they represent. Both public and private schools (Catholic, Protestant, Hindu, Muslim, Jewish, Montessori, and others) are supported provided they meet (sometimes very specific) requirements that are defined under the law. The result is that approximately 70 percent of Dutch children attend a school that operates under private auspices.

But the Dutch constitution also states in its first paragraph that education will be a subject of continuous concern and oversight for the government. This paragraph is interpreted to mean that the national government may intervene in schools if a curriculum or a school practice is thought to contradict national interests. The conflict between clergymen (who argued for the freedom of education clause in the nineteenth and early twentieth centuries) and merchants (those responsible for the long-standing tradition of promoting national economic vitality) was resolved in the constitutional change of 1917—but only temporarily. In practice the tension between freedom of education and the responsible oversight of the government has meant that every proposed educational policy undergoes extended consultations of all actors before any decision is made.[1] This consultation process ensures that "freedom of education" and "interests of the economic state" are balanced and satisfactory to virtually every interested group. In practice, this also means that policymaking in education is extremely slow and conservative in its aspirations.

A System in Structural Transition

In the late spring of 2010, the Dutch parliament voted the "Goed Onderwijs, Goed Bestuur" (Good Education, Good Governance) bill into law. The intent was to establish a system in which autonomous school boards, both public and private, were give full responsibility for all aspects of school life: curriculum, instruction, quality, student performance, teachers' hiring and firing, governance, accountability, and so on.[2] This legislative event marked the end of a long policy development process that began in 1979 when the Dutch Association of Catholic School Boards published a paper called "Building the Relatively Autonomous School" (NKSR, 1979). This apparently innocuous publication unleashed a long debate in which the focus was primarily on how to reduce the influence of the central government, leaving the schools free to manage themselves with fewer constraints. The demand of Catholic schools for more freedom from regulation spread to the Protestant and nonsectarian private schools and into the public sector. The idea that the government's role was to "steer at a distance" rather than to regulate the details of school operations was firmly embedded in policy conversations by the early 1990s (Louis, Teichler, & Bodstrom, 1991).

The plea for more autonomy by the public (nondenominational) school boards coincided with the government's early enchantment with New Public Management (NPM) in the 1980s. The consequence was not, however, more autonomous *schools* (in the sense of the Danish freestanding schools, described in chapter four). Instead, based on input from the denominational school boards associations, the result was more autonomy for *school boards*, which were encouraged to take a more entrepreneurial stance by managing their resources more wisely and efficiently, and growing their resources by recruiting more students. The law that was implemented in 2010 may be regarded as an adjustment in the longstanding discussions about the balance of freedom and state interests, with a long-term consequence of increasing the influence of a management level (the school board) that mediates between the individual school and the national legislature and Ministry of Education.

The public debates around school governance may, therefore, be characterized as both moralistic (what is good education, and whether good governance can create better, more responsive schools) and individualistic (education should become a marketplace where institutions compete for clients and aim for ongoing growth). The former argument appealed to the denominational schools and their political parties; the latter perspective reflected the growing influence of liberal thinking and the liberal party.[3]

Forty Years of Education Policies

Until the 1970s, the role of the Ministry of Education was to distribute funding with very clear regulations on expenditures. That changed dramatically when the Netherlands entered a period of strong economic growth and became aware of the need for a well-trained labor force. A white paper that outlined the future of the education system, written by an influential Social Democratic minister, set the ministry on an active and constructive role in shaping a new approach to education (Kemenade, 1975). Supported by the centrist Christian Democrats, the Conourennota outlined an approach to boosting the overall quality of education while improving access to education for all and increasing equity for students from low socioeconomic backgrounds (Leune, 1999). For 20 years, a variety of mandatory national reforms were initiated by parliament: kindergarten and primary education were integrated into one system of eight years of primary education; education was made compulsory till the age of 16 (later raised to 18); experiments with changes in the highly selective secondary education schools were made.[4] All of these changes were structural, and were regarded as consistent with the government's obligation to organize schools in the national interest. The government was, however, prohibited by the constitution with reform initiatives that affected the interior life of the school, particularly curriculum and pedagogy.

Parallel to these reforms the department was looking for a helping hand to convince the nonpublic schools to accept the need to change content and instruction. They found their lever in the funding of a well-defined "support system," composed of quasi-autonomous nongovernmental institutions that developed and delivered curricula, teacher and school leader training, tests and testing services, and tailored consultancy to both private and public schools and school boards.[5] This support system was formalized by a law that was adopted in 1986 (WOV—"Wet op de Onderwijsverzorging" or Law on Educational Support) and adjusted in 1997 (Wet Subsidiering Onderwijsondersteunende Activiteiten). The support system was intended to provide inducements for the private schools to engage with the national reform agenda without forcing them to do so, and capacity building in the form of professional development. An interesting feature of both laws is that they included a set termination date—almost as if another shift in the government's role in the education system was predictable. The 1997 adjustment indicated such a shift: before then the government was funding specific *institutions* and after 1997 it subsidized *activities*. As a consequence other agencies could also receive funding to support government policies. For the organizations that were part of this support system (operating both on local and national levels) it meant a gradual process of adaptation to a real market in which they had to compete with outsiders. As a consequence, private for-profit consulting agencies such as KPMG and Ernst & Young entered the market; staff of the local or national organizations left to start competing firms; and school boards learned how to negotiate the best possible deal.

A driving force behind the emerging strategies for reshaping the educational system was the spread of the NPM paradigm in Dutch governmental policies. The need for a new approach to the role and function of the national government in education was obvious—at the one hand the successfully implemented "education for all" strategies made the open-ended funding of schools a major risk for the nations' budget; on the other hand, the economic crisis of the 1980s made the government look for another approach of managing public services. NPM, compared to other public management theories, is more oriented toward outcomes and efficiency through better management of public budget—and was therefore consistent with the preferences of the "merchants." Efficiency is achieved, in theory, by applying private-sector economic and leadership models to organizations in the public sector. NPM addresses beneficiaries of public services much like customers, and conversely citizens as shareholders. The main hypothesis in the NPM-reform waves in the Netherlands was that a market orientation in the public sector would lead to greater cost efficiency for governments, without having negative side effects on other objectives and considerations. At the same time, in education it was consistent with the political reality of a firm opposition to more direct influence by the government by the religious school sectors (the "clergy"), which made it a reasonable compromise.

A critical event in the process toward more autonomous school boards was the so-called Schevenings Agreement in 1993, when the government, the school boards, the unions, and the parents' associations created a covenant whose principle was decentralization and deconcentration. Different parties viewed it differently—some saw it as moving toward a market system, others emphasized the importance of democratic participation at lower levels, while still others were supportive of stronger school boards and local governance mechanisms for the education sector.

But based on this loose covenant, an overhaul of the system has been gradually implemented.

The Current State of the System

Although engaged in continuous compromise, the Dutch (relatively) autonomous schools and the government need each other desperately in order to make the educational sector work. The government has a constitutional obligation to monitor the quality of education but cannot intervene without the agreements with relevant partners in the education arena: school boards, unions, parents, and students. But these partners are dependent on the regulatory powers and funding from the government. Introduction of the NPM paradigm generated major changes in the relationships of these partners. These relationships, as they exist currently, can be visually portrayed using an adaptation of the model developed by McKevitt (1998) (figure 5.1).

One of the major consequences of the shift toward NPM in the Netherlands was unanticipated at the time of the 1993 Schevenings Agreement. Until the beginning of the twenty-first century, the principle of semiautonomous schools meant that each school (through the principal) had a more or less direct link with the government. Many schools were governed by a small autonomous board, composed of lay unpaid volunteers who provided governance oversight, but did not involve themselves with day-to-day issues in the school. With the delegation of more management responsibility to schools, a large number of schools in the Netherlands became quite vulnerable: they were simply too small to

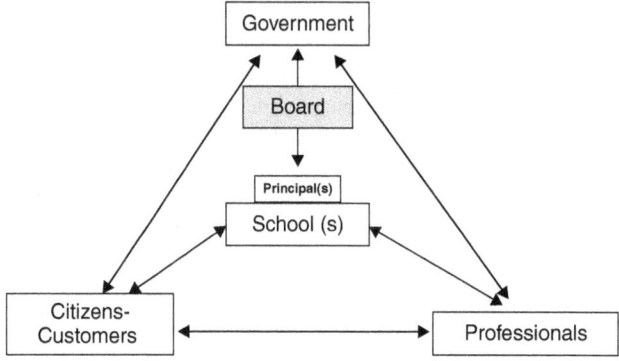

Figure 5.1 Relationship between partners in the education arena.

develop the capacities for strong financial and personnel management that the new model assumed.

The consequence was that schools increasingly banded together to form alignments with a larger role for a more professionalized intermediary board, which was expected to engage in financial and other management support. As a side role of increasing board size, they also took on the role of negotiating with the government and buffering schools' direct interventions. The government deals directly with the board; principals no longer have direct access to the government. Larger boards also took on additional management responsibilities, particularly in supervising principals.

In this regard, it is now the school board policies that define the degree of autonomy for the school, which has become highly variable between boards. In a study on the status of school autonomy in Europe, the European Union reports that in many instances it is not possible to determine the autonomy of a Dutch school since the school's competent authority (e.g., the board) can delegate responsibilities. Since this is not standardized by either law or custom, it is therefore not possible to determine which tasks are delegated or not (Eurydice, 2007a).

Another consequence is a major shift in the role of the principal. Particularly in primary schools, but also in smaller secondary schools, the position of the principal in his or her team was largely that of *primus inter pares* (first among equals), or a "head teacher." In the new management model characterized by strong school boards, the principal became the intermediary between the board and other school professionals.

As the influence and position of school boards has grown, they have become more actively involved in school policies, and therefore in (micro-) politics both inside the organization but also locally and regionally. This is most apparent when social, health, and education sector interests collide. Both sectors are given responsibility for the well-being of each child. The ensuing complicated negotiation procedures have, however, been driven by the reality of the students in systems that are not yet aligned, and that are simultaneously competing for shrinking national funding.

That brings us to the citizens—who also are clients in the new NPM model. As a client, they are encouraged to demand the best possible services from their schools; as citizens they have been promised lower taxes due to the introduction of NPM and its efficiency-driven strategies. Of course this creates tensions between them and educational professionals, who understand that good cooperation with parents is extremely beneficial for students but do not want to be bossed around by parents or other community members who act as consumers. Boards are not always in a position to protect teachers in this regard. Unlike intermediary units in other countries (the United States, the United Kingdom, and Canada), the boards are voluntary associations that are not necessarily based on a geographical area or municipality. As schools banded together (or were recruited by boards), they were sometimes scattered across a wide area, with no geographic cohesion or citizen base.

The increasing role of school boards has also affected the teaching professionals' experience directly. In the past, teacher salaries and working conditions were part of the government's role in providing oversight to the educational system to ensure quality. Now these responsibilities have been delegated to the school boards, and they no longer can rely on the government (or their national unions) to ensure that their income and working conditions will be similar to a school located in the same region. They have to deal with their board, and collective bargaining has, to a large extent, become a more or less decentralized responsibility. Bronneman-Helmers (2011), in an analysis of Dutch educational policies between 1990 and 2010, concluded that teachers have lost authority regardless of claims that they are the key to school performance.

The introduction of NPM in the education system forced both the government and the schools to redefine the arenas where consultations between the government and educational organizations took place. The government no longer wants to talk with representatives of each denominational group, but prefers to deal with larger bodies that represent the interests of all schools for primary, secondary, vocational, and tertiary education. For each of these sectors a new national council, which has as its major function the negotiating of conditions for implementation of national policies, was initiated (and funded). These associations quite naturally are dominated by the larger school boards—a given that forced many schools to give up their independence and merge with other schools into organizations under one board.

The Political Culture

Looking at the broader picture of the way the Dutch do things in education politics is fundamentally grounded in the constitution and its emphasis on freedom of choice, which is, in turn, premised on the importance of the freedom of parents to choose a religious or nonreligious education for their child. Choice is not seriously contested by any group or political party; it remains the one feature of the educational system on which there is genuine consensus rather than the compromises that are reached in order to foster improvements and change that will satisfy both the clergy and the merchants.

The most important underlying practice, in education as in other social spheres, is commonly known as the "polder model"—or the willingness to put aside differences to reach a conclusion that is not consensus, but a workable compromise.[6] The term "polder model" emerged in the 1980s to describe the manner of reaching an agreement about economic policies, but quickly became adopted to describe a particularly Dutch way of reaching a decision in spite of enduring differences. While there are shifts over time in who is included in consultation (e.g., student organizations have recently been included in regular consultations about policies affecting education and youth), the underlying assumption is that representation occurs through association in corporate groups that are recognized partners.

While there have been some shifts in the locus of power over educational policy, there has long been recognition that the central government can act only when representatives of local schools (now school boards) are willing to engage with policies. The notion of "freedom of education" has always been interpreted to mean that parents can choose the school that they prefer for their child, but it also means that local schools are largely free to educate children as they see fit, in line with parental preferences. The government can mandate certain structures and some financial principles, but their policies are "soft"—meaning that they rely on agreement and inducements to effect change. The government has limited direct influence over any given school; they must work through the boards and through consensus building around new initiatives. "Virtually no policy has been formulated over last 20 years covering the entire education system and educational context. Government policy in these areas is effectively the sum of the policy pursued in relation to the individual sectors" (Bronneman-Helmers, 2011, p. 444). One consequence of decentralism and openness is that the process of decision-making in education is extremely slow—but also limited in the ability to set a long-term agenda. Government coalitions change frequently, and the polder model means that big visions for change cannot be achieved. One example is the stated commitment by all governments for over 30 years to increased equality of opportunity couples with a recognized inability to create policies that make a big difference for the typical underprivileged student. The association between parental social status and measures of student achievement revealed by international tests like PISA and TIMMS is relatively high (OECD, 2005, 2010b). Public concern over segregation (Islamic schools that are exclusively chosen by immigrant families from Turkey and Morocco) is accompanied by "we can't do anything about it." This concern about, but willingness to live with, ambiguous tensions that cannot be fully resolved exemplifies some of the contradictions that occur as a result of the "polder model" form of consensus building.

An emphasis on efficiency is great and predates the embedding of the NPM philosophy into all parties. The Dutch pride themselves on the fact that their system of education is not very costly, but produces "good results" both in public opinion and on international tests. The inefficiencies in the system that accrue from having a system of parental choice and many autonomous schools are moderated by the kind of structural constraints that are legally allowed (requiring schools to be of a certain size in order to be founded and remain open). As a consequence, the competition between schools for students, although low key, was present well before NPM.

Key actors, in addition to the minister and state secretary of education, are largely corporate groups. As noted, these shift over time: the earlier "umbrella organizations" that represented different denominations have been replaced by the councils for primary, secondary, vocational, and tertiary education. Unions remain strong, but tend to partner with the representatives of education employers to maximize their influence. Parent associations have influence largely through the other groups, but can be very important behind the scenes. The major point is that there is no single center of power; rather, there are many actors who must be consulted at many levels.

In a system like the Dutch, it is difficult for the government to have a large direct influence on quality. The inspectorate, a quasi-autonomous agency responsible for school quality, has shifted its role on several occasions over the last 50 years, but is the primary lever for ensuring oversight beyond the responsibilities of the school board. However, its influence is only one of many, and efforts to promote quality through testing have not created significant changes because the tests are not high stakes for schools, but only for students.

In sum, a recent parliamentary inquiry into the effects of Dutch educational policies over the last several decades concluded (quite reasonably) that little had been attempted and possibly less accomplished (CommissieParlementairOnderzoekOnderwijsvernieuwingen, 2008). This self-reflective criticism was an acknowledgment that the Dutch way of creating educational policies constrains an active powerful role for the government and provides many actors in the system with the tools to create their own distinctive futures. Still, the system works: quality is generally high, most schools function reasonably well, and parents are generally very supportive of their children's schools. Compromise rather than consensus has worked reasonably well, and there are few who would argue that major changes are needed: the system may not be perfect, but it is "good enough."

From the governments point of view, the success of the new system that gives a legal framework to the slow evolution of a school board dominated system of coordination is mainly that the budget is in complete control. The downside is that each national ambition will have to be negotiated with the councils, the school boards, and the unions. The system, as always, is in a slow transition, in which all parties are involved in negotiating the meaning of their roles.

Table 5.1   Framework for analyzing state political cultures: The Netherlands

Dimensions of political culture	
Openness	Very open. Everyone expects consultation (Polder model/overleg traditions). Consultation is formalized, with recognized interest groups funded by the government to act as partners. Limited openness to individual lobbying outside of the "corporatist" structure
Decentralism	Highly decentralized; currently school boards hire and fire, set many employment conditions (within national employment policies), and are responsible for all resource allocation except physical plants. School boards are autonomous (public school boards must be separate from municipal government) and in most cases are appointed (not elected).
Rationalism	Limited—largely incremental. There is an evolutionary but largely unplanned shift toward more decentralization of formal authority. Most reforms are system adjustments designed to modify identified problems with the formal structure
Egalitarianism/ equity	Egalitarian rhetoric is prevalent but limited by the "freedom of education" clause
Efficiency	Very high. Emphasis on limiting financial investments in education is supported by good performance of Dutch students on international examinations. Emphasis on mergers over the last 25 years was motivated by efficiency more than quality
Actors/influence	Corporate representation through interest groups. Interest groups form fluid coalitions to influence policies. There is no single center of influence
Quality	Rhetorical emphasis on quality; limited government efforts to stimulate quality through expansions in the required testing system and shifts in the role of inspection to place more emphasis on school inspection. The only formal definition of quality indicators is in the law governing the inspectorate, which identified 9 dimensions on which schools (and the system) are to be inspected. The inspectorate elaborated these dimensions into a quality grid of 10 aspects and 85 indicators
Choice	Choice is a key feature of policy, embedded in the constitution. There are tensions between choice, efficiency, and equity, which are acknowledged but viewed as dilemmas that always will be part of the system. Local initiatives will have to find ways to deal with these dilemmas

To give one example, in the spring of 2011 the minister of education (Marja van Bijsterveld) announced in parliament that she planned to reduce vacations for school staff by one week, and to make staff use this week for development work. In unison, school boards and unions told her that this was not her prerogative any longer—it was the school boards' responsibility to discuss this kind of measures with the unions nationally and also a variety of implementation strategies locally if they concluded that it was both relevant and doable to do so. But we also see the reverse: carefully drafted and consulted plans to boost the quality of teachers have great support from professionals and boards alike.

The school boards are, in turn, still struggling to understand the full consequences of their autonomy. Quality control and good education are now linked with good governance, and it will be the board that has to define what the benchmark is for "good" (Ten Have, Hiemstra, & van-Velzen, 2009). That makes them the owners of the dilemmas we have indicated in the overview at the beginning of this chapter. But the school boards are now facing problems arising from being entrepreneurs in the public sector. Growth through consolidation and competition among school boards is an obvious option, but the debate on this dimension of the NPM paradigm is now in full force. There is some evidence that this paradigm may lead to an ethical crisis in the profession, and recent incidents in which school board chairmen granted themselves salaries higher than a Dutch prime minister have added to the current controversies. But these incidents and the ongoing controversies point to a long-standing tradition in the educational sector: the moral standard in Dutch education has always encouraged more students to learn more for less money, while still preserving freedom of choice (Biemans, 2010). In terms of Elazar's definition (see chapters one and eight) the highly individualistic tendencies in Dutch politics seem to be moderated to a large extent by its moralistic roots (table 5.1).

Notes

1. The consultative process was streamlined in the 1960s through the 1980s by the presence of "umbrella organizations" that represented the interests of particular sectors—public, Catholic, Protestant, and nonreligious private schools. Umbrella organizations brought the interests of the schools in their group into ongoing regular consultations with the ministry. The influence of these groups has declined, for reasons that will become apparent in this chapter.
2. The only exception is the physical school building where the local community still plays a decisive role.

3. What has been somewhat lost in this conversation of the last two decades of the twentieth century, however, is the voice of the Social Democrats, who had long sought to create a more egalitarian and comprehensive system, and to undo the tracking system that fed students, at the age of 11, into a variety of university preparatory levels or several vocational tracks. However, not all Dutch Social Democrats have been fully supportive of a comprehensive and nontracked system for all students because they too support the constitutional provision for "freedom of education."
4. These were never fully implemented due to lack of popular support.
5. For secondary schools, the support system was organized into sectors, reflecting the strong political influence of the private Catholic and Protestant school associations. For primary schools, the system was located in the municipalities and was nonsectarian.
6. A popular explanation of both the term and the reason this decision-making style works so well in the Netherlands is the unique situation created by the fact that a large part of the country consists of polders (bodies of land surrounded by dikes) below sea level. Ever since the Middle Ages, competing or even warring cities in the same polder were forced to set aside their differences to maintain the polder dikes.

6

Flanders (Belgium): Regulated Anarchy in Catholic and Public Education

Geert Devos

Introduction

The kingdom of Belgium is divided into three distinct regions, which, since the early 1970s, have increasing autonomy. Although there is a king, a Belgian prime minister, and a national parliament, Flanders has its own parliament, an official language (Dutch), and full responsibility for health, education, and social welfare policies for its population of six million.[1] Because there is no national education system in Belgium (the Belgian federal authority is only responsible for three educational issues: the start and end of compulsory education, minimum conditions for obtaining a diploma, and education staff pensions), this book has chosen to treat Flanders as if it were a distinct country. The authority responsible for education in Flanders is the Flemish Community.

Throughout its history Flanders has been continuously occupied by larger European powers (France, Spain, Germany, and others), and during the early twentieth century it was dominated by the French-speaking elite from the Southern region until after World War II. Not surprisingly, the Flemish still have a mixed attitude toward the natural capital of Brussels, where Flemings are a residential minority and where their distinctive concerns are subsumed in the multilingual conflicts that increasingly dominate Belgian political life. The history of the region has resulted in a tendency for Flemish citizens to distrust every kind of public authority, and to see the state as a source of potential oppression rather than a symbol of national pride. This suspicious attitude toward the state and public authority is reflected in an educational system headed by a government that has limited power in one of the most decentralized educational systems of Europe (Eurydice, 2007a).

Key Policy Events

With the founding of the kingdom of Belgium in 1830, freedom of education was recognized as a constitutional right. Nevertheless, this principle has been subject to many conflicts and so-called school wars. These conflicts are part of the cultural and political history of Belgium during the nineteenth and twentieth centuries with particularly critical disputes in 1850, 1879, and 1951. The key question in each of the conflicts was: Who is entitled to organize education? This century-long period of intense conflict ended with the "'School Pact" in November 1959. This agreement represents a milestone in Belgian educational history and has defined the basic principles of the education system since then.

The pact is twofold. First it guarantees the right for everyone to organize education and to establish institutions for this purpose. Schools that satisfy the governmental conditions are recognized and their staff is funded by the government in an equal way, independent of the public or private nature of the governing body. This governing body (or school board) is a key concept in Flemish education. Governing bodies enjoy considerable autonomy. They are entirely free in the choice of teaching methods and are allowed to base their education on a specific philosophy or religion. They can also determine their own curriculum and timetables as well as hire and fire staff. Second, the constitutional right of freedom of education guarantees parents the access to a school of their choice (public or private) within a reasonable distance from their home.

The School Pact of 1959 created a political balance between the representatives of the public and private (Catholic) schools, which is continuously tested. The governing bodies of the public and private (Catholic) schools in Flanders are organized in educational networks, which promote common interests and concerns.[2] Since the School Pact Flemish educational policy has been characterized by a constant search for areas of accord between these educational networks. This search for political consensus has resulted in a stable, almost static educational system, where fundamental change is rare.

In 1989, a major constitutional reform represented the final step that institutionalized the Belgian federal-state model. The Flemish and the French-speaking community gained almost complete autonomy in several matters, including education. Together with this constitutional reform the authority of the national minister of education also became even more limited. Prior to 1989 the minister exercised limited political authority over all schools and was the governing authority for all the public schools. With the final decentralization of authority to the regions, the minister of education no longer has this governing power. Instead, a new governing agency was created, the Autonomous Council of the Education Community. In other words, all schools achieved a similar level of autonomy with respect to the national Ministry of Education.

Another result of the 1989 state reform and its educational autonomy provisions occurred in the Flemish school quality review system and illustrates the continuing efforts to create compromise between government policies and the powerful Catholic educational network. The Flemish minister of education reached a consensus about the reform of the quality review system among the representatives of the different networks after intense consultations. In 1991, the government developed attainment targets for primary and secondary education, which identified the minimum goals for all schools in the Flemish region. There are both subject-related and cross-curricular attainment targets that pertain to knowledge, insight, attitudes, and skills. Every school governing body is obligated to address the attainment targets in the curriculum for their schools. However, the way in which the schools attain these targets remains entirely the province of the governing bodies. In addition, schools can decide to establish higher standards than those stipulated by the government. The Flemish educational inspectorate was given the task of assessing the implementation of the attainment targets through school audits. Instead of supervising individual teachers, as was the case previously, the inspectorate audits schools to monitor whether the curriculum reflected the established targets.

The School Pact of 1959 guaranteed equal funding for the staff of Catholic schools, but until 2007 operating costs remained the responsibility of the educational network. Public schools thus received more operating funds than Catholic schools. In 2007, funding for operational costs was also equalized between all schools. The main principle underlying this reform is that each pupil carries a similar lump sum "funding backpack" to the school of his or her choice. In addition, schools (regardless of denomination) that enroll low-income students receive additional funds.

Key Actors

The history of Flemish education points to two main actors: the Flemish government, which sets out the general legal framework and the minimal conditions for education and funding, and the powerful Catholic educational network, which represents 60 percent of the students in primary education and 75 percent in secondary education. Due to the School Pact and the subsequent interpretations of the constitutional freedom of education clause—and also because of its size—no decision in Flemish education that is perceived to be fundamentally against the will of the Catholic educational network can be enacted. This network is represented by an "umbrella agency" (VSKO). The power of the president of VSKO is very considerable, although dependent on the goodwill of the Catholic governing bodies that constitute the network that the VSKO represents (Devos, 1995). Catholic dioceses and congregations have organized many different legal governing bodies, all of which are represented by the VSKO. However, the VSKO itself is not a governing body, but only a representative of governing bodies. Therefore, the VSKO must continuously consult numerous other actors in order to maintain their support.

Other important actors in Flemish education policy are the umbrella organizations representing the two public educational networks, the network of the Flemish community, GO, and the network of the local public authorities (OVSG for the municipalities and POV for the provinces). As these networks are not as large as the Catholic educational network, their influence is accordingly less. Moreover, all policy actors we interviewed for this study confirmed the important role that the president of the Catholic educational network plays in Flemish educational policy. This role is important not only because of the structural importance of Catholic education, but also because of the charismatic personality of the president.

The other key actor in Flemish educational policy is the government, represented by the minister of education, his or her cabinet, and the civil service in the ministry. In Flanders, all ministers have a personal cabinet, which traditionally has a lot of political influence. This cabinet is typically a collection of temporarily appointed expert advisors, selected by the minister. The head of the cabinet has a very powerful position but, like the minister, disappears from the political stage when the minister is no longer in office. The cabinet reflects the typical balance of power arrangements described earlier, with the presence of an expert from the Catholic educational network as a key member in the current Social Democratic minister's cabinet. All other cabinet members are Social Democrats, traditionally supporters of the public schools. The role of the Catholic expert is to guarantee that no policy decisions that radically go against the will of Catholic education are prepared. This does not mean that the Catholic network has to agree to everything the minister decides, but they are able to ensure that measures that go against the Catholic interests do not enter active policy discussions.

The civil service in the ministry has a more permanent role than the minister's cabinet, and is becoming increasingly influential. Until the

1990s, the civil service had limited influence on policy development, but in the last 20 years ministers have decreased the role and the size of the politically appointed cabinet, and have increasingly involved the civil service. Many new civil servants were attracted or promoted, and administrative systems were modernized. Some informants even suggested that in the last decade the civil service staff has become the master of the policy development process, with a revolving cast of ministers consigned to executing the policies that the civil service prepared during the previous year. Others saw a shift in the authority structure within the civil service, with a clearer public administration performance appraisal system reducing the independence of civil servants in middle management positions. In either case, there is general agreement that the more prominent role of the administration is paralleled by a policy that is more based on research and objective data, which are often analyzed and summarized by the civil service rather than politically appointed experts.

The teacher unions are also key players in Flemish education. Although their importance has been reduced during the last decade, they remain dominant in all personnel-related policy issues. Union representatives have indicated that increased data-driven policymaking and the importance of national and international scientific research in policy decisions has made them more dependent on the expertise of the ministry's civil service.

According to representatives of education stakeholders, within the subtle power shifts described earlier an important voice is being lost. Many of them mentioned that it has become more difficult to mobilize members of various interest groups for collective action in the educational policy arena. They claim these members are reluctant to protest government proposals because they fear that participation of their followers will be limited. In conjunction with the agreement about the role of the major network leaders, and a more active civil service, there is a sense among different stakeholders that participatory democratic voice in education may be diminishing. This may be, perhaps, a consequence of a period of stability since the ending of the "school wars" and increasing trust that each group's interests will be protected.

Political Culture in Action

The language of New Public Management (NPM) has entered educational policy discussions in Flemish education, but in ways that reflect its typical political culture. Two key components of output management and quality control that have evolved recently in Flanders are the policy of school inspection and the introduction of student tests developed by the government.

A New Role for the Inspectorate

As noted earlier, the inspectorate is responsible for school audits and evaluates if schools implement the attainment targets. Until recently the inspection audits were limited and did not include any recommendations in case of a negative evaluation. Since 2007 the inspectorate can also require a school to consult a pedagogical support agency in case of a negative audit.

The opinion of our interviewees about the new inspectorate role varies depending on their sector affiliation. Catholic representatives claim that the inspectorate goes too far in its recommendations and should limit itself to the control of the attainment targets. Although the inspectorate is not permitted to make recommendations about the way the schools want to attain the minimum goals, representatives of the Catholic school sector claim that they often do, and that this violates the freedom of education laws. Non-Catholic representatives see this differently, and support the expanded role of the inspectorate. School audits not only result in a positive or negative evaluation, but also in useful recommendations. Moreover, they suggest that the inspectorate should develop clearer policies about sanctions for weak schools. The argument is that there are very few highly negative school evaluations, and that having a credible sanctioning authority that respects school autonomy except under specific conditions would be preferable over adding regulations to achieve the same effect.

This different view is typical for Flemish education and reflects the permanent tension between a government that tries to make its mark on the educational field by implementing an effective quality control system, and the Catholic educational network that holds on to its autonomy in the provision of education. This illustrates the apparently permanent struggle between more systemic policy levers (mandates and structural reform) supported by the government and public-sector schools, and bottom-up policy levers (capacity and inducement policy) promoted by the Catholic educational network.

Government-Sponsored Student Tests

The second key component in the quality control system that has changed recently is the introduction of governmental student tests. In recent years, Flemish government has developed two kinds of student tests: "probing tests" to monitor if Flemish schools attain the minimum goals for a specific subject and the so-called parallel tests that schools can use on a voluntary basis to check if their students meet the attainment targets. The parallel tests result in a school feedback report that compares the individual school result with the average test result of other Flemish schools that have also voluntarily taken the tests. Neither of these tests is mandatory, and the results of both, at the school level, are not made public. Officially, the "parallel tests" are meant to stimulate internal quality control and school self-evaluation. Again, opinions on the use of these tests differ.

The Catholic educational network argues that the inspectorate uses tests in an illegitimate way. Although the parallel tests are not mandatory, schools are supposed to inform the inspectorate of the test results in case they have used the tests. Therefore, according to Catholic representatives many schools use the tests to make a positive impression on the inspectorate in case of a school audit. Catholic schools increasingly use the government's parallel tests instead of the well-established tests developed by the Catholic network. Representatives outside the Catholic network have a different opinion. They consider the governmental parallel tests as important components in the improvement of educational quality and the internal quality control of schools. Public educational networks see these tests as an additional instrument for the pedagogical improvement of their own schools. There is consensus on one aspect of government testing, however: all interviewees rejected the public release of test results, and agreed that this would lead to increased stigmatization of schools with many low-income students. In addition, they saw no benefits of public ranking of schools for improving the quality of education in general.

In this analysis of recent policy issues on quality control and output management we notice that Flemish education is characterized more and more by elements of NPM. However, the strength of the Catholic educational network has resisted fundamental changes in governmental authority, which does not permit the development of a comprehensive system that links targets and accountability. Freedom of education remains guaranteed. The struggle between the governmental authority and the Catholic educational network striving for school autonomy continues.

Equal Opportunity Policy

One of the major educational issues of the past decade is the equal opportunity policy. The repeated success in the 1990s of the extreme right-wing party, Vlaams Blok, which raised issues of immigration and security, led to an increased attention to immigrant students and low-income students in general. In 2000, the Liberal minister of education launched an equal opportunity policy based on two components: creating a more equal distribution of low-income students among schools, and providing inducements for additional educational support for low-income students. His successor, a Social Democrat, supported and continued this policy initiative, and provided additional justification based on the PISA results of 2003, which indicated that Flemish education had one of the highest average scores in the OECD, but the largest disparity in achievement between students from different social sectors. This finding was affirmed in PISA 2009 (OECD, 2009).

With the support of the president of the Catholic education network, the Flemish minister invested substantially in the equal opportunity policy. Characteristically, however, freedom of education was not restricted. Therefore, the equal opportunity policy was driven by incentives rather than requirements. This allowed the decentralized school governing bodies to avoid the admission of low-income students if they wished to. By general agreement the result of a decade of equal opportunity policy is that additional attention is paid to the guidance and support of low-income students, which is an important achievement. However, the policy's aspiration to achieve a more equal distribution of low-income students among schools has failed, and social segregation between schools has even increased. Schools and governing bodies continue to create public profiles that hint at their exclusivity. Inequality remains a structural characteristic of Flemish education.

Summary

Educational policy in Flanders is characterized by a government with limited power searching for a balance between the interests of the Catholic and public educational networks. Policy is the result of many consultations and negotiations among the government, the educational networks, and the unions. The three fundamental elements of the educational policy culture in Flanders are a commitment to philosophical and religious pluralism, minimal government control over schools, and parental choice. These add up, on paper, to an approach that is consistent with many of the tenets of NPM, but is premised on a deeply rooted market mechanism that preceded the development of the NPM "movement" and the increased influence of transnational agencies. In other words, the alignment of Flemish policies with NPM is accidental rather than deliberate. Philosophical pluralism and free school choice are considered to be the cornerstones of educational quality in the Flemish system. Education in Flanders means more than instruction: it also includes the transmission of norms and values. This provides a foundation for the continuation

Table 6.1 Framework for analyzing state political culture: Flanders

Dimensions of political culture	
Openness	Public authority is weak, governments are distrusted and freedom of education is a cornerstone of the educational system. Networks and associations have easy access to government policy discussions; citizens have access to the largely autonomous local school governing bodies Unions have a strong voice in all personnel matters.
Decentralism	Highly decentralized as a result of the constitutional right of freedom of education. Concern for school autonomy is constant and government efforts to enhance their authority have failed
Rationalism	The Civil Service has become a source of data for decisions, and other actors have become more dependent on the administration to gain the necessary information to prepare policy issues. This evolution had no effect on the fundamental relations between the government and educational networks, which oppose comprehensive reforms
Egalitarianism/equity	Equal opportunity policy is an important educational issue, but social segregation has not diminished. Government initiatives to redistribute low-income students more equally among schools have failed, as governing bodies still can influence the enrollment of lower-class students. An incentive policy that provides more support for these students has had limited impact on the social profiles of many schools
Efficiency	Not on the policy agenda: the existence of Catholic and public educational networks and the freedom of education have led to an abundant supply of schools and programs in the same municipality. Attempts to reduce the number of schools and to rationalize the school supply have systematically failed Schools are funded according to the number of students they have. This mechanism prevents the system from too much bureaucratic inefficiency, but has not led to system efficiency
Quality	Freedom of education and school choice are viewed as the best mechanism for quality The competing networks stand for certain values, which, for the public, are also related to educational quality The government requires schools to guarantee that their students meet attainment targets. Quality is here defined as conformity with specific requirements to find out if the schools implement the attainment targets. The inspectorate conducts school audits to assess perceived system quality
Choice	The most dominant value in the educational policy culture is choice, which is associated with perceived system quality. Everyone has the right to organize education and all parents are guaranteed the choice between Catholic and public schools within a reasonable distance from their home

of distinct educational networks that provide their own education and autonomy for individual schools.

In line with international trends, the government has introduced standardized student tests. However, most stakeholders consider these tests to be too narrow to provide a useful indicator of educational quality. Moreover, there is general agreement that these test results should not be made public. The fear of school ranking, let alone the ranking of networks, is so deeply rooted in Flemish culture that the educational system will only allow a very controlled, limited use of standardized tests.

The dominance of philosophical pluralism and parental choice has considerable consequences for the inequality between schools. The system in general and the Flemish authority in particular are still struggling with these effects. Many reform efforts in the past and in the future can be related to attempts to reduce inequality in the educational system. This remains a precarious enterprise since reducing inequality means reforming substantially the fundamental elements of the educational culture in Flanders (table 6.1).

Notes

1. Flanders also has significant autonomous responsibilities for economic planning and development, and is permitted to establish some international treaties in its own name, but these topics will not be covered in this chapter. These independent responsibilities substantiate our decision to treat Flanders as if it were a country rather than a province in the context of educational policy cultures.
2. The Catholic governing bodies are organized in a single network. They are represented by a separate umbrella organization that represents their interests and that provides coordinating and educational services to the Catholic schools. The public schools are organized in two different networks. One network represents local public authorities as governing bodies like the municipalities and the provinces that act as governing bodies with a separate umbrella organization for the municipalities and an umbrella organization for the provinces. The other public educational network comprises so-called state schools, for which agency acting for the Flemish community is the governing body.

7

Austria's Balancing Act: Walking the Tightrope between Federalism and Centralization

Michael Schratz

Introduction

School systems in German-speaking countries are facing new challenges, which confront the old problem of balancing the center and periphery. Austria, Germany, and Switzerland are united by language, but their social fabrics are affected by very different historical circumstances. While Austria and Germany have their roots in formerly influential monarchies, Switzerland is rooted in a strong direct democracy where citizens should have full influence on the state. Each of the three countries has a framework of a federal parliamentary democratic republic, but their experiences in the late nineteenth and twentieth centuries have led to very different models for how these function in practice. The Swiss Federal Constitution limits federal influence in the formulation of domestic policy and emphasizes the roles of private enterprise and cantonal government. Germany is a parliamentary federal republic that consists of thirteen states (*Bundesländer*) and three city states, only seven of which existed before the end of World War II, and which were only fully joined in 1990. After the fall of the Austro-Hungarian Empire (1918) the Austrian Republic underwent several dramatically different political phases until it became what is now known as the Second Austrian Republic (1945–present).

Over the course of recent history, Austria changed from a large, powerful, multiethnic, centrally regulated empire to a small democratic country trying to construct a new identity within a Europe that is also changing rapidly. It has developed into a federal state of nine provinces with distinct historical identities, but is, at the same time, characterized by the cultural residue of centralized thinking in national policymaking. One person interviewed for this chapter referred to Austria as "the most centralized federal state—or the most federal centralized state." This chapter highlights the issues facing a country that has a very short history of democratic policymaking in education, making the transition from autocratic to more democratic system development.

A Bureaucratic Heritage

Empress Maria Theresa introduced compulsory schooling as early as 1774, and used the tools that were available to her to ensure that it happened: "The bureaucracy that Maria Theresa and Joseph II had created infiltrated every corner of Austrian life. Ostensibly the administration's mission was to extend uniformity throughout the empire, westernizing the non-German peoples and regimenting everyone to obey edicts of the crown" (Johnston, 1984, #150, 45). This penetration of a centralized regime has outlived two world wars and still influences educational policymaking in Austria.

In 1918, after World War I, the school system of the monarchy dominated a slow transition of school laws during the so-called First Republic. After the *Anschluss* in 1938, and the incorporation of Austria into the Third Reich, German law governed education. After 1945, when Austria was still occupied by the Allied forces, the school laws of the First Republic were briefly reintroduced, before another phase of transition of school laws began with full independence in 1955. It is not unreasonable to say that Austria has experienced a very short history of democratic policymaking during the so-called Second Republic.

A number of significant laws that reflect the policy culture in educational policymaking have been enacted since then. In 1962 a parliamentary decision was made that school laws should be treated like constitutional laws, requiring a two-third majority for laws to pass. This measure prevents sudden changes by minority governments while also safeguarding the interests of the political parties and the provinces. The result, of course, is that national changes of any magnitude come about slowly, if at all. The School Education Act of 1974 (SchUG: Schulunterrichtsgesetz) introduced the present law on teaching and learning in Austrian schools, which defines the core curriculum framework but also gives teachers, parents, and students power in decision-making at both classroom and school levels.

As a consequence of the turbulent history of the modern Austria, influenced by fierce Habsburg rulers, the subsequent strong antimonarchism, and the turmoil of two world wars with four allied forces leaving their imprints on a newly formed "neutral state," the present Austrian education system is, on the surface, highly bureaucratic, engaged in detailed regulation of inputs and operations, hierarchically organized, and minimally focused on outputs. The strong desire to avoid too much concentration of power at the center has resulted in provincial structures that parallel those at the national level. There are also many actors, numerous equivalent agencies with limited coordination in tasks and responsibilities. According to the OECD's (2010b, #151) indicators, this has resulted in Austria having one of the most expensive education systems in the world, while producing only average results on international tests.

The basic structures of the system are depicted in figure 7.1, which illustrates the complexity of policymaking; this is highly influenced by the tensions between federal decision-making and strong political influence of provincial administration. The complexity of policymaking in the thicket of the multilayered system with competing influences of the actors involved (see figure 7.1) suggests that policy decisions can neither solely be made on the national level nor on the provincial (*Länder*) level. This often leads to tensions or even confrontations between the ministry and key educational actors in the nine provinces. System changes are highly dependent on a balancing act between center and periphery with the actors involved at either end vying to gain more political weight. These power struggles are further complicated by the enduring tensions among those bureaucrats (at federal and state levels) who are endeavoring to maintain the existing system and innovators at both levels who are struggling toward reform. At least one observer has noted that these endemic tensions result in a historical propensity to adopt a "muddling-through" attitude:

> Accompanying ubiquitous bureaucracy was [...] a willingness to bend rules by overlooking infractions. Inefficiency in enforcing edicts became known as Schlamperei, meaning laxity or muddle. In the minds of many Austrians, Schlamperei symbolized the opposite of Prussian efficiency, offering at once a source of strength and weakness. (Johnston, 1984 #150, 22)
> When Victor Adler called Austria's government *"ein durch Schlamperei gemilderter Absolutismus"* (Absolutism mitigated by Schlamperei), he meant to praise the humanizing impact of anti-Prussian *laissez-vivre*. (Ibid., p. 23)

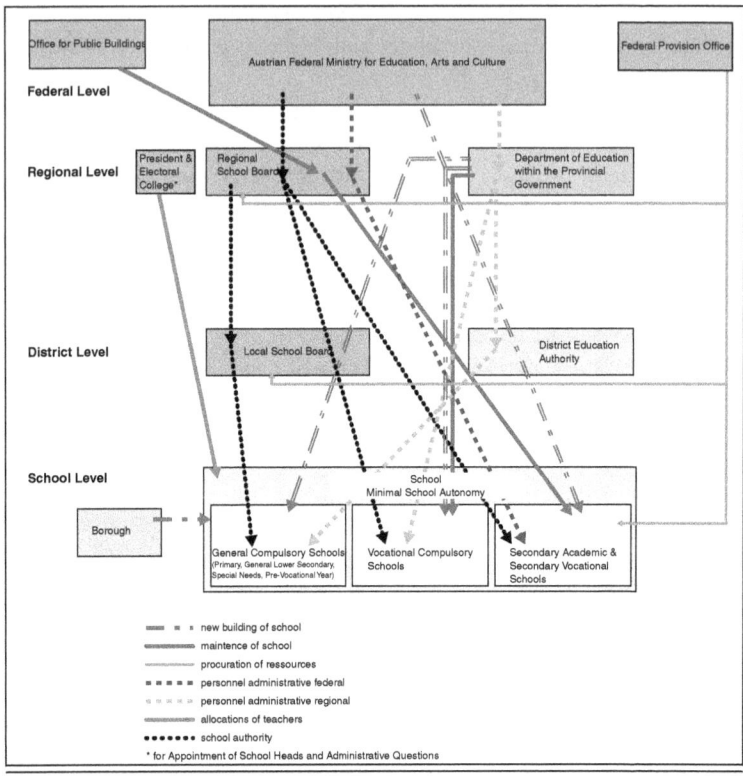

Figure 7.1 Overview of the Austrian school administration (simplified version) (Schmid, Hafner, & Pirolt, 2007 #152, 77).

Respondents interviewed for this chapter generally expressed similar sentiments.

The strength of this historical attitude is that individual leadership potential can create innovative developments both at the national and regional levels—as long as they do not disrupt the bureaucracy. The weakness of the dominant policy culture lies in the difficulty of developing cohesive reform initiatives, which makes widespread sustainable change difficult. Therefore, when answering the question "What metaphor, image, or analogy comes to your mind when you think of the educational policy environment of your country?" all persons interviewed for this study referred to images of slowly moving animals, such as a sedate elephant or a snail, or objects, such as a slowly moving tank molasses in winter. Others referred to the story of the hare and the tortoise to explain the difficulty in policy work, which involves expending a lot of energy with no certainty of winning.

All respondents saw a need to oppose the strong legacy of a hierarchical system by increasing autonomy, not only through increased responsibility at the provincial level, but also through increased autonomy for schools. It was agreed that the final responsibility for defining objectives and assuring quality rests with the ministry. At the other end, schools should be responsible for the organization of teaching and learning processes and should have the necessary freedom of curricular, financial, and personnel issues.

External Pressure for System Renewal

That Austria has a centralized frame for thinking about educational policy is unquestioned. There was equally strong consensus among respondents that Austrian society values social cohesion, trust, and stability in organizational structures. This stability has been built not only on a strong centralized bureaucracy, but also on the bureaucracy's tendency to extensively consult with and include the many groups and organizations with a "legitimate" interest in educational decisions. The centralized consultative process makes it difficult to reach the necessary majority for significant changes. Therefore all respondents in the Austrian strand of the project regard school administration in its present form as outdated, since the comparatively high expenses (input) produce only average results (output), a fact that had been publicly discussed after the publication of the PISA results and follow-up OECD analyses.

The overall trust in the stable quality of the Austrian school system was disrupted by the first international comparative studies and PISA in particular, which demonstrated that the education system has so far not achieved what it was supposed to. The prevailing tendency toward stasis, however, did not immediately lead to radical changes, as indicated by the following quote:

> The official reactions to the poor PISA test results 2003 in Austria and Germany was reminiscent of a highly talented student who succeeded in muddling through for years but whose poor achievement was suddenly exposed after an important exam. The responsible politicians took on the role of enraged parents who angrily approached the examination board to file complaints ranging from the completely unsuitable exam tasks their child had to solve to mistakes made in the corrections. (Salcher, 2009 #153,195 [author's translation])

The pressure for political action, fueled by regional and national media, increased, and brought public attention to the way in which structures and processes stymie change in Austrian educational policy. Moreover, new research brought to light the increasing number of immigrant children who were failing in the Austrian system, which stirred discussions about how to support children with home languages other than German. These debates led, in turn, to policy debates about whether German-language instruction should be compulsory in preschool or kindergarten, particularly for immigrant children and/or those with additional support needs.

The concern about limited government activities increasing focused in on a rich mix of previously unrelated educational problems that were made visible by both international testing and national research. Demands increased for more comprehensive and coherent solutions to salve the affronts to national pride. The thicket of interwoven policy-making strands and the tensions between federal and regional actors in school administration made it difficult, however, to meet these demands within existing agencies. The response was to create a brand new agency to assume responsibility for quality. In 2008, the BIFIE (Federal Institute for Educational Research, Innovation and Development of the Austrian School System) was founded with the mandate of educational monitoring, quality development, and national reporting in the Austrian school system. Its mission is to support all system levels in their endeavor to ensure that the quality of educational processes are monitored and continually improved. The present activities concentrate on standard setting and testing and the introduction of a centralized school leaving exam (Matura).

The options for inducements in Austria are quite limited (extra money for German-language teaching or offering supervision on longer school-opening hours), and the previous focus on bottom-up improvement through school-based involvement has seen limited payoff. The novel policy lever of standardized testing, on the other hand, has opened a new chapter of centralization of school reform in Austria. The BIFIE's mission also provides another new approach because of its mandate to support improvement. Therefore capacity building is emerging as a strong policy lever in system development. One example is the Austrian *Leadership Academy* (LEA), which the previous minister of education (People's Party) initiated and the present one (Social Democratic Party) utilizes to strengthen system development on all levels throughout Austria (Schley & Schratz, 2011, #71; Stoll, Moorman, & Rahm, 2008, #102). Still, in spite of these indications that Austria is open to outside influences and stimuli, the strong preference for slow (or no) change has not been deeply shaken.

Dimensions of Austrian Policy Culture

The strong influence of the social partnership structures, partisan politics, the (teachers') union, and the teacher representatives means that participation mainly takes place through representative agencies. Parents, students, research(ers), and other (less formally organized) actors have little voice (Schmid, Hafner, & Pirolt, 2007). This focus on developing representation and consultation with recognized groups has contributed to the country's stability and growth after World War II. Growing ideological differences among the major parties (historically the People's Party and Social Democratic Party, nowadays with growing influence two more parties, the Freedom Party and the Greens) means that negotiations between political actors often leads to political "compromise," which results in limited reforms that are half-heartedly introduced. The constitutional requirement that major education-related decisions require a two-third majority in parliament further restricts the possibility for individuals or smaller and less well-established groups to gain a voice.

The Austrian system is neither centralized nor decentralized, but a hybrid. The hybrid model is, however, still centralized when viewed from the perspective of an individual school. The federal system of education governance requires the national government to set the framework and the provincial governments to enact the detailed legislation. The federal government has full responsibility concerning the employment and the conditions of teachers and other staff working in schools. However, responsibility for the actual employment is more complex, with provincial governments responsible for staffing some schools (primary, secondary modern, polytechnic, and vocational schools), while others (the general academic-track lower and upper secondary schools, as well as vocational upper secondary schools leading to the school-leaving Matura examination) are administered at the federal level. Although there has been a shift toward more decentralization and deregulation (Schratz & Hartmann, 2009, #105), local school autonomy is still limited in scope. School heads, who are selected by either the region or federal level, have only limited authority over budgets, curriculum, and personnel.

Like other German-speaking countries, Austria is under pressure to align its national and regional structures in order to save money. However, the policy context described in section 2 makes it very difficult to introduce coherent national approaches to school system. Reform initiatives are small in scale and heterogeneous, and often create overload problems as actors at different levels of the system try to sort out their meaning and requirements. This fragmentation leads to a sense of irritation, confusion, and uncertainty, deenergizing effort through fragmentation, creating leadership dilemmas, and pulling the key actors into different directions between *sollen* (obligation) and *wollen* (aspiration) (Schratz, 2003, #104). The Austrian system, like the German, separates students into alternative streams or tracks at an early age. In general, the public is supportive of this policy, based on an argument that it allows all students to succeed, but in different ways. However, one consequence is that, again like Germany, the schools tend to reproduce the social and economic differences that students bring with them from their families (Haider & Schreiner, 2006, #103). While this has been well established by research and has resulted in serious policy debates about how to minimize disparities and social injustice, comprehensive structural solutions are not on the table. The current minister of education has, however, initiated a reform policy with the aim of reorienting the instructional and organizational system of teaching and learning for 10- to 14-year-olds. Softening or eliminating early tracking is one of the core elements in this development work, which builds on a framework in fostering as well as challenging all children, irrespective of their social, cultural, and language background or their individual performance in the early primary school years. The debates have not, however, changed the basic commitment to a system of tracking, but have only shifted the decision point to the end of lower secondary level.

Austrian educational policy decisions have resulted in an eclectic mix of reform initiatives, which cause an overload problem by layering policies upon policies. This has often led to the situation that school reform does not reach the classroom door. The main reason for the missing sustainability of reform initiatives seems to lie in the dysfunction of a political culture, which develops reform models and tries to implement them by means of (limited) prescriptive strategies rather than by looking within schools for what is needed to create change. Policy failure is often attributed to the top-down model's lack of penetration into the hearts and minds of school professionals. To date, the contradictory and parallel paths of decision-making, reflected in figure 7.1, cannot be challenged due to the two-third majority constitutional requirement.

School quality has, in Austria, typically been thought of holistically, based on the general "goodness criteria" assumption that was outlined in chapter one. Quality was regarded as stemming from the appropriate (and caring) allocation of students to a curriculum and program of study that would prepare them to be effective adults. The assumption of quality was premised on the belief that good teachers make a good educational system, and the belief that well-trained Austrian teachers were more than up to the task. Although the Austrian school system has traditionally been very centralized, teachers in the classroom have had the freedom of choice regarding whatever they choose as relevant within the open framework of the national curriculum. There has been minimal external control apart from the inspectors of schools who, in practice, rarely "inspect" or supervise individual teachers during their careers. Recent reform movements, as a reaction to Austria's average achievement in international rankings, as described previously, have shifted the conversations to incorporate an accountability debate. Professional approaches to accountability encompass both the implementation of standards and professional control of site-based management as it applies to the practices of teachers and school leaders as well as control of entry into teacher education, but the notion of site-based management (as opposed to the traditional emphasis on teacher quality and autonomy) is not supported by structures and procedures.

Although compulsory schooling was introduced as early as 1774 to offer every citizen of the Austrian Hungarian Empire educational opportunities, today's Austrian school system has paid limited attention to an equity perspective that is measured by increased opportunities for social

Table 7.1 Framework for analyzing state political culture: Austria

Dimensions of political culture

Openness	Moderately open, but constrained by the focus on participating through existing formal representative groups. Few opportunities for participation outside these groups
Decentralism	A mixed model, but more centralized (at either the federal or the provincial level) than decentralized
Rationalism	Comprehensive reform policies are difficult to enact; most national initiatives are limited in scope and not necessarily integrated into a larger framework
Egalitarianism/equity	Recent concern for demonstrably inequitable outcomes has resulted in some efforts to reduce early tracking. Public commitment to a tracked system is not seriously challenged
Efficiency	In spite of serious issues related to funding, eliminating the systemic inefficiency of duplicative systems at federal, regional, and lower levels is not a policy priority
Quality	Quality is traditionally thought of as embodied in a well-trained teacher workforce; questions about quality as measure by international tests are challenging the older perspective
Choice	Choice is largely made within the school system, as students are assigned to various streams or tracks. Limited attention is paid to parental choice of schools, privatization, or the role of markets

mobility. While the reasons for this are complex, one is clearly structural. The historic roots of the upper secondary Gymnasium track reflect a philosophical commitment to a classical curriculum for the bourgeoisie. The high number of students from parents with an academic background shows that the Gymnasium has become the reproductive instrument of educating middle- and upper-class members of society. Internal and external forces are mustering to question the demonstrably unequal outcomes of the tracking system but demand has been limited to changes in the lower secondary level in order to avoid social segregation (table 7.1).

Note

I thank Helmut Seel (2010, #114) for providing me with an insightful historical overview and my interview partners for their stimulating responses, which formed the basis for this chapter.

8

The More Things Change, the More They Stay the Same: The English Case

Karen Seashore Louis and John MacBeath

Introduction

The English seem to delight in the policy process. Along with a deeply embedded tradition of public debating and argumentation, there is a historical focus (evident in the popularity of Shakespeare's histories) on the role leaders play in visibly shaping national identity. The importance of ceremony and the articulation of clearly defined roles and titles has never been more apparent than during the recent royal wedding, but these public events, which emphasize ceremony and tradition, fail to reveal a deeper aspect of the political culture that is rooted in a combination of individualism and a high tolerance for risk-taking and innovation (Hofstede, 1991). This older traditional persists side by side with a modern tradition that looks to the role of government in supporting basic needs, "cradle to grave" (as Prime Minister Clement Atlee phrased it when he took office after World War II).

The role of national governments as policy leaders in education is, however, a relatively recent phenomenon. Until the last part of the twentieth century, education (unlike health or other social services) was largely the province of local education authorities who provided the oversight of schools within their area. In addition to the strong local focus, there was considerable emphasis on the role of professionals as guides to the system, with teachers and head teachers having considerable leeway to develop schools and classroom learning as they saw fit. Since the last decades of the past century, however, national governments, both Labour and Conservative, have engaged in a concerted effort to give educational policy a significance that puts it on the same footing as other major social sectors such as housing and health.

The Roots of Today's System

The modern English system was defined in the 1944 Education Act by clearly distinguishing primary and secondary education, and providing public support for secondary schools for all students. In addition, it established the Ministry of Education as a distinct entity with significant administrative authority. The policy environment for education remained, however, quiescent until 1988, when the "Thatcher Revolution" delivered a new vision of education in an omnibus bill that changed everything:

> Twenty years ago, [the secretary of education] delivered the single most important piece of education legislation for England, Wales and Northern Ireland since the war . . . National curriculum? Still here. Key stages? Still here. Testing at [ages] 7, 11 and 14, with published results? Ditto. The power to let headteachers take control of their budgets? Ditto still . . . (Woodward, 2008)

While there were a number of parliamentary actions in the subsequent years, most of them involved minor changes to the 1988 act. The one exception was the 1992 Schools Act, which established the possibility of quasi-autonomous government units (known as Quangos) that operate outside the ministry, including OFSTED (Office for Standards in Education), a schools inspection unit whose purposes involved improving school quality and accountability.

The election of a Labour government in 1997 was accompanied by an increasing number of white papers and commission reports on education, suggesting that more big changes might be in the offing. In particular, the teachers and head teachers associations expected that a Labour government would realign the responsibility for developing innovative programs to improve education by giving professionals greater voice, while local communities hoped that the local education authorities, substantially weakened in the 1988 act, would regain some authority over finances. These expectations were, however, unrealized, as the new government's proposals built on the foundation laid by the Conservatives, most surprisingly and significantly retaining the highly unpopular inspection regime OFSTED (Bangs, MacBeath, & Galton, 2010).

The Labour government started, in 1998, with an omnibus bill that revised some of the elements of the 1988 Act[1] while initiating two new targeted initiatives. The Literacy and Numeracy Strategy was accompanied by extensive curriculum requirements, professional development, and mandated teaching strategies. Rather than promoting more freedom for professional decisions in the classroom, the strategy rested on the assumption that the relatively weak performance of British schools on international test results would be improved only by a focused and prescriptive approach.[2] A second new initiative was to target resources for educational improvement on "Education Action Zones" (high poverty areas with low school test performance). Both of these initiatives could, in retrospect, be viewed as building on, rather than substantially altering, the 1988 act (Mead, 2008).

Who Initiates and Who Decides?

A review of both the key parliamentary actions noted earlier, and others viewed as less critical by respondents interviewed, lead to one important conclusion: There are few cooks in the English educational policy kitchen, despite a relatively broad and ongoing process of consultation and advice seeking. Kenneth Baker, education secretary under Margaret Thatcher, is unchallenged as the key actor in formulating the 1988 bill that has shaped the education sector since that time, although the underlying role of a number of conservative "think tanks" such as the Institute for Economic Affairs and the Adam Smith Society made their own contributions. What is notable about the 1988 bill was the relative rapidity with which it was developed and introduced, seen widely as bearing the personal signature of one man, whose focus was on parental choice, per capita funding, local managerial control, and independence from local education authorities (Pierson, 1998). Baker's ideas were equally influential in his reshaping of the inspection system in the act that was to follow in 1992.

The number of actors associated with Labour's 1998 act was slightly larger, but the main influences were limited to a number of key participants whose names are associated with the "brain trust" appointments by the prime minister. The position of secretary of education was stable and influential for most of the decade-long Conservative regime, but under the Labour government the most powerful positions were typically in advisory roles.[3] What is notable is the reliance placed on key individuals who were, at the time, unelected, but who had more influence than the secretaries of education who (under the British system) were required to be members of parliament. Several of our respondents and at least one published source claimed that one advisor, Andrew Adonis, effectively ran education policy from his office at 10 Downing Street under four successive education secretaries (Beckett, 2005). While one of the first initiatives under the Labour government in 1997 was to set up a Task Force with a broad range of advisers from key agencies, from business, from schools, and from academia, these representatives expressed continuing frustration that their presence was largely cosmetic and that decisions had already been taken within the "kitchen cabinet"—an inner circle of policy advisors whose influence trumped other advisory and consultancy bodies (Bangs, MacBeath, and Galton, 2010).

Interviews and published materials are consistent in noting the absence of significant actors outside of the trusted members of both the Conservative and Labour prime ministers' "kitchen cabinets." Over the same period, the role of the civil service has, according to a number of actors, been diluted as the influence of appointed advisors has increased. In sum, a notable feature of the political culture that has characterized the national educational system in England is the power of a relatively small, elite, and often unelected group of actors, exercising influence on policy over a considerable period of time.

Political Culture in Action

The greater educational policy activism that has emerged in England over the last several decades reflects a strong commitment to the ideals underlying New Public Management (NPM) that has been consistent across both Conservative and Labour governments. The 1988 Education Act, which established the framework for a national curriculum and greater school autonomy, was based primarily on (Conservative) political principles rather than on a strong educational platform. The subsequent 1992 Act that established OFSTED (inspection), while intended to provide public accountability for educational services, contested its own accountability to government ("only to God" as the chairman of the Government Select Committee said in interview). Many of the policies espoused by the Conservatives received minor facelifts under Labor, albeit couched in new terminologies and language. The major change was that Labour added to the Tory accountability changes were improvement targets. Labour's literacy and numeracy initiative also had a clearer focus on improving classroom experiences, but the emphasis was on changes that would lead to rapid improvement on the new targets.

The story of continuity across governments with markedly different political platforms is best illustrated by a specific example: the case of schools that were permitted to "opt out" of the local education authority system and that received direct funding (and oversight) from the national government. These were first initiated under the Conservatives in 1988, with the title of "grant maintained schools," which were officially independent and allowed to set their own admissions criteria. This policy received a facelift under Labor, couched in new terminologies and language. Grant maintained schools were eliminated early in the Labour government, but were replaced shortly thereafter with "Academies," which shared many features, including direct funding and the opportunity for businesses and religious groups to sponsor them. The Academies were initiated through amendments to the authorization of City Technical Colleges that were also part of an earlier conservative act. The chief architect of the Academies, a consistently influential advisor to the prime minister, promoted them as an alternative pathway for poorly performing low-income students. Academies were given leeway for innovation and self-direction, free from local authority control, with school-site governance and funded directly by the national government. Their espoused purpose was slightly different and couched in the "improved outcomes and equity through competition" language favored by New Labour, but the underlying assumptions were quite similar to the erstwhile grant-maintained schools. The academies are supported by the recent Conservative/Liberal Coalition government, and have been expanded to become the preferred form of secondary schooling.

Governing by Regulation Produces Fundamental Change

The parliamentary history and the specific example discussed earlier tell only part of the story, however. Respondents agree that most educational policies in England are not articulated in laws, but are administrative (regulatory) in nature. The law gives broad powers to the prime minister and the secretary of education. Between 1988 and 2004, most parliamentary actions are viewed as adaptations of new details in the fundamental structures. However, as a teacher or head teacher working in a school, the initiatives that have emerged are far more numerous than is suggested by the major bills. Statutory instruments (SIs) are used to make orders of general application. They need not go before parliament (although parliament can object to them). Regulations can be made and imposed by the secretary. Circulars are documents sent out by government departments for information and comment, often by parliament, but public debate about them is rare. Many of these instruments are detailed in their expectations of what schools must do in order to implement or comply with regulation. Acts are often intended to put a legal basis under initiatives that have already been administratively implemented, while parliamentary committees provide gentle corrective feedback.

The changes in English education over the past 20 years have been fundamental and are unlikely to be fully overturned by the recently elected coalition government as they are largely consistent with principles established by the Conservatives as long ago as 1944. Policymakers in all the major political parties appear to agree that improvement in education should not be left in the hands of those closest to the action—teachers, school heads, and local authority advisers ("the usual suspects")—but steered from the center. An example of how fundamental this assumption is may be found in the current coalition government's proposal for "free schools run by parents and consortia who wish to opt out of local government control." Only 24 schools were approved to open in September 2011, and these were subjected to rigorous national government controls.[4]

Where Conservative and Labour governments have differed is in the degree of intervention in school management and accountability, with Labour proposing attainment targets, more specific national curriculum, and priorities for particular groups of students and regions. However, many of these interventionist efforts were promoted under an NPM rhetoric that is acceptable to Conservatives (improved management, value for cost, etc.). Differences in policy tend to be around the margins, although the fiscal policies of the current government in response to economic crisis have resulted in cutbacks to programs targeted at disadvantaged children that were sponsored under Labour.

How the Elite Works

The prevalence of elite insiders who are generalists but are called on to chair commissions and inquiries is notable, as is the recurrence of a limited number of actors over long periods of time. One example is Lord Ron Dearing, who was deputy secretary on Nationalised Industry Matters in the Callaghan and Thatcher administrations. He chaired three independent and influential education commissions during his career (1993, 1997, and 2006), each of which influenced government policy. His background, however, was in the postal service, and later in the higher education sector.

A major change over the last 50 years is in how the elite is formed and carries out its work. We might characterize this as a shift from corporate elitism to entrepreneurial elitism. Up to and after World War II, the government consulted with the heads of groups that were considered to be key stakeholders (unions, local government associations, etc.), with the elite in the civil service, and, occasionally, universities. Members of these groups might, therefore, have been considered as second-tier players in the policy game. This pattern has shifted toward an entrepreneurial, elite consultation model, in which individuals, often with positional influence, compete for opportunities to serve and to be heard. Compared to many of the other countries in Europe, academics have played a minimal role as members of the elite. A residue of suspicion of academics, many of whom have been highly critical of educational initiatives over the last 30 or more years, has meant that money previously given to universities for applied R&D is now directed to consultant organizations. Universities play a major role in evaluation and knowledge generation, but do not have much direct influence on policy.

Summary

There is evidence that the patterns of educational policymaking established over the past 30 years, which are summarized in table 8.1, mimic those that went before it in the other social sectors, and will probably

Table 8.1 Framework for analyzing state political culture: England

Dimensions of political culture	
Openness	Many groups and individuals give advice on policy; "White" and "Green" papers are published, as well as dozens of reports. Advisors are drawn from universities, bodies such as OFSTED, and from "think tanks" and commercial consulting firms. There is a strong sense that educational policymaking occurs as a contest of ideas. However, getting access to a network of real influence is not easy; the circle is relatively closed and entry is based on elaborated (personal) networks
Decentralism	Highly quiescent and largely decentralized until 1988. Since then, the assumption of both parties was that the national governments should make policy, and individual schools should carry out the policies
Rationalism	Highly rational: Government passes few acts, engages in a great deal of evaluation and assessment of the effects of programs and policies, and makes frequent adjustments based on both the knowledge generated within the government/Quangos and outside (externally funded studies). Emphasis on knowledge production and use of research/evaluation is increasing, but has always characterized the "White Paper"/"Green Paper" process

Continued

Table 8.1 *(Continued)*

Dimensions of political culture	
Egalitarianism/ equity	—Public pronouncements about the need, and elaborate reorganizations of ministries, but not as prominent feature of conversations and reports. There is acknowledged class-based bias within the government school system. There is discussion about improving the educational opportunities of immigrants, largely through co-location of services and targeted development
Efficiency	—Strong efficiency emphasis is characterized by accountability for increased funding and by auditing of effective management of resources. New Public Management philosophy emphasizes the need for competition and privatization of some services to make them more efficient. Strong emphasis on education as human capital formation
Actors/ Influence	—Who is most influential varies:(ministers and civil service under Thatcher; Quangos and advisors under Labour and coalition governments). The presence of elite nonparliamentary, nonministerial actors continues the tradition of elite influence. Parliament has a modest role in educational policy. The consultative strength of unions has been attenuated, while traditional civil service functions and analyses (white papers) are increasingly delegated to chosen advisers
Quality	—Quality has largely been defined in terms of test results, although there is renewed attention to the condition of school physical plants and health and safety measures. Quality is also measured by high-stakes inspection
Choice	—Choice has driven many policies, along with standards. The names given to choice schools have changed, but initiatives to increase choice have been persistent. The underlying belief for both Tories and Labour is that competition will lead to improvement

continue. Like its predecessor governments, the coalition government of 2010 hit the ground running with a series of rapid reforms, but most of them have involved reintroducing or shaping programs that are variations on old themes: creating schools that have more freedom from local government and a continued concerted focus on standards, curriculum, and testing. Like the Labour government before it, it wished to be seen as consulting widely, and it appointed a group of four key academics to conduct a radical curriculum review. Their latitude for advice has been constrained within the National Curriculum framework that was established in 1992, which limited their potential influence. The English case therefore suggests that even in a country where public debate and parliamentary contestation are the red meat of politics and policymaking, much of the media ruckus over "radical new policies" is, as Shakespeare said, "full of sound and fury, signifying nothing" (*Macbeth*, Scene V). Rather, the much deeper tradition of relying on a small number of advisors to the elected head of the state trumps dramatic orations about open and participatory processes.

Notes

This chapter is based on interviews with several dozen key policy actors that were conducted independently by the two authors as part of separate projects.

1. Grant maintained schools, which were established in 1988 as funded directly by the national government, and reporting to a private board of directors, were allowed to set their own admissions standards. They were eliminated in 1998.
2. An external evaluation of the Literacy and Numeracy strategy indicated that it had a significant effect, but that the results were spotty and hard to maintain over time (Earl et al., 2005).
3. The tenure of secretaries of education under Blair was typically quite short. During his time in office, there were six secretaries. Key unelected educational advisors served, however, for much longer periods. One of the most influential was Michael Barber, who served as a head of the Policy and Standards unit within the Ministry and in other senior advisory positions from 1997 to 2005. Also noted as influential in the years during which the Blair policies evolved were David Miliband (head of the prime minister's "Policy Unit" of unelected advisors from 1997–2001) and Andrew Adonis (also a member of the "Policy Unit").
4. The actuality of free schools has fallen short of the aspirations of the current government coalition, perhaps due to the first free schools having been established by entrepreneurs, head teachers, business, and other groups rather than by parents as originally envisaged.

9

E Pluribus Unum? Dissonance in US Educational Political Culture

Karen Seashore Louis

Introduction

The musical, *1776*, popularized a deeply embedded belief that the United States became a country when several colonies declared their independence from England. The legal basis for cooperation was not, however, fully accomplished until 1790, when a limited and highly contested constitution was ratified by all of the colonies. Two features of this early history are critical. First, the constitution does not mention education and a rapidly passed addendum, the Bill of Rights, laid out the responsibilities of the federal government but implicitly left education as a responsibility of the states.[1] Second, the Bill of Rights explicitly indicates that the government may not promote any religion, which means that the United States is the only Western country that provides no financial support to religious schools and forbids any teaching of religion (other than in history classes) in public education.[2]

These two bedrock principles, embedded in a constitution that can only be amended by a vote of two-thirds of the state or reinterpreted by a decision of the Supreme Court, is critical to understanding educational policy in the United States. Among the many consequences, for example, was the uncontested decision by slave-holding states to prohibit education for people who were not free,[3] the continued tension between widespread preferences for religious education despite consistent Supreme Court decisions that overrode state and local preferences for prayer in the schools, and the enormous variability in educational standards (including preparation and licensing of professionals, funding, participation, achievement, and curriculum) among the 50 states. To give just one example, one may have been a teacher or principal in one state for many years, but moving to another state can be a challenge for many educators, who may have to pass new tests or take new courses in order to qualify in the state next door.[4] Similarly, there are no required grade configurations or timetables for schools, nor any examinations that apply to students in all states.[5] Arguably, education is still the only major public institution in the United States where agreements that occurred more than two centuries ago continue to be fueled by clear preferences for maintaining difference over achieving uniformity.

Antecedents of US Political Culture

In most regards, the United States exhibits the kind of regional variation that one expects in most large countries, as well as unifying features including a powerful national media. Even most conservative populists tend to agree that the United States needs a national foreign policy and military, that some uniformity in licensing and monitoring health care providers is critical, that roads and bridges must meet safety standards, and that the elderly and people who lose their jobs need a social support system. Outsiders look at the raucous and divided system of governance at the national level, with its deliberately competing bases of power between the executive, the Congress, and the courts, as odd but understandable—and generalize what they know to US political culture in general. However, as Congressman Tip O'Neill from Massachusetts said in the 1980s, in the United States "[a]ll politics is local" and *most* decisions that affect the lives of *most* Americans are not made in Washington.[6] While one may disagree with the Congressman, the resonance of this quote is indicative of the general mistrust that many people (including those on the political left) feel for the federal government.

This reductionist perspective ignores, however, some systematic variations in US political culture. In 1970, a political scientist proposed that there were three identifiable broad political subcultures that were regionally embedded (Elazar, 1970). With limited empirical evidence, he traced these differences to the deeper history of the way in which the country was populated in its early years, which he later elaborated with more empirical (although still impressionistic) work (Elazar, 1984).

In the Southern states (slaveholding prior to the Civil War), the economic and political system was based on large agrarian enterprises controlled by a few wealthy families. Over time, even when the economic basis shifted, the assumption that a traditional pattern of governance and decision-making that deferred to the more educated owning class emerged, which Elazar labeled "Traditional." In the modern era, the traditional culture in these states tends to value continuity and the status quo, assigning responsibility to more powerful (and often generationally stable) groups from multiple sectors to determine whether change is needed in order to protect common interests. Perhaps the most critical characteristic of the traditional political cultures is the tendency to defer to authority (Almond & Verba, 1965). This relates to current educational policies in a very explicit way: The states that are often categorized as traditional are more likely to have centralized educational policy systems that govern local choices of textbooks, teachers, and finances—but those states also typically allocate limited funding from state coffers, and have lower teacher salaries.

In the original New England states, small business and individual agricultural enterprises were (and are) more common, and the region developed an approach to governance that involved consensual decision-making and a focus on localized participation—a pattern that Elazar called "Moralistic." In its modern form, the moralistic political culture (which is also found in states in which a large proportion of the population is of Scandinavian origins) places an emphasis on the role of government in fostering the common good, and supports a broader commitment to economic and social interventions. The contemporary artifacts of this political culture are a tendency to be at the forefront of examining, and at times legislating, more equitable educational financing systems and fostering public discussions about what constitutes a "good education." At the same time, considerable leeway is given to local schools around a wide range of decisions that are not part of the state's legal authority.

The century of westward migration, accompanied by the continued influx of many new immigrant groups from non-English-speaking countries through the first part of the twentieth century, resulted in a more diverse population that competed for land and political influence, and resulted in the emergence of a political culture that Elazar called "Individualistic." Individualistic political cultures emphasize a marketplace model of governance, with competing interests emerging to reflect particular perspectives on who should benefit from the limited state interventions. In current educational policy, more individualistic states have tended to be relatively slow to articulate statewide policies regarding both funding and governance of schools, and have been, until recently, largely uncritical of wide variations in educational opportunities and standards. Many individualistic states are permissive about requirements for private education and homeschooling, and provide limited state oversight for schools that are not publicly funded.[7] Educational policy is, in fact, often a minor element of political deliberations.

The Legacy of Regional Variations

Elazar's regional perspective on political cultures in the United States have been both affirmed and contested in the research literature. Some have pointed out that few states consistently exhibit the characteristics of a single type, and that it is more realistic to look at the degree to which a state shows characteristics of one or another (Sharkansky, 1969). This approach, which looks at empirical evidence (e.g., about voting behavior, or responses to policies that are determined by states, such as capital punishment), has confirmed that dominant political cultures do exist to some extent (Fitzpatrick & Hero, 1988; Norrander, 2000). Others argue that increasing population mobility within the US regional variations may lead to a decline in distinctive political cultures (Baker, 1990). Nevertheless, the prevailing perspective appears to support the notion that these three types shed light on the enormous variability in educational policies that can be confusing to outside observers.

The finding that political cultures vary by state and affect the development of educational policies was confirmed in the 1980s (Wirt, Mitchell, & Marshall, 1988), and a more recent comparative study of ten US states argued that these embedded political cultures have influenced the way in which current pressures for accountability have been incorporated into public discussions and law (Louis et al., 2008). This variability will be explored further in chapter thirteen.

The Effects of "Separation of Powers" on Political Culture and Education

Like the European countries that are part of this book, the US educational system has also gone through major upheavals since the end of World War II. These, however, rarely emerged from the executive or legislative branches of the federal government. The most significant changes developed from challenges to the historical interpretation of the constitution by the third branch of government, which is the federal court system. These court rulings have created radical changes in some parts of the educational system, while affecting others in relatively minimal ways.

The Supreme Court played a minimal role in disrupting state preferences and control until 1954, with the decision that is universally referred to as "Brown v. Board of Education." The ruling, based on a case brought by parents from Topeka, Kansas, stated explicitly that separate educational facilities for white and other children were inherently unequal and unconstitutional. This ruling led to more than 20 years of conflict, as segregated schools and universities across the country were required to integrate.[8] The responses, in both the north and south, were often violent, and disrupted the long-accepted reality that affluent, predominantly white parents lived in affluent, predominantly white neighborhoods that had predominantly white schools. In many urban areas, the result was greater use of private schools and "white flight" to residential enclaves outside of the scope of integration efforts (Clark, 1987). The magnitude of the effects of the court on these changes is empirically questionable (Rossell, 1975), but the impact on the public imagination is enduring.

In many ways, the responses of states to this long period of turmoil reflected their political cultures as well as their histories with school segregation. For example, in the traditional states (often those with de jure school segregation), elites tended to continue their centralized role in directing public schools, although now providing lower funding and overlooking the increasing role of segregated private schools (Kruse, 2005). In more moralistic states, such as Massachusetts (which prohibited school segregation in 1855) and Washington, violence was lower, and suburban (largely white) communities participated in voluntary school desegregation efforts, which reflected a broader discussion about the desirability of more residential integration. In many states, de facto educational segregation issues are being raised again as a consequence of rates of immigration that have more than doubled in the last 20 years.

Brown v. Board of Education created a new role for the federal government, which had a constitutional obligation to enforce integration. In 1965, the US Congress passed the Elementary and Secondary Education Act, which provided funds to schools with high proportions of low-income and minority students. This act was particularly significant because it represented the first "general support" federal funds for state and locally run schools. Like all subsequent federal funding, the money was given to the states, which had the responsibility of determining how it would be administered. Similarly critical decisions were made in subsequent Supreme Court decisions that required schools to provide educational opportunities to children with special needs (learning disabilities and physical handicaps), and to those who could not speak English. Again, the Congress affirmed the court decisions and provided some funding to support state efforts to comply.

The economic repercussions were significant. In the mid-1950s, the federal government's financial support for schools were largely limited to the provision of surplus commodities for school lunch programs, which were viewed as an efficient way of dealing with hunger and were administered by the Department of Agriculture. By the early 1980s and after two decades of sustained federal funding for various court-mandated programs, the percentage of federal support for K-12 education had risen to nearly 5 percent; by 2008, the federal share had increased to about 9 percent, largely due to increased funding for early childhood education and support for low-income schools. No state is obligated to agree to abide by federal educational initiatives other than those that are required by the courts—but if they accept federal funding, it comes with compliance strings. Federal funding is not equal across states, however, and ranges from more than 16 percent in Louisiana (one of the poorest states) to 5 percent or less in Massachusetts and New Jersey. While the federal share of the funding pie is trivial compared to most other countries, it is large enough that no state has voluntarily agreed to forgo it, and it provides a lever for national initiatives to influence state and local behavior.

Federal funding has not changed the enormous disparities in financial support for education both between and within states. In 2008, on average a state provided 46 percent of the funding for schools, while the local communities provided 45 percent. The variation between states ranges, however, from a high of 86 percent state funding in Hawaii and Vermont, to a low of less than 35 percent in Illinois, South Dakota, Florida, Nevada, and Missouri.[9] Similarly, the differences in average total funding state and local sources per student ranged from lows of less than $10,000 per student in some relatively low-income states (Alabama, Florida, Mississippi, North Carolina, Tennessee—all more "traditional" states) to highs of over $15,000 per student in other states that are also less affluent (Vermont, Maine, Rhode Island—states that are ranked as more "moralistic"). While the relative affluence of a state's economy has some bearing on educational expenditures, much of the differences appear to be based on policy choices that vary to some extent by political culture.[10]

Persistent Controversies About Education and Religion

The United States has a much higher proportion of citizens who are actively involved in religious organizations than in most high-wealth countries: Some argue that the disconnection between church and state is responsible for the enormous proliferation of autonomous churches and spiritual practice groups ranging from small Zoroastrian groups to Evangelical Christians who meet in "mega churches." While it is difficult to measure religious participation, at least one source suggests that more than 50 percent of the population adheres to some formal religious group (ARDA, 2011), and attend religious services once a month or more (Wald & Calhoun-Brown, 2009). Religious participation is, however, highly regional, and variable within states.[11] Some religious denominations have developed networks of private schools, which serve most of the roughly 10 percent of the total US student population. There is no government subsidy to these students or institutions; parents must pay the full tuition costs.

Conflict over the role of religion in schools has been persistent and also tied to regional differences. Communities with a dominant and active religious affiliation historically tended to practice religious observances in schools with limited objection, but beginning in the 1950s, the Supreme Court consistently rules against previously accepted school religious observances such as prayers or posters displaying the Ten Commandments. The "bright line" separating religion and schools has been contested in elections as well as in the courts, as some states grapple with the insistence of religious groups that alternatives to evolution be included in the curriculum. The religious wars in schools extend to topics that might be uncontroversial elsewhere, such as teaching students how to clarify or examine the values underlying legislation or historical events, or using moments of silence in classrooms in place of prayers.

This issue has become increasingly fraught in recent years, as policymakers in some states have attempted to find ways of providing public funding for students to attend religiously affiliated schools, but most of these, when passed, have been ruled illegal in either state or federal courts. Parents who are frustrated with the lack of religious values in schools are increasingly choosing to teach their children at home, which is allowed in most states: the percentage of homeschooled children increased by about 75 percent between 1999 and 2007 to include nearly 3 percent of school-age children, and about 40 percent of those who chose this option reported that religious or moral reasons motivated them (NCES, 2008).

Religious controversies have served as a catalyst for a growing sense of disconnection between schools and parents. But it has not been the only factor. Inner city parents who have felt betrayed by public schools have long enrolled their children in Catholic schools for the discipline and focused curriculum, even if they are indifferent to the specific religious values they espouse.[12] Likewise, the rise of charter schools is often viewed as a way for parents to express their desire for a school whose values match their own: although charter schools are public and thus prohibited from teaching religion, they are often based on a clearer set of values than the local public schools.

Political Culture and Education in the United States: A Summary

For every generalization that one may make about schooling in the United States, there are at least ten exceptions (out of fifty states). The role of the nation-state, while clearly limited by the constitution, is not a fully settled matter. Many educators tend to support more unity among the

Table 9.1 Framework for analyzing state political culture: The United States

Dimensions of political culture	
Openness	Variable between states: traditional states are dominated by elites; individualistic states tend to foster participation by interest groups; moralistic states tend to encourage "grass roots" participation
Decentralism	The system is constitutionally highly decentralized, with limited authority to make systemic changes based on constitutional issues decided by the Supreme Court; power over education resides with the 50 states. Moralistic and individualistic states tend to be decentralized; traditional states more centralized
Rationalism	Highly variable; depends on deep political history. Some states have pursued constructive and evolving comprehensive reform programs; others pay minimal attention to legislating educational policy. Rationalism is not clearly associated with the three culture types
Egalitarianism/equity	Key issues (desegregation and inclusion of special education students) are decided nationally, through Supreme Court decisions (usually later backed up with legislation); high between-state variability in focus on equity, both in resource allocation and attention to equitable opportunities and outcomes. Egalitarianism is most prominent in moralistic states, and is less prominent in traditional and individualistic states
Efficiency	Efficiency is not a key issue in many states, but is critical in others. Efficiency tends to be defined in terms of reducing nonteaching personnel and overall costs. Efficiency is most likely to be associated with individualistic states
Quality	The importance of quality as a factor in policy varies between states. Some highly decentralized states delegate most considerations of quality to local communities. Emphasis on quality tends to be limited to standardized test results. Quality is not clearly associated with the three culture types
Choice	Choice is highly politicized. Most states allow charter schools (publically funded schools that are not part of a local school district) but vary in their support of alternatives such as charters or homeschooling. Choice discussions are most prominent in individualistic states

states, particularly around the development of some common standards and funding addressed to equity, but much of the action they propose is to stimulate voluntary changes rather than enact national laws. Both conservatives and liberals typically find a great deal to dislike about legislative and executive policies that move beyond providing supplementary funding that is largely controlled by the states, so new "national initiatives" tend to provide a short-term stimulus that can be easily undone. Every few years there is a proposal in Congress to abolish the Department of Education, and The No Child Left Behind Act, which is the presumed wedge for a more muscular federal role in education, has produced such bipartisan dissatisfaction that any new authorization is likely to require less from states. Some of the key decisions that contribute to this persistent tension are summarized in table 9.1

There are other countries that are equally decentralized, but the United States may be unique in its acceptance of widely varying practices, policies, and student-learning outcomes from one state to the next. The only area of consensus is the preference for a limited role for national educational policy.

Notes

1. The Tenth Amendment indicates that all powers not delegated to the federal government "are reserved to the States, respectively, or to the people."
2. The First Amendment states that "Congress shall make no law respecting an establishment of religion, or prohibiting the free exercise thereof; or abridging the freedom of speech, or of the press; or the right of the people peaceably to assemble, and to petition the government for a redress of grievances."
3. The legal constraint was only resolved as part of the aftermath of the Civil War.
4. Interstate agreements to respect licenses are voluntary. In most cases, however, it involves, at minimum, administrative review and paperwork.
5. Participation in the National Assessment of Educational Progress, which is federally funded, is voluntary and has no consequences for states, districts, schools, or students.
6. O'Neill (1987) attributed this famous quote to his father's advice after the only election that he ever lost.
7. http://www.associatedcontent.com/article/1913414/homeschool_friendly_states_to_live.html.
8. Court decisions outlawed both de jure (established by law) and de facto (a result of racial residence patterns) segregation.
9. Where state funding is low, education funding is typically based on local property taxes, which because they are highly visible and locally determined are subject to frequent voter contest. Where it is higher, it is typically funded through state income tax.

10. The comparisons presented here come from a report compiled by the National Educational Association, a public teachers' union, and are based on available public data (NEA, 2009).
11. Alabama (a southern state) has a participation rate of nearly 75 percent, most of which are Southern Baptists; the participation rate in Massachusetts (a Northern state) is similar, but the majority is Roman Catholic. In contrast, the participation rate in Colorado is just over 50 percent, and is split between a much wider variety of denominations (ARDA, 2011).
12. Nearly 15 percent of Catholic school students are not Catholic (http://www.ncea.org/news/annualdatareport.asp). Nonwhite students make up 32 percent of Catholic school enrollment, compared with 46 percent in public schools.

Part III

The Cross-Country Studies

As part of the project that led to this book, the authors met on a number of occasions to examine emerging results. While discussing the data that resulted in the country cases in part two, we could not avoid making comparisons, each of which raised interesting issues with respect to our framework as well as new questions that will be discussed briefly in chapter fourteen. In the end, we decided that a cross-government analysis that used all of our cases was too complex to result in any conclusions that were not superficial, and that the value of our work was grounded in providing deeper insight through case studies. That is how we arrived at the idea of a limited number of paired cases that could illustrate some of the emerging ideas that we found most interesting. The pairs that are presented in this section were not formed by throwing a dice, but reflect our consensus that we had something to offer through each that extends what is known about political cultures and policies.

The Austria and Flanders combination is important because both represent relatively new national entities. Austria began a new life as an independent country in 1955 and Flanders has evolved into an relatively independent part of a new federal state since the early 1970s. In both countries a national government is regarded with caution (if not distrust), so education is highly decentralized, albeit in different ways. We will see in chapter ten that these similarities are not sufficient to compensate for some powerful dissimilarities that impact the way education policy is made. (The issue of the relative age of a government's political culture will also come up in chapter fifteen, where Gábor Halász will comment on the situation in Eastern Europe.)

We chose to contrast England and the Netherlands because New Public Management language was taken up very quickly in both countries and has driven efforts to change the public sector's structure and governance for at least 25 years. As we considered the effects of political culture on policy initiatives in each country, we found that in one case the basic structure of the educational system remained stable (England), while in the other (the Netherlands) a whole new structure emerged over a 30-year period. But even though we can observe changes in the Dutch system's structure, the new arrangement shares many traits with the system that was described in very old policy texts.

In our discussions we came to the conclusion that we needed to understand the differences between the Scandinavian countries if we want to understand the successes of their education systems. We also heard from the Swedish and Danish participants that they were not as similar as most people thought. These two countries have different systems based on different philosophies of teaching and learning, and are, as was made apparent in chapter three, quite different in their historical approach to educational reform. We found, however, that there are similarities in political culture that results in increasing similarities in educational policies.

Last but not least, we wanted to contrast two states in the United States. We chose North Carolina and Nebraska, in part because they illustrate the wide variety of political cultures that exist within the country, and also because they are rarely in the news (even within the United States) except during election years. Comparing these two states gave us a better insight into the possible impacts of political culture at a subnational level in a country where states have considerable autonomy, but somewhat less than Flanders. In the United States, a common federal pressure is apparent in all 50 states, but regional political cultures and a larger degree of state autonomy have shaped implementation and the resulting reforms.

10

Reform in Stable Systems (Austria and Belgium [Flanders]): The Impossible Dream?

Geert Devos and Michael Schratz

Introduction: Pride and Prejudice in Quality Measures

Policy cultures are closely related to the sociohistorical context of a country, and that is why mere policy borrowing does not work easily. Nevertheless, recent global interventions, such as international testing of student learning, have had a similar effect on school systems around the developed world. The intersection of local history with a strong reaction to international test results will be used in this chapter to compare the policy cultures in Austria and Flanders,[1] which share a long tradition of resistance against public ranking or comparisons among schools. Although the two small countries have different histories and different cultural contexts, they share some important similarities in policy cultures. Their educational systems are based on stability and conflict avoidance. Consequently, national decisions to change educational policy are met by resistance from stakeholder groups, which results in compromises that minimize the pressure to change. In spite of this culture of stakeholder and local control, global system interventions in the form of large-scale assessments have led to paradigmatic changes in the political landscape in both systems.

We take it for granted that all stakeholders strive for high quality in their respective education systems: we assume that parents want the best education for their children and that the actors on all levels of the system try to offer them the best education possible. In Austria, the school system is structured with distinct career paths for students who are judged to have different abilities and ambitions. The schools in Austria may be locally managed, but these career paths and the age of entrance to them is set at the national level. In Flanders, the freedom of parents to choose the best school for their child is considered a mechanism to spur educational quality. Since schools are funded according to their number of students, they do their best to attract more students.

In Austria, the government decides what constitutes a good school; in Flanders, schools, and indirectly parents, play the primary role in the definition of quality. Although the Flemish government defines the minimum goals that all schools must meet, the schools decide how they attain these goals. Although one might expect, armed with this knowledge, that Austria would be more receptive to national testing in order to evaluate school quality, a long tradition of local autonomy has resulted in a resistance to testing that is similar to that in Flanders. In both systems, the desire of policymakers in the central government to use national and international tests to shape and improve education has been indirect and slow.

This long tradition of resistance to national testing in both countries has been nurtured by a national myth and an underlying fear that this set of beliefs could be destroyed by excessive outside influence. In Austria the national myth is focused on a conviction that a multitracked school system tailored to the individual student is the ideal way to guarantee the best education for all children. Starting the streaming of students at the age of ten makes it one of the few countries in the world believing in early selection as a philosophy and as having an educational value of its own. In Flanders, the national educational myth is that the Catholic and non-sectarian schools are equal in quality: Any objective comparison between them might result in labeling one as better than another, reawakening the old but still simmering conflicts and tensions that were identified in chapter six. An additional concern about tests is related to the belief that Flemish schools are responsible for more than transmitting knowledge and skills: education is about religious or philosophical values, citizenship, and providing guidance to young people to become responsible adults. There is a consensus in Flanders that these valued elements in education are impossible to measure, and that quality comparisons based on limited "objective" testing would undermine their importance.

This chapter illustrates how the two educational political systems deal with the structural weakness of their central governments and manage the various opposing actors in the periphery in order to drive reform forward. We first elaborate on the significance of the historic events that have shaped their educational policies; second, we examine how these different paths lead to the common tradition in resisting national tests; and third, we describe initiatives that have acted as drivers for change in spite of a tendency of both systems toward stasis.

History and Educational Policies

Austria

Austria needed political stability after World War II to recover from the damages caused by the turmoil of the Nazi regime. The destruction caused by the total domination of one political party led to a political philosophy aimed at preventing a recurrence. This "Second Republic" was built on social cohesion, trust, and stability in organizational structures. By the time the Allies left in 1955, Austria was relieved to be a neutral state with a growing economic prosperity built on maintaining the status quo and avoiding conflict.

Austria had become a federal state with a very strong identity in the provinces, which continues to lead to tensions and even confrontations between the central government and its partners in the different Länder. The permanent strain between center and region leads to difficulty in implementing national policies without significant "interference" on the part of the Länder. Reform cannot be undertaken without involving political actors in the Bundesländer and obtaining their agreement to inhibit counterproductive activity. These continuous negotiations produce a delicate balance between center and periphery. As a consequence of this tradition in Austria's policy culture, there are many actors, numerous parallel structures, and little congruence in task-orientation and responsibility.

In the educational sector, the fear of ideological domination was addressed by a parliamentary decision in 1962 requiring a two-thirds majority to pass laws affecting schools. This measure prevents sudden changes by minority governments (or even most majority governments) while also safeguarding the interests of the political parties. This has resulted in a school system with many consultative processes with groups and organizations that have a right to be involved—a condition that often makes it difficult to reach the necessary majority for significant changes.

Austria has two dominant political parties, the Peoples Party and the Social Democrats, which are often unable to agree on educational policy. Neither can muster the two-thirds majority required to proceed without significant compromise. An example of how this system plays out in policy was the attempts of the Social Democrats, when in power, to reform the heavily tracked middle school system where students enter Hauptshule or Gymnasium for grades five–eight. A parliamentary agreement was not possible, so the minister of education, a Social Democrat, negotiated directly with each of the nine provinces: four responded and agreed to adopt the "Neue Mittleshule" (NMS). The model was communicated centrally, but further developed through dialogues with key actors at the Länder level, which added distinctive imprints and a provincial face and identity. Moreover, the individual Länder labeled the NMS according to the names of the provinces (e.g., VMS for the Vorarlberg Middle School or SMS for the Styrian Middle School) to emphasize their uniqueness within a centralized school reform. As a consequence, the two-track system remained in place as a national policy, but a new type of school was introduced in a way that added more complexity to an already complicated structure.

Flanders

In Flanders the long history of conflict between public and Catholic education during the nineteenth and twentieth centuries came to an end with the School Pact of 1959. This Pact was a truce in which the foundations of Flemish education for the modern era were settled. Both sides agreed not to criticize the efforts or outcomes of the other, or to lobby to change the public funding system. The School Pact contained guarantees for the freedom of education, which reinforced elements of the Belgian constitution. The Pact stated that all schools, private or public, religious or secular, that meet governmental conditions are recognized and funded by the government in a similar way. Parents were guaranteed the choice of a public or private school within a reasonable distance of their home. Since the School Pact of 1959, Flemish education has been characterized by a constant struggle to maintain this balance. All policy measures introduced since then have had to walk this tightrope between the two separate educational networks.

Public education in Flanders consists of two different educational networks: a "local" educational network, in which municipalities and provinces are governing bodies, and a "national educational network" of which an agency representing Flanders is the governing body. *Catholic education* is represented by another network, which is headed by a governing body from the Catholic school sector. Flemish educational policy is the result of negotiations and compromises between these three networks, the government, and the unions, which also play an important role in educational policy, especially in personnel issues. As unions are also organized within the networks, the number of key stakeholders is high. Moreover, all these stakeholders continuously consult with their members in order to maintain their legitimacy. Policy making is laborious and fundamental change is rare because all the stakeholders are concerned primarily with looking out for their own interests. Policymaking can move forward only when there is significant agreement between the different groups.

One underlying principle to maintain equality and balance has been that school networks should not be compared. Occasionally some suggest that Catholic schools are better schools, but these suggestions are immediately countered by the assertion that Catholic schools do not recruit their fair share of lower-income students.

Governmental power is inherently limited in this process of negotiations around educational policy. Schools in both networks must meet the Flemish attainment targets, which are monitored by an inspectorate, but, apart from this, governing bodies determine their own curriculum and timetables, evaluate students as they choose, and select and evaluate staff using their own criteria. This reality limits the policy options available to the government. Top-down levers, such as mandates, laws, and system change, which are used to effect educational changes in most countries, are not available in Flanders because it might alter the balance created by the School Pact of 1959 and threaten the power of the networks. Change must emerge from the bottom up through professional development and capacity building, and inducement policies that provide financial aid for specific objectives. However, the funds for capacity building and inducements are, by custom, managed by the educational networks and the governing bodies, which further limits the ability of the government to reform the basic structure of the system (Devos, 2008).

Summary

The educational systems in both countries have evolved through balance and compromise. School laws in Austria must be approved by the two major parties (People's Party and Social Democrats); in Flanders all laws must respect the interests of public and Catholic education and the basic principle of parental choice. In both countries, these fundamentals of the policy culture preclude major policy changes. Moreover, in both countries policymaking is characterized by required consultations with a wide variety of stakeholder groups and organizations. Both countries are characterized by weak central authority that is unable to mandate significant changes unilaterally. Central influence depends on the goodwill and cooperation of different actors (educational networks in Flanders and Länder in Austria). These actors have flexibility to interpret policy as they implement it, which leads to a complicated and differentiated educational landscape that is also remarkably stable.

Finding Systemic Drivers for Change

Both Austria and Flanders have been keen participants in international studies like PISA. Their results are published widely, carefully monitored by educators, the media, scientists, and ministers. At the very least, the results have an impact on discussions of educational policies in both countries. Whereas Flanders has scored highly in the PISA studies to date (unlike the French speaking community in Belgium), Austria has fallen below the average OECD results. What they have in common, however, is that both scored as two of the most unequal systems among the OECD countries. Both countries had Social Democratic ministers of education who viewed the inequality revealed by the PISA results with alarm, and used them to justify the introduction of new equity policies, which, in line with their respective policy cultures, used different levers to initiate change.

The new equity policy in Flanders was based on two components: a student care policy that provided additional funding to schools with low-income students, and a student redistribution policy that aimed to more equally allocate low-income students between schools. Because central mandates are not possible, the policy used inducements—the promise of additional funding—to encourage schools to increase their enrollment of lower SES students. To facilitate the desired result, the government created platforms for the governing bodies of local schools to consult with one another regarding the redistribution of students. In keeping with the Flemish culture of local autonomy, however, these platforms were advisory with no real authority, and the eventual decision about the admission of students remained with an individual school's governing body. Schools were officially prohibited from refusing students based on their social background, but unofficially some schools created mechanisms that served to exclude them: a low SES student might be "advised" that they fell below the school's educational standards, or were informed about expensive extracurricular activities in ways that suggested they would never really belong. This then became the fate of the twin components of the Flemish equal opportunity policy: schools accepted the student care funds for the low SES students they already had while creating barriers to thwart a more vigorous redistribution policy.[2]

In Austria, there are also limited ways of providing inducements to bring about change toward more school-based involvement in innovation. National policymakers soon learn how difficult it is to get policy decisions into practice, and quickly try to find ways to build capacity for change by reaching out to actors who may be willing to try something new as a way of nudging the system in a different direction. For example, rather than try to move the whole system toward a new type of lower secondary school that provides more equal opportunities, the current minister of education introduced it using a law that permits reform experiments that include a maximum of 10 percent of the schools. A core element of the *Neue Mittelschule* is dismantling the system that tracks children at an early age, while building on a pedagogic framework intended to challenge all children, irrespective of their social, cultural, and language background or their performance at the end of primary school. Shifting decisions about tracks or streams from the end of primary school to the end of lower secondary school was also intended to foster integration of immigrant and special needs students, who were almost invariably assigned to the lower streams at the beginning of their secondary education. Within three years, the success of the experimental schools led to parental pressure to turn more *Hauptschulen* into *Neue Mittelschulen*. For the minister, the removal of tracking in lower secondary education was a first step toward comprehensive education reform in Austria, but the decision to implement this major change had to come from below.

Another example of how voluntary capacity building is used to create system-wide change is the *Austrian Leadership Academy* (LEA), which was initiated in 2004 by the then minister of education as an effort to enhance the innovative capacities of educational leadership on all levels. Two researchers were invited by the ministry to set up the academy to reflect a new paradigm of both personal and institutional leadership for improvement on all levels of the school system. This resulted in a program that takes quality leadership as a starting point for systemic innovation, and applies a new understanding of theory and practice transforming the educational system (Schley & Schratz, 2011). A focus on creating a critical mass that is knowledgeable about reform ideas and has enhanced capacity for advocating for essential change processes has fostered a different kind of discussion on the local level.[3] Encouraging networks among graduates of the Academy on the regional and national levels enhances dissemination of new practices. Creating leadership as a lever for systems development is, again, a bottom up process stimulated by central support for experiments and voluntary capacity building.

National Testing Regimes Take Over?

The Flemish education has been very stable since the School Pact in 1959, and all new policy initiatives and reforms have respected this delicate agreement. Governing bodies are authorized to develop their own tests to evaluate their students, and national standardized tests are viewed as a threat to this feature of school autonomy. Nonetheless, the Flemish government has recently introduced tests that enable schools to compare/benchmark themselves with other schools but, as a nod to autonomy, they are not mandatory and the results are not made public.

Several forces have encouraged the use of these tests. First, international studies, like PISA and TIMMS, have a high impact in discussions about Flemish education, and have promoted the idea of objective tests as a quality measure. Second, scientific research focused on internal and external quality control paved the path for policymakers to promote common assessment tools. A British-educated education minister, who held his position between 2004 and 2009, was eager to use scientific research findings and objective data and encouraged their use. A third important force was the more active role of the ministry's civil service staff, which has been modernizing since the 1990s. Members of parliament who used to justify their proposals mainly with ideological or political arguments have become more used to considering the data provided by the ministry's staff.

Balancing the forces that have stimulated the use of national tests are sources of resistance. The Catholic educational network forcefully opposes increased use of the tests, which are viewed as a fundamental challenge to their autonomy and freedom of education. The Catholic system has, for decades, used its own tests to compare and monitor its own schools, and to indicate where interventions may be needed. They see no need for additional tests or to compare their schools with those outside their own network. As a result, the national tests are seldom used in Catholic schools. A further limitation when national tests are used is the lack of publicly available data: the test results are meant for internal use by the schools tested, although schools are expected to inform the inspectorate of the results during school audits. One consequence of limited use and the private nature of the data is that the tests cannot be used for any systematic research about the Flemish educational system that might lead to other suggestions for improvement.

Austria also has a history of school autonomy in the post–World War II era, although this evolved without a formal agreement comparable to the School Pact in Flanders. With a long tradition of well-trained teachers, Austrians have been largely satisfied with their performance in comparative international studies. National policy focused on "input orientation" to promote equal opportunity and ensure the coverage of content. This complacency was shattered by the unfavorable results of TIMMS (2007) and PISA (2003 and later administrations of the tests). While the schools and teachers' unions were satisfied with their relationship with the state, school reformers and politicians saw a need to shift from an input focus to a quality assurance/output focus that included student performance. Although the state had developed highly functional lines of communication for transmitting expectations about input, and the technical capacity to measure student outcomes, schools and unions are resistant to this shift in emphasis.

The government has developed standards that describe what pupils in year 4 (in German, reading, writing, and mathematics) and students in year 8 (in mathematics, German, English, and science) should know and be able to do. Standards monitoring tests were developed and conducted by the BIFIE (Federal Institute of Educational Research, Innovation and Development of the Austrian Educational Sector), an agency affiliated with the Ministry of Education. Regular monitoring of these competencies is intended to help improve the overall quality of teaching and learning.

The implementation has placed strict limits on the use of test results. The standards are also expected to serve as an instrument of self-evaluation for teachers and schools. They are not aimed at changing the way in which schools present their profiles to prospective families, or as challenges to teachers' autonomy to choose instructional methods. Instead, their goal is to provide soft guidelines that shift the emphasis of teaching toward output orientation. Students' grades are not supposed to be affected by national standards and monitoring, which reflects the long tradition in resisting national testing. Students and their parents are notified of individual results but teachers and the school administration receive only the anonymous results of their classes as feedback about the effectiveness of their teaching and suggested areas for improvement. A higher stakes development related to national testing is the introduction of the centralized Matura, a school-leaving exam after year 12 of schooling, which is in the pilot phase at the time of publication of this book. However, the Matura is intended only as a high-stakes test for students, and not for schools.

There have been national debates about centralizing testing at certain stages in the career of a student. Opponents of output standards argue that because learning is an individual activity it is unrealistic to apply the same outcome criteria to a heterogeneous cohort of young people.[4] From this point of view, input standards would be a fairer means to ensure equality of opportunity. The counterargument is that the principles of personalized education and differentiated instruction should be realized for all learners. The way to achieve standardized learning outcomes need not be uniform; standards in fact do not prescribe instructional procedures but leave instructional decisions to the teacher.

Teacher unions regard standards, as well as the new centralized Matura examination, as problematic. They argue that these developments could lead to "teaching to the test" and leave little time to respond to students' interests and interdisciplinary pursuits; holistic learner profiles generated by schools would likely be neglected. Moreover, teachers fear that testing could jeopardize their autonomy, and the powerful Austrian teacher unions are concerned that external examinations might be used to evaluate teachers' performance as well as that of their students.

Language, Policies, and Political Culture . . .

The influence of New Public Management ideas that focus on increasing standardization of student learning outcomes is significant in both educational systems. The international trend to focus on national student assessments, benchmarked to the curriculum, has led both countries to introduce tests developed by the Ministries of Education or outsourced agencies. Both countries share a similar reserved attitude toward the use of these tests. The tests can be used to monitor the educational system and to provide schools with performance feedback, but their full potential to create a more accountable system is limited because test results are not made public, they are not used to rate or rank schools, and they do not affect student grades. In the planned Austrian Matura (school-leaving exam after upper secondary education) only certain elements will be centralized, and the teachers will continue to mark the students' work, which will allow them to retain some local professional control.

Change Does Not Come Easily

Since the direct influence of central authority in both countries is weak and policy measures depend on the consent of many different actors outside the parliament and ministry, educational reform is not characterized by effective mandates or comprehensive restructuring plans. In Flanders, mandates are not really mandates but suggestions with reward structures attached, allowing local actors to subvert the intentions of national policy where they conflict with local preferences. In Austria, the long tradition of local autonomy has led to direction from the national level that is only modestly coherent and is effective only when a critical mass of support has been cultivated. School autonomy has a stronger legal status in Flanders, but local resistance in both countries has stymied national efforts to create systemic reform. This makes more radical change possible—but it is rare, episodic, and often localized.

So, change is difficult, but not impossible. Both countries, influenced by international trends, have recently developed national tests to measure student achievement. This is totally new in their political culture of decentralization and school autonomy. Opposition to national testing that is grounded in basic value assumptions about education, and supported by the traditions of decentralized decision-making, has, however, limited the use of tests and blunted corrective policy initiatives that might be stimulated by new data. Autonomy and internal quality control remains important in both Flanders and Austria, although pressure to allow the tests as an external measure of quality is increasing.

Despite important similarities in their educational political cultures, there are significant differences in how they formulate and implement national policy in an environment that resists central authority. In Flanders, an important change in educational policy was the inducement initiative, which provided extra funds for students from low-income families. The driving forces for this change were two policymakers in key positions (the minister of education and the head of the Catholic educational network) and the PISA studies indicating the high inequality between schools. Capacity building in Flanders has, however, proved to be a disappointingly weak lever for change, as professional development is outsourced to the educational networks, which can reinterpret the mandates as they wish.

In contrast, Austria has not chosen to use funding inducements to cajole local stakeholders into meaningful reform, but has focused on national (voluntary) capacity building. An Austrian-wide Leadership Academy was initiated by the Minister of Education in 2004 and developed by "objective, impartial researchers." Principals and people in other key management positions from the different Länder participated on a large scale in this academy, which has led to the creation of new alliances for innovation and change. Rather than safeguarding the interests of the Länder they come from, the participants of the *Leadership Academy* or *Neue Mittelschule* made use of the knowledge they gained to improve their own work—in the case of the Leadership Academy through more vigorous system leadership, and in the case of the middle school by learning from each other about how to deal with mixed ability grouping.

The common Flemish and Austrian culture of stability, conflict avoidance, and the continuous search for compromises between the different parties involved has slowed reform. The intervention of key individuals (ministers of education in both countries, the head of the Catholic educational network in Flanders, and the two academics who designed the Leadership Academy in Austria) has led to meaningful changes in both educational systems. In Flanders the change has not been radical. Although significantly more support is provided for schools with students with low SES, the social segregation these policies were designed to reduce remains in place due to school autonomy. In Austria progress still runs slowly like a "sedate elephant" or a "snail," to use the metaphors actually provided by interviewees. Nonetheless, school leadership has brought new impetus to the reform agenda of individual schools and capacity building in the *Neue Mittelschulen* has begun to change the learning culture.

As for the impact of New Public Management, the introduction of tests has led to some incremental changes. However, deep-rooted cultural mechanisms in both countries continue to successfully promote decentralization and stability as the most highly valued sources of educational quality. The fears of stakeholders that publication and comparison of test results will undermine their autonomy and influence may indeed be well founded; if and when this does happen, a more fundamental change of the political and educational cultures of each country may not be far behind.

Notes

1. The Flemish community has its own autonomous education system in Belgium and is therefore treated as a country for the purposes of comparison——see chapter six.
2. The Catholic educational network supported the policy and worked with the minister to enact it. It did not, however, pressure its schools to comply because this would have required undermining the autonomy of individual schools within the network.
3. Every year two new cohorts join the Leadership Academy, each consisting of 250–300 school principals and other key people in managerial positions. There are not seven "generations" of graduates.
4. Heterogeneity is, of course, increased by the still dominant tracking system, which separates students at age ten.

11

Political Cultures in England and the Netherlands: Similar Discourse, Different Results

Karen Seashore Louis and Boudewijn van Velzen

Introduction

We determined early in this project that we wanted to compare the English and Dutch political cultures because the language of New Public Management (NPM) has been prominent in educational discussions there for several decades. NPM has engaged ministers and other key political figures, and there is also evidence of policy borrowing, particularly in explicit interactions among officials in the Netherlands discussing the significance of English initiatives for reform in the Dutch context. However, the consequences of efforts to create a more "modern," streamlined, and efficient system in the two countries are very different.

In England, where most schools were public and governed by local education authorities, NPM resulted in efforts by the national government to create systemic changes in structures and policies that required competition within the public school sector to create quality education. In the Netherlands, where most schools were small and 70 percent "private" (but government-funded) efforts to create incentives for greater efficiency led to the growth of intermediate coordinating units that constrain the ability of the central government to enact significant systemic reform. Therefore, the main question that we will explore in this chapter is: Does a country's political culture explain how parliaments and elected officials have responded to the call to apply the principles of NPM to education?

Introduction

Our data collection for this chapter was similar to that in the other countries with one exception: both authors were involved in the interviews in the Netherlands, and from the beginning we made attempts to ensure that the actors we interviewed in each country represented similar positions within both the formal and informal structure. As "outsiders" to the political structures (neither author has an advisory position to any government agency; the first author was not a citizen of either country), we had an apparent neutrality with regard to the policies of particular governments and/or coalitions. The issues that intrigued us emerged from several observations made by our respondents: first, policymaking initiatives in both countries have shifted, over time, between central governments and intermediate or local agencies—but the direction of the shift is toward more centralization in England and more decentralization in the Netherlands. Second, the rise of international and national standards and accountability language, driven by NPM, has challenged the patchwork of local, municipal, and local education authority/school board preferences that shaped educational policies in both countries in the post–World War II era. Finally, although the use of NPM-flavored language is similar between the two countries, the broad characteristics of the policymaking process have not been disrupted in spite of several changes in the political parties that control parliament.

England and NPM: Market Language, Central Control

As was indicated in chapter eight, the English political culture may be characterized as "traditional" (Elazar, 1970). However, not all traditional cultures are characterized by a focus on the language of NPM. For example, although North Carolina (chapter nine) was also characterized as traditional, the standards and accountability movement in that state do not rely extensively on the language of efficiency and reform of public services that characterizes NPM. In this section we will briefly summarize the way in which the decentralized and variable English system, which historically placed little emphasis on either efficiency or standardized best practices, emerged as an advocate of NPM.

Background to NPM in England

Until the middle of the twentieth century, there were few parliamentary initiatives defining educational standards and structures. Two major acts created "the modern system" that has become both more standardized and more focused on centrally initiated experiments that are designed to create improvements. The 1944 Education Act was, according to all respondents, a defining change in English education because it created national definitions for the basic strands in English education (e.g., primary and different types of secondary schools) while at the same time creating more equal access to government schools. The act created a system from what had been previously an agglomeration of locally run and identified schools. Equally important to the story of NPM in England was the 1988 Education Act, which introduced school governing bodies independent from local education authorities (LEAs), a national curriculum, public reporting of school test results, and greater parental choice. The 1988 act was introduced to the public with statements that presaged the evolving NPM language of the years to come. The goal of the act was greater central control by the government *and* market principles that would make individual schools responsible for offering an education package that would attract students. The notion that markets would be tied to publicly available measures of school effectiveness eroded the role of the local education authorities (Gillard, 2011).

In 1992, a new education schools act introduced the Office of Standards in Education (OFSTED) that stressed external quality control and provided the government with the authority to close schools that didn't meet the national criteria. This further increased the national focus on a particular model of effectiveness linked to national tests. Like emerging movements in other countries, a great deal of emphasis was placed on the need for a greater variety of schools and the importance of competition to foster quality (DfEE, 1997). The public rollout of the 1992 act was framed with an emphasis on market-driven language (West & Penning, 2002).

NPM is Entrenched; Regulation Increases

The 1998 School Standards and Framework Act, introduced under a Labour government, legislated a national literacy strategy and "attainment targets" that all students and schools should meet. Thus, rather than rely on the role of the market (which allowed parents to choose schools on the basis of their test results) the government determined the standards but, as noted in a 1997 white paper, would not determine school structures and procedures. Nevertheless, the report, which set forth the outlines of the Labour Party's approach, drew on NPM language, and argued that it was compatible with a focus on quality classrooms. Marrying market-driven and competition-based strategies with government-mandated standards that determined how teachers work was the new path forward:

> It was right, in the 1980s, to introduce the National Curriculum . . . It was right to set up more effective management systems, to develop a more effective inspection system, and to provide more systematic information to parents. These changes were necessary and useful. We will keep and develop them. But they are not enough . . . but we face new challenges at home and from international competitors . . . They do not rely on market forces alone, and neither should we. It is now time to get to the heart of raising standards—improving the quality of teaching and learning. (DfEE, 1997, p. 11)[1]

The link between the market, classroom, and standards was, in the view of this report, reciprocal, and later initiatives, while reflecting the Labour government's efforts to increase opportunities for less affluent children, consistently supported choice, privatization of a variety of aspects of the educational system (including responsibility for school-building facilities), the ability of schools to select students, and the critical role of the government in establishing quality control. While the language of free markets for parents (and the responsibility for governance at the school level) was well established, the government was nevertheless increasing its regulatory approach to education. The report pointed to a huge increase in the number of statutory regulations that were created by all ministries, and urged that the government take a lighter tough: "Head teachers welcomed a House of Lords committee report which urged [the Minister of Education] to stop deluging schools with new regulations. In 2008 schools in England received 79 policy consultations and more than 300 announcements from the Department for Children, Schools and Families" (Shepard, 2009). To give just one example, while the interviews for this study were being conducted in 2008, a group of school leaders reported that they had just received a directive from the Department for Children Schools and Families[2] that they were required to examine all of the lunches that children brought from home, and to remove any items that might be considered unhealthy (primarily sweets). A colleague, who was on the board of a school, received a similar letter indicating that she was responsible, as a board member, for ensuring that this new regulation was implemented. According to critics, such requirements often required immediate implementation, and allowed no time for comment.

The focus on markets did not, however, decrease. A singular shift in the late 1990s through 2007 was the effort to marry market forces and equity initiatives. The Excellence in Schools report (DfEE, 1997) emphasized the importance of targeting resources to areas characterized by high poverty, and later the importance of requiring greater collaboration between education and human services. At the same time, however, there was increased autonomy for schools, including allowing them to select a proportion of their students on the basis of aptitude and previous performance in schools. One important school improvement initiative that used a market approach to create equity was the "specialist schools" initiative. This program allowed comprehensive secondary schools, particularly in urban areas, to change to new and more entrepreneurial models, which involved a more specialized focus to the curriculum (business, arts, technology, etc.):

> Schools would achieve specialist status by raising £50,000 in business sponsorship, setting improvement targets and involving the local community. In return they would get a £100,000 capital grant and £120 extra per pupil per year for at least four years and would be allowed to select up to ten per cent of their intake on the basis of aptitude. (Gillard, 2011, chapter 10)[3]

The specialist schools conversion was a centerpiece of the London Challenge initiative, which was designed to target low-performing schools in some parts of the city. It was, however, also intended for all schools and, at the end of 2009, approximately 88 percent of government-funded secondary schools had taken the bait.[4] In sum, the NPM language infused all initiatives and white papers from 1988 till the present days with an increasing emphasis placed on business language, control through testing and numbers, and experimentation with alternative approaches to improving opportunities for children from less-advantaged areas.

At roughly the same time a more extreme form of market-and-privatization became law: The Education and Inspections Act of 2006 stipulated yet another variation on the idea of schools becoming more independent by designating an option for all schools to become "trust schools." The trust school was characterized by its links with an external partner(s) who would, essentially "own" the school, employ the staff, and create its own governance system. These external partners would appoint the majority of the governors, own the school's assets, employ it's staff, set admission arrangements, and be able to apply for additional flexibilities constrained only by the national curriculum and testing schemes.[5]

A remarkable feature of the English system was the sheer variety of school types that parents (and supporters) confronted by the beginning of 2010. According to a website designed to help ordinary citizens work their way through the maze of government agencies, the education system supports 11 different types of schools that operate with government funding: Community schools, foundation and trust schools, voluntary aided schools, voluntary controlled schools, specialist schools, academies, city technology colleges, community and foundation specialist schools, faith schools, grammar schools, and maintained boarding schools. Each of these different types has variants, and different funding and governance structures. Some of these school types are not entirely new, but have arisen from the persistence of older systems that (pre-1944) have continued to function inside an increasingly centralized national system, while others are the legacy of efforts to "tweak" and create market incentives for improvement.[6] This list does not include Sixth Form Colleges, which provide the last years of secondary education for students who will go to university, or independent schools that receive no government support. These results indicate that the seemingly contradictory policies of markets, privatization, and centrally mandated standards and assessments have been successful.

State-School Relationships

When, in 1944, the national government announced that it had a role to play in developing a framework for the educational system, governance was still largely through local education authorities. The reform that was envisioned in 1988 was one in which the national agencies would maintain full responsibility for quality and funding, while the individual schools had increased room to become actors in a new market. The role of local education authorities was decreased and in the case of London, eliminated, while the roles and responsibilities of school-governing bodies and school heads were increased. That the government was able to choose a new model and move so quickly toward that vision is due to England's parliamentary system. One influential advisor summarized the contrast with the American system: "'Once Britain's prime minister is elected, he has a majority in Parliament and it's much easier to change things,' Sir Michael [Barber] said. 'In contrast, the founding fathers [in the United States] created a political culture where you have to get consensus from competing factions'" (qtd in Dillon, 2007). This is not to say that the process has always been smooth or even logical. The growth of regulations has undermined the role of broader public consultation in determining educational policies, and parliament appears to have been increasingly excluded from serious debates and consultation. A member of the education committee in parliament remarked, for example, that they were rarely consulted before acts were introduced, and that the committee's role was typically confined to evaluating the effects of government action after the fact. The teacher unions, which had traditionally been part of the larger pattern of consultation prior to introducing acts, had, according to several respondents, a declining role, with little or no representation in discussions about the future of education during the first decade of the twenty-first century. Another respondent in the interviews noted that many new educational regulations, as well as the basic frameworks for parliamentary acts, were determined over dinner, with fewer than 20 trusted advisors and representatives from the growing quasi-government organizations in attendance.[7] Representatives of the scholarly community indicated that their role as advisors had been replaced by private consulting firms. A respondent from one of these consulting firms concurred that policy analysis and evaluation was increasingly outsourced to private agencies rather than to universities.

What is remarkable about the English incorporation of market-driven language/privatization and centralized control is the degree to which it has persisted across prime ministers and education ministers and advisors who have little in common politically. In spite of the evidence that the centralized policies put into effect under different governments have improved the quality of education for many children in England, many educators and most of the left have been disappointed in the changes that have occurred over the past 25 years. Peter Mortimore (2009), the former director of the prestigious Institute of Education in London, stated:

> Much needed to be done . . . And many teachers wanted to help improve schools and make our society more equal. But, instead of the formulation of a long-term improvement plan based on the two big questions—what sort of education system is suitable for a modern society, and how can excellence and equity be made to work together—schools got top-down diktat. Successive ministers, and especially their advisers, thought they knew "what works." They cherry-picked research, suppressed evaluations that gave them answers they did not want, and compounded the mess. Trusting teachers—which is what ministers do in the best-performing countries—was not on the agenda.

The Netherlands and NPM: Market Language, Corporate Influence, and the Need for Consensus

The most critical event in modern Dutch educational history was the 1917 "Pacification" agreement, which produced a constitution that recognizes both public education schools and publicly funded "private schools." The implementation of the new constitution also resulted in the establishment of a Ministry of Education, whose function was primarily to ensure compliance to the detailed and complicated laws and regulations that were passed as a part of the agreement.

About 30 percent of the Dutch schools are public, with the remaining 70 percent being publicly funded private schools with a wide variety of religious or pedagogic orientations.[8] Parents choose the school they prefer; if in their community such a school is not available, local communities are obligated to provide transport to a nearby school that meets parents' criteria. Parents or their representatives are also free to start a school and request for funding if there is evidence that a sufficient number of students may have an interest in such a school.[9]

The role of the Dutch government in the middle of the twentieth century can be described as "distributive": as long as the schools met the limited criteria for quality outlined in the law, it provided funding. It monitored curriculum in public schools (together with local government), but had minimal control over curriculum in private schools. The laissez-faire approach to supporting schools changed in the early 1970s. Fired up by an activist social-democrat minister, and with support from the Christian Democrats in parliament, the government assumed a constructive and innovative role. That coalition made it possible to adopt a series of major reforms, and weakly defined "attainment targets" for all publicly funded schools were introduced. Control over curriculum by the government remained a contested issue, especially in the case of private schools. Nevertheless, a general feeling developed that the government was becoming a partner with teachers and parents in guiding the "inner life" of school.

NPM in The Netherlands

The Catholic School Board Association (NKSR) played a significant role in introducing NPM ideas into the Dutch educational system. As the NKSR heard about the difficulties that some of their member schools encountered as part of implementing the national reforms, and also about the schools' desire to remain as independent as possible, the idea of the "semi-autonomous" school was introduced into national policy discussions. The main driver of this idea was an OECD research program that indicated that effective educational innovation begins with the school as the unit of change rather than starting with the system (van Velzen et al., 1985). This assumption is now controversial, as governments look for ways to move their entire systems toward new goals in a more coherent way, but at the time the conversation was largely about the failure of previous system reforms to create any significant change in classrooms in a variety of countries. In the Netherlands, the government, school boards, and unions entered a process of discussion that culminated in 1993 in a binding covenant rather than in a specific legislative act. Critical features in this covenant were:

- Less extensive and simplified rules and regulations from the national government.
- More independence for school boards.
- Greater accountability of schools (and their boards) to the national government.

The full implementation of the process that began with this 1993 covenant was not finalized until the end of the first decade of the twenty-first century: in 2010 the "Goed Onderwijs, Goed Bestuur" (good education, good governance) bill passed parliament, which gave school boards the full responsibility and accountability for all dimensions of school life—finances, personnel, curriculum, pedagogy, professional development, and equipment. Funding is "lump sum" based on enrollment.[10]

The process we have described earlier started out in the 1980s, stimulated by the NKSR's assertion that a decentralized approach to reform was needed to create better conditions for school improvement and innovation, but ended up with public conversations focused on efficiency and effectiveness. In the decades it took to complete the discussions, the Dutch economy suffered from several economic shocks, including the most recent worldwide economic crisis, which created financial constraints for the government. Coalitions—both center-left and center-right (and one unusual left-right coalition)—slowly embraced NPM as the tool to make significant cuts in the generous support for all public services. When this approach was married to the traditional emphasis on "freedom of education," a peculiarly Dutch form of NPM emerged.

In education, the new emphasis on efficiency was introduced by a Social Democratic education minister (Jo Ritzen), who introduced the first significant limits on school size as part of the eligibility criterion for public funding. For the first time, small schools were told to grow, merge—or close. This, in addition to other incentives, created a wave of voluntary mergers of small schools into larger organizations (usually not housed in the same building, but relabeled as a "school") because it was felt that size would help to ensure survival under the new financial conditions. These larger organizational units—in some cases very large—created a need for new governance models and management. A semiautonomous primary school of one hundred students required little administration that couldn't be provided by a principal and parents; a large consolidated upper secondary vocational school that enrolled several thousand students required more management levels between the teaching staff and those on the top, and an expanded role for school boards. The increasing size of the average school was accompanied by another shift that, in the early 1990s, appeared rather subtle. No longer was the focus only on the autonomy of small *schools*—it was also on autonomy for the *school boards* that managed groups of schools. In less than a decade, the view of school management changed, and principals began to be seen as "middle managers" rather than as "first among equals."

Lump sum distribution of public funds with increased freedom for schools and their boards to decide how to use it also triggered reflections about the governance of public education. Most public schools were governed by city or village councils and were subject to the considerations of local politics. Why, it was asked, should the private schools enjoy quasiautonomy while the public schools did not? Today all public schools are also governed by independent school boards who operate at arm's length from the local elected officials. The only restriction on their authority is that they cannot decide to close a school without consulting with local authorities because by law public education must be an accessible option for all students.

While throughout the twentieth century the religiously orientated and nondenominational schools on national level were organized in powerful "umbrella organizations" with direct access to the minister of education, under the new conditions school boards organized themselves in sector-specific national associations for primary, secondary, and vocational education. The old umbrella organizations still exist but have less influence in discussions about education policies. These shifts occurred gradually, not as a result of comprehensive legislative policies but of more subtle changes in the political definitions of what constitutes "freedom of education." In fact, a recent parliamentary report argued that formal policies were inconsequential drivers of educational change, in large measure because they were piecemeal and unfocused (Parliament, 2008). One consequence of the increasing influence of school boards and the decreasing influence of older representative groups is that the national debate about education policy became even more fragmented (Bronneman-Helmers, 2011). The days of a national government vision on the nation's future education, which briefly held the public and parliament's attention in the 1970s, are over. Or as Marc Chavannes (2009, p. 10) in his study on the privatization of Dutch politics, put it: "The government no longer believes in government."

Similarities in Political Language; Differences in Policy Outcomes

Although NPM has permeated the debate on what constitutes "good governance" in many countries, England and the Netherlands are among those governments that have embraced this paradigm with the greatest passion. The persistence in focusing on privatization as a means to increase efficiency and effectiveness, the importance of accountability in governance, and the importance of standards have, in both countries, persisted across parliaments of remarkably different party composition.

This tendency is apparent not only in education but in other sectors as well. For example, the European Union has promoted an open and fair competition between providers of transportation services in order to guarantee the best possible services at the lowest possible price for all citizens. The NPM-based argument is that infrastructure should be separated from train services, and that principle has forced major changes in the organization of the once mighty national railroad companies. However, Germany, France, Belgium, and Italy have separated their infrastructure and services but have created a coordinating organization to ensure that they remain linked for the purposes of major management decisions. Only the United Kingdom and the Netherlands have created one organization that is responsible for infrastructure and have opened a process for public tenders for companies interested in delivering services to the public (Leijendekker, 2011). As any citizen in these two countries can tell you, rail transportation has not become uniformly better since 1991, despite hefty fines for providers who did not meet government standards in the Netherland and as demonstrated by a breakdown of the UK railroad system in 2002. Interestingly enough, the Swiss (who are not part of EU) never thought of separating infrastructure and services—and nevertheless have the best-performing company in Europe, which is highly appreciated by its clients for its cost effectiveness.[11]

Some Similarities

"Good governance" on a national level today means that the role of the government is to provide policy frameworks, funding, and accountability mechanisms. Local education authorities (England) and school boards (The Netherlands) are expected to ensure that policies and procedures produce the results that are defined in more or less detail. In both countries however we can see how difficult it is for a government to sit and wait to see what the teachers, school leaders, and students in all those schools will do—so indirect efforts to intervene in the professional realm of teachers may be observed in abundance in both countries. Nationally developed and monitored exams that impact school curricula and teaching are a highly popular intervention.[12] In both countries we see that the authorities and media (often supported by "research") question teachers' competence, often with disregard for the fact that Dutch teacher shortages forced school boards to hire nonlicensed teachers and there are serious difficulties in recruiting highly qualified teachers to some areas and some schools in England. An NPM-based intervention is becoming more widely discussed in both countries to opt for performance pay schemes, despite evidence that this in unlikely to contribute to better results (Goodman & Turner, 2010; Springer et al., 2010).

In both countries the shift to local control has led increasingly to consideration of accountability. England has developed a "balanced score card" that links finances, activities, and results. In the Netherlands the government focuses on financial accountability but school boards develop their own in balanced score card procedure, which puts schools in the same position as their English colleagues. For practitioners it comes down to more control on both process and outcome, although the source of the pressure is the national government in England, and the "autonomous school board" in the Netherlands. One Dutch observer notes that the language of NPM has eroded the trust between teachers and school managers, and between "the public" (as represented by the media) and schools (Cools, 2005).

NPM Effects are Different

Notwithstanding the similarities in language used by ministers, top civil servants, researchers, and corporate consultants who play a role at the national level in both countries, the effects are quite different. Political cultures, as they have existed for decades or longer, still shape the political process and outcomes will therefore vary. In England, reform policies and efforts at innovation are still largely channeled not only from the elected parliament, but from a small group of advisors who have considerable administrative as well as legal authority. Under both Conservative and Labour governments in England, for example, many schools were officially given more autonomy, which was followed by an intricate web of regulations to guide processes and outcomes. Schools were assisted by government-induced remodeling strategies; they were required to participate in a national literacy and numeracy initiative that mandated curriculum, professional development, and allocations of instructional time.

Schools had to coordinate with other human service organizations at the local level and were "incentivized" to engage in a variety of initiatives to increase equitable outcomes. Or, if that failed, they were expected to turn themselves into "academies" based on government frameworks. The focus of English policies was on mandates and system change, which were backed up, in many cases, by professional development to increase fidelity to government intent.

In contrast, school reform initiatives in the Netherlands are preceded by a government announcement that it will only define an expected outcome ("the what") and not interfere with the process ("the how"). In the Netherlands, schools have traditionally been given a great deal of latitude over curriculum, hiring and firing of teachers, and organizational processes; this freedom to make decisions without government interference has increased over the past few decades, and now includes most financial decisions, human resource policies, and salaries. Independent school boards have full responsibility. The inspectorate has also revised its procedures to create more flexibility for school boards—it basically restricts its concerns to determine if the quality control mechanisms of the board are in place and operating.

In addition to the formal governance structures and responsibilities, the process of change remains distinctive. In the Netherlands there is a continued emphasis on incremental and adaptive change, using inducements and capacity building, while avoiding mandates or centrally directed structural change. The period from 1970 till 1990, when the government took a more assertive role in setting a reform vision, was an outlier in Dutch education. Changes develop gradually after broad consultations with many stakeholders: while the specific groups to be consulted shift gradually over time, the basic process has changed very little. In England there is a continued emphasis on broad system change. The government is given the responsibility to initiate these, and to develop the specifics of multiple initiatives with consultants and unelected advisors. Subsequent consultation with stakeholders is mostly local and limited.

In other words, similarities in language and policy rhetoric, and some of the popular solutions to perennial educational problems (like teacher quality), can obscure fundamental differences in policy processes, and even major outcomes. In addition, it does not help to account for the different policy instruments that are most commonly used to try and achieve the government's intent. What struck us most was that even landslide changes in the elected government may have only limited impact on the major directions taken in education policies, and in the way policies are developed (tables 11.1 and 11.2).

Table 11.1 English and Dutch political cultures compared

Enduring political cultures: A comparative summary	England	The Netherlands
Openness	Relatively closed	Relatively open
Decentralism	Centralized	Balanced, gradually implemented since 1990
Rationalism	Rationalized/comprehensive	Rationalized/comprehensive for accountability; limited in leadership
Egalitarianism	Moderate emphasis; focus on "zones" or underperforming areas	Moderate emphasis; focus on school finance equalization
Efficiency	Strong emphasis on efficiency; thematic and embedded in policy	Little emphasis on efficiency, and much on financial accountability
Quality	High emphasis on quality; many national policies to promote and assess quality	High emphasis on quality; responsibility shared between state and school boards
Choice	Moderate emphasis on choice	Strong emphasis on choice

Table 11.2 English and Dutch policy levers compared

Choice of policy levers	England	The Netherlands
Mandates	Many mandates; most with some funding	Limited emphasis on mandates; state funding *indirectly through independent school boards*
System change	Strong/persistent efforts	Moderate initiatives, introduced gradually over more than 25 years; largely uncoordinated and often "bottom up" responses to government actions
Capacity building	Strong emphasis on state-funded capacity building	School or privately funded capacity building—government provides indirect financial support
Inducements	Limited	Covenants often imply inducements for schools

Notes

1. Note that the name of the government agency responsible for education changed with some regularity during this period. In the late 1990s, it was also known as the Department of Education and Employment. The current government has changed the name back to Department for Education.

2. The national agency responsible for education has changed its name on a regular basis as noted earlier.
3. http://www.educationengland.org.uk/history/chapter10.html.
4. There is little evidence that this policy has undermined equity, and modest evidence suggesting that the quality of performance in the areas of specialization has improved (Castle & Evans, 2006).
5. Note that trusts were required to be nonprofit.
6. http://www.direct.gov.uk/en/Parents/Schoolslearninganddevelopment/ChoosingASchool/DG_4016312.
7. The individual who made this comment was one of those who attended the meetings.
8. There are a small number of private, tuition-based schools. Most serve international populations.
9. The number of families required to start a school has increased. The current law requires between 200 and 350 students before government funding is allocated. The increase in required numbers has limited the start-up of new schools.
10. Schools receive supplementary funding when their enrollments include students whose education is more expensive, such as non-native Dutch children, those with special education needs, and so on.
11. But there is always an upside to report—the former national Dutch railroad company is taking over rail connections in the United Kingdom and making large and so far successful investments there.
12. In the Netherlands the reliability and validity of the school-designed portion of the final school-leaving exams is being seriously questioned, which of course impacts the feeling of trust teachers and schools experience.

12

Examining the Myth of Nordic Uniformity: The Production of Educational Policy in Denmark and Sweden

Mats Ekholm and Lejf Moos

Introduction

Danes and Swedes have a sibling relationship, made increasingly close by the recently completed bridge connecting Copenhagen and Malmö. Like siblings, the countries often joke that their close relative is too lazy or too serious to do a needed task well. In this chapter we avoid such pleasantries, and focus exclusively on differences and similarities in the ways educational policies are produced, enacted, and accounted for.

The initiation of an educational political issue, the policy preparations or the construction of premises for decision making, the decision-making itself, and the follow up on decisions are used as a basis for our understanding of the policy process (Moos, 2009a). Our examination of policymaking suggests that, in spite of the efforts on the part of the two governments to differentiate themselves and to establish a unique profile in educational reform, the underlying similarity in the political cultures has been minimally disrupted. We conclude that the rhetoric of New Public Management (NPM) has been far more visible in Denmark than in Sweden, but that the consequences in terms of real change are less obvious.

Roots of Today's Political Systems

Denmark and Sweden have an intertwined history. In the fifteenth century they were linked in a weak union that was broken up at the end of the first quarter of the sixteenth century. Following the breakup of this union, Sweden and Denmark endured the next three centuries with mutual animosity and several wars. The peace of 1814 has held for the last two centuries.

Several disastrous rounds of warfare between Denmark and Prussia in the nineteenth century marked the end of Denmark as a significant force in Europe. These defeats, coupled with an economic crisis that hit farmers hard during the middle of the nineteenth century, caused Danes to lose faith in the national government and focus on local democracy. One effect was the emergence of a strong cooperative movement. In a parallel development, it was decided that all parents were responsible for having their children educated in public or private schools or at home. It is still the case and thus approximately 15 percent of all students attend private schools, and home schooling is allowed.

Sweden has avoided war since 1814. During the nineteenth century this country went through a development that took it from being a poor country based on agriculture to a wealthy state with strong industries and access to abundant natural resources like lumber and iron ore. As wealth grew, the government created an effective national transportation network. The population grew faster than the wealth, however, and Sweden became an emigrant country starting in the mid-nineteenth century, eventually sending nearly a quarter of its population to other countries (primarily the United States). The poor conditions of the late nineteenth century led to the birth of a workers' movement that included strong cooperative associations for marketing and buying goods. From 1842 participation in a common folk school was made compulsory, but local control of buildings and teacher recruitment made quality and participation spotty. Around that time the state took over the responsibility for teachers' salaries and also took on a more active role in guiding the content of basic education. Private schools were, therefore, almost invisible in Sweden during most of the twentieth century.

The Threads of Educational Policy Come Together

Educational policy has been an issue at the national level in both countries for several centuries. The history of educational policy is, however, different in the two countries, with more emphasis on local influence in Denmark and on national influence in Sweden, but both countries ended up with centralized systems in middle of the 1900s. In both countries the state employed the teachers, negotiated pay and duties, and set rules for the work. The state also formulated curriculum frameworks, and specified the school schedule (including holidays), the number of hours of teaching in each class and subject area, and attainment targets. The targets were more detailed in Sweden than in Denmark, which left room for local (municipal and school) interpretations. In both, the state controlled examinations directly and made inspections through regional advisers. As the state was a main actor on the educational scene, strong traditions that ensured educational issues were to be dealt with by the national parliament and by the government were developed.

In spite of the high level of centralization in two relatively small countries (Denmark grew from 2.5 million in 1900 to 5.6 million inhabitants in 2010 and Sweden from 5.1 million to 9.4 million inhabitants), a spirit of openness in political procedures was also developing. As modern parliamentary processes emerged in the early twentieth century, there was an expectation of broad participation in educational policy discussions among all political parties and groups, and stakeholders and practitioners, who are represented through the associations and unions. Participation was not limited to elections, but also included engagement in the initiation of policies and in the construction of premises for decision-making as well as follow up debate and implementation. In keeping with emerging differences in political culture, participation in Sweden occurred more often at the national level, while there was an expectation of more participation at the local level in Denmark.

During the middle of the twentieth century, the national political arena in both countries was used to transform the school system from one based on selection and differentiation of students to one that reflected the value of a common comprehensive curriculum and equality. After 1962, all Swedish children attended a grundskola for nine years, with no streaming or differentiation. In Denmark, all children were expected to attend a nonstreamed comprehensive Folkeskole for ten years. During the same period both countries made extensive changes of the basic administrative structures. In Denmark the many small *sognekommuns* were merged into larger units, which became economically strong enough to support a modern Folkeskole. By 1974, the number of kommuns was reduced to 275, and this was further reduced to 98 in 2007. Sweden went from a structure of around 2,500 local municipalities in the late 1940s where each one had its own school board to a system with 276 kommuns in 1976.[1]

The general trend of the mid-to-late twentieth-century educational policies has been to advance social justice in a comprehensive and non-streamed school in both countries. In Denmark, the Social Democrats, the Liberals, and the Social Liberals have supported this trend since 1903, when a new "middle-school" served as a temporary transitional link between the basic school and the gymnasium and thus the basis for the modern comprehensive school ("Enhedsskolen"). By 1937 middle school was made exam-free, and schools in more rural and remote areas were upgraded. In Sweden the Liberal party was a driving force in the early twentieth century to create a more comprehensive school. From the 1920s the Social Democrats emerged as politically important, and the two parties supported each other in modernizing the school system. Together with the agrarian parties, they created the momentum for the parliamentary decision in 1949 that fostered a decade of experimentation leading to the fully comprehensive grundskola model in 1962.

These trends toward a fully comprehensive system continued in both countries through the rest of the twentieth century. In 1958 the Danish middle school was incorporated into the basic school with a "soft streaming" at the end of grade seven, leaving all students in one school but in different classes for the last three years. In 1975 the streaming was further softened, and in 1993 streaming was abolished totally. All students attended the same classes in which teachers were expected to differentiate their instruction to meet the needs of students.[2] In Sweden the different specialties within the upper secondary schools (covering 16- to 19-year-olds) were also brought together under the same organizational roof in 1986.

At roughly the same time, a rather major system transformation took place in Sweden, as the highly centralized school system was transformed into a decentralized version that looks more like the traditional Danish system. Sweden also followed Denmark in adopting a new policy that supported "free" schools that operate outside of the municipal governance systems. During the same period, some Danish initiatives moved in the opposite direction, with some recentralizing of curriculum details, and a shift of accountability beyond the boundaries of the municipalities. This occurred over time and was accompanied by a diminution of the role of "Bildung" and an increase in an emphasis on more goal-oriented teaching and was formulated in the Act on School in 2006 ("Consolidation Act No. 170 of 2. June 2006," Act on Folkeskole 2006).[3] The act allowed the long tradition of "dispensation" to permit municipalities to reintroduce streaming if local school boards and the municipal council sought to do so. This aspect of the law married the Danish commitment to local educational autonomy with an emerging concern about the capacity of a fully comprehensive system to meet economic needs.

In both countries, new policies in education have traditionally involved nonpoliticians in all stages of preparation and debate. Beyond this commonality, however, the efforts to transform administrative educational systems were made under rather different political circumstances. In Denmark the period after World War II until 2001 is characterized by coalition politics: no one party nor steady coalition of parties have ever held permanent majorities in parliament. Instead, they must find majorities by negotiating with a broad range of smaller parties. From the 1950s through the 1990s, a variety of coalitions between liberals and social democrats were built. In contrast, between the end of World War II and 2006, in Sweden one party (the Social Democrats) was in power 50 out of the 60 years. During this time, the Social Democrats pursued a tradition of unanimous cooperation in decision-making within education, which was designed to maintain stability and keep the country's eye on the future.

Different Paths for Education Policymaking

Stability in Swedish politics and fragmentation and less stability in Denmark appear to have resulted in different approaches to the development of educational policies. The Swedes have been more in favor of formulating central curriculum (Läroplans) in which the will of the central political actors (influenced by the consultative process) is expressed. In these documents central goals are formulated, combined with detailed syllabus for different school subjects together with guidelines for the use of time for different subjects. This preference has thwarted a number of efforts (in 1962, 1969, and 1975) to decentralize more responsibility for the details to the schools.[4] At the same time, however, politicians also stated that Swedish schools should be directed by central guidelines as before. The political intent was signaled in the four different editions of the Läroplan developed during the second half of the twentieth century, in which the number of pages devoted to mandated directions decreased from 410 in 1962 to 63 in 1994.

Teachers and school leaders were not the only consumers of the Swedish Läroplan: the most important were the authors of textbooks, whose content was carefully vetted by a national agency. This agency was closed in 1992, and the local schools are entrusted with the selection of learning materials. However, the authors of textbooks remain just as eager to base their texts on the Läroplan, since schools continue to use the text of the Läroplan in spite of their increased freedom to choose materials and texts.

Swedes have also used central testing to clarify their educational policy needs and goals more frequently than the Danes. When the grundskola was introduced in Sweden, the school system not only got a new structure, but a new student assessment system as well. A seven-point scale based on teachers' holistic appraisal of the quality of knowledge that the students had absorbed was changed into a five-point scale, where teachers were asked to rate students in relation to national standards—a difficult task for a teacher who worked in one kommun with one group of students. As one basis for the assessment, teachers could rely on standardized tests. In 1997 Swedish politicians again changed their minds and a new assessment system was introduced. To support the new marking system, national tests to determine whether students reached certain criteria were developed. Today, national subject guidelines contain descriptions of the criteria for achieving the different steps of the grading system, and give examples of what students should know at each grade level.

In Denmark, the path between national policy and local schools is less direct. Denmark never developed an attachment to texts based on the national curriculum, and texts tend to be less detailed and therefore require local curriculum work. No state agency has monitored textbooks. In addition, Denmark had not used national testing to set standards for schools and students until the last year of the schooling. Although the Swedish Läroplan has slimmed down, the description of subject knowledge requirements has always been less detailed and strict in Denmark. Danish politicians have shown more trust in teachers, school leaders, municipal school authorities, and politicians. In contrast to Sweden, it was assumed that the local level had the capacity to effectively interpret the political signals that were given in parliament and by the government.

Beginning in 1992, a shift occurred in Denmark that moved it more in the direction of Sweden. As finances and personnel management was decentralized from state to municipalities and for some parts further on to schools, other aspects were recentralizing. National curricula were gradually made more detailed, some national testing was implemented, and a semi-independent oversight agency, The School Agency, was formed (but merged with the ministry again in 2011) early in this century. These changes occurred as the Danish government has become more attentive to the advice and perspectives of transnational agencies, like the OECD and the European Commission.

Sweden Follows Denmark in the Distribution of Responsibilities

In Sweden, however, politicians are beginning to follow in the footsteps of their Danish colleagues by showed trust in the schools and the professionals who work there. The Swedish parliament's decision in the early 1990s to change the balance of responsibility among the state, kommun, and schools was premised on the capacity of local people to manage budgets well. The kommuns receive a lump sum of money that they distribute to their schools, but the schools are responsible for determining how that money will be used to educate students. The money that the school has at its disposal is used for salaries, learning materials, student transportation, student meals, and for all other aspects of school life. At the same time as this large trust was given to the kommuns and the schools, the state monitors whether students' learning reaches the goals that are formulated in the central Läroplan.

At the same time as the Swedish state loosened its grip over school funding and budgets, it strengthened its requirements in other areas. The Swedish Läroplan and the subject curricula of today are documents that need to be interpreted by teachers and school leaders on each school. Each school is expected to formulate a local working plan in which it explains how it will realize the central guidelines in their specific situation. Each school is also expected to make an assessment of the quality of its inner work and find out to what degree it has reached the aims for the students. During the first decade of the twenty-first century schools presented an annual quality review report to the kommun, and the kommun reported on the quality of its schools to the National Agency of Education. This information is openly available on the Internet, along with the ninth grade marks and the results of national tests for each grundskola.

In Sweden, this shift in the distribution of responsibility in the school system was foreshadowed by earlier decisions to prepare the school leaders to cope with the new responsibilities. Compulsory school leader training was introduced in the mid-1970s (Ekholm, 2007). Professional development for teachers and school leaders has been a characteristic of the Swedish approach to policy implementation for a long time. For example, the introduction of the most recent Läroplan was accompanied by 5 days of orientation, study, and discussion about the implications for the classroom. Currently, all grundskola and gymanasie teachers have 13 days for professional development, including days that are allocated to shared activities at the school level. A focus on professional development as a tool for policy implementation is less characteristic of Denmark, which has no compulsory training for school leaders and where education authorities rarely use the available professional development days as a vehicle for policy implementation.

The most important policy initiatives of the last decade have their origins in decisions that were made in the 1970s, 1980s, and early 1990s, when Sweden began to follow the lead of the decentralized Danes. Step by step the Swedes followed the Danish example, shifting an increasing responsibility for interpreting the overarching educational goals to the local kommuns and schools. Like the Danes, the salaries of Swedish school employees are now decided at the local level, within a framework that is negotiated nationally by the government and the unions. As in Denmark, it is the kommuns that make decisions about how to organize the use of time in schools, and on school buildings. Again, as in Denmark, many of these responsibilities are delegated to the rektor (principal) of the school. The Danish principle—that decisions should, insofar as possible, be made by those who must comply with them—is becoming institutionalized.

Influence is a Two-Way Street: What Does Denmark Learn from Sweden?

Educational stakeholders themselves in Denmark don't see their world through the same eyes. The Danes who were interviewed suggested that there is a broad agreement that the influence of the stakeholders has changed so that the teachers' union has lost influence and the Ministry of Finance and the inspectorate have gained influence. There is also agreement that, perhaps to an even greater extent, the end users, the "customers" of the school product, have gained influence. There is, however, a feeling of uncertainty, as old alliances have been broken in recent years. This development is due to the fact that the center-right government with a stable backing from the populist Danish Folks Party was able, for ten years, to act as if it was a majority government, without engaging in the complex rituals of negotiation that are more characteristic of Danish educational policymaking. Since the interviews were conducted, the national elections resulted in a coalition dominated by the Social Democrats, so readjustments are occurring. However, some of the changes are part of the slow evolution that is similar to what we have documented in Sweden.

The tide of Danish opinion supports modest centralizing trends.[5] There is agreement between the Conservatives and the Social Democrats that the increased use of centralized steering tools in the educational sector is needed. The Conservatives back this trend because they want more focus on the reading and numeracy; the Social Democrats because they argue that the goal of greater equality is better served with common goals and national adaptive tests rather than allowing each municipality to determine whether students have been well served. The trend is also approved of in many of the municipalities, where Liberal mayors are increasingly winning elections. This increasing consensus among the political parties reflects the long Swedish experience with educational policymaking.

Changing Partners in the Consultative Process

Swedish Social Democrats dominated educational policymaking for many years, even though they rarely had a parliamentary majority. Rather than forming a coalition, they chose to work through broadly representative committees to build consensus around new proposals before decisions were taken. During the periods when they were not the dominant party, the new policies introduced by the coalitions were respected when they returned to power. Because of the consultation process, differences between the Swedish political parties around education issues are not very dramatic. Even the current center-right coalition has made only modest changes to the initiatives to increase the focus on achievement results at the kommun and school level.

In Sweden the National Association of Kommuns has limited influence over the development of educational policies, which are now legally vested in national conversations and local political negotiations within the kommun. In Denmark, the influence of the National Association of Kommunes is generally regarded by stakeholders as declining. It cannot speak on behalf of all municipalities because there are differences of opinion among its members on educational issues. Increasing bureaucratization within the organization has reduced its appeal as a democratically run organization, and it has contentious and somewhat unproductive conflicts with the national government over who will control the schools. However the association still negotiates personnel salaries and working conditions in partnership with the unions on a national as well as on a municipal level, and thus has some indirect influence.

Other middle-level organizations in both countries have also lost influence during the last few decades. The LOs (National Union of Unions) in both countries are not very influential when it comes to the comprehensive school, but they eagerly participate in policy discussions about the upper secondary level. In Sweden, other national associations, such as those representing parents, have lost much of their old influence in the educational political discussion. According to some, the Danish parents' organization, School-and-Society, has become stronger and more influential, but it is difficult to find specific areas where they have influenced discussions in a forceful way. The associations of leaders with the field of child care and for schools are important players when it comes to the implementation of agreements and laws in the schools in both countries, but not in initiating new policies.

Recent Policies that Illustrate Fundamental Policy Processes

While it is usual to think that the world is changing rapidly when new policy proposals are debated in the media, by the unions, and among teachers, even a short step back allows us to see the apparent turmoil in a different light. Two cases that we present here both show the degree to which efforts to shift the policies toward greater adherence to NPM principles are confronted with the realities of how things are done in Sweden and Denmark.

A Recent NPM-Inspired Political Initiative in Denmark

In January 2010 the prime minister of Denmark appointed an ad hoc committee to unveil the strengths and weaknesses of the Folkeskole and to submit recommendations with a view to making the Danish Folkeskole among the top five nations in the global competition. He called the group of six people the Flying Squad of the Folkeskole. Two teachers of the Folkeskole, a principal of a Folkeskole, a superintendent of a school area, a Swedish researcher of education, and a managing director of a research institute were chosen for the task. The squad made a tour around the Danish Folkeskole system during the spring of 2010, visiting 20 schools in different areas of the country and speaking to hundreds of committed teachers, headmasters, politicians, administrators, pupils, parents, and others. It consulted organizations, researchers, and institutions of education that have a vested interest in and knowledge about the Folkeskole. The squad also developed a number of surveys and included existing research and knowledge about the Folkeskole that was integrated into a report delivered to the prime minister in June 2010 (Folkeskole, 2010). In the fall, the usual round of consultations associated with the Danish policymaking process commenced. However, the consultation revealed that building a partnership with stakeholders around the implementation of the report's recommendations would not be easy, and education largely fell off the prime minister's policy agenda. Perhaps the only outcome of the report has been to illustrate how difficult it is to shift educational policy in Denmark. The report stimulated a discussion about whether a "league table" of school test results should be made public. A majority of stakeholders were against it, but in the summer of 2011 the minister of education published the test results. The minister was replaced only a few months later as a result of a parliamentary election.

Some Recent Political Events in Sweden

In Sweden the Social Democrats used their long tenure during most of the 1950s–1990s to take the initiative in the educational political field. This included not only the slow implementation of the comprehensive school model, but also the major shift in governance that has been described earlier in chapter three. This shift was challenged by the deep budget cuts of the 1990s, but the Social Democrats responded to the distress in school budgets by allocating additional special funding from 2001 to 2006 to the kommuns to be used for employment of teachers.

This initiative challenged the new distribution of power between the state and the kommuns as the state prescribed what the money could be used for. Because the strengthening of the educational budget of the kommuns was seen as a shared interest, the kommuns accepted. From 1999 to 2002 the government also distributed large amounts of money to the kommuns to strengthen adult education and the government offered professional development fund to grundskola and the gymnasie schools to support the use of computers in education. The teams of teachers that participated in these educational events were also given a personal computer to make it easier to use them in educational settings. In sum, although in theory the national government allocates funds, and kommmuns decide how to use them, the national government has been busy ensuring that its educational policies are carried out with incentive funding.

Other major policy issues illustrate that the "hands off" decentralization has never fully replaced the older system of central steering. This is illustrated by several important political decisions that occurred after decentralization. For example, national responsibility for preschool education has increased. In 1998, responsibility for preschools authority was transferred to the Ministry of Education from the Ministry of Health and Social Welfare, and a central Läroplan for preschool activities was developed. As in the case with schools, the kommuns are responsible for the work and life that appears in preschools but they must now follow the central learning guidelines. Revisions to the central Läroplans for the grundskola and the gymnasie were introduced in 1994, and the marking system change (as described earlier). In 1998 the first group of students that were marked in this new way reached grade nine of the grundskola and statistics about their results were presented. Since then the shortcoming of the grund schools to make every student capable of going directly to the gymnasie school (10–11 percent of a year group does not directly qualify) is a recurrent theme for political discussions, reinforcing the role of the national government as the "overseer" of educational quality.

This latter role has received increasing prominence as the discussion of Sweden's position on international tests increased. At the end of 1990s the largest newspaper of Sweden (*Dagens Nyheter*) started a campaign designed to show the weaknesses in Swedish school standards, but in subject matter knowledge and social norms. During the last decade many discussions have been held in Sweden at the national level about the interpretation of the results of the international comparative studies by the IEA and OECD. These discussions have been fueled in the media by critical views of the school system. The ongoing quality debates have been taken up vigorously by both more and less conservative politicians. Overall, however, these debates occur on the surface of public conversations and have very limited impact on major educational political initiatives. In many ways, Swedes see the issues raised by international agencies like the OECD and the EU as harmonious with the questions and policies that Sweden has been working on for more than 50 years. The country sees little need to develop new norms or initiate radical change.

Patterns of Educational Policy Production in the Two Countries

There are similarities as well as differences in the Danish and Swedish policy histories. Overall, those we interviewed and our analysis lead us to conclude that, in spite of different histories, educational policy processes in Sweden and Denmark are more similar than different, and are, if anything, converging rather than diverging. In neither country has the strong market nor privatization rhetoric that characterizes NPM had a major impact, although there are clearly influences that have been adapted to fit within the specific contexts and immediate political considerations facing both countries. Both countries tend to have "soft" versions of testing, national standards and accountability procedures that fit within their existing processes and which have been adjusted, but not dramatically, as a result of policy discussions over the last decade.

Openness

There is a long tradition of openness in the political processes of both countries, and this has not changed. Both have multiple active political parties and involve stakeholders of many kinds. Openness has been formalized as key parliamentary practice, like the right of extended public hearings/consultations before legislation is passed in parliament. More important is the tradition of consultation prior to the formalizing of a parliamentary bill.

Another channel for openness is the national, standing and ad hoc committees. In Denmark there are more ad hoc committees than in Sweden, and there was a tendency over the last decade to reduce the number of committees and to include more representatives that are appointed by the government. The core of the system remains, however. In Sweden researchers are more often used as experts on standing committees, and there is a more embedded tradition of formal experimentation and adjustments with policies during implementation. In both countries, there have been some changes in the influence of various representative groups, which always creates grumbling, but others have become influential. When a proposition is agreed upon after political negations and a white paper is written, in both countries it is sent to relevant stakeholders for consultation. In Denmark the standing committees receive proposals that used to be negotiated by and prepared in detail in ad hoc networks of, for example, politicians, civil servants, union leaders, researchers, and so on (Torfing, 2004). In Sweden political initiatives often are taken within the political parties or are made by the unions. In both countries proposals have been developed through a long process of public discussions that are often inspired by transnational agencies (e.g., the OECD or the EU Commission) through "peer pressure" or "the open method of coordination" (Pedersen, 2010). The influences from the international agencies have together with attitude alterations of importance for the policy processes in modern society (Lindvall & Rothstein, 2006) caused a rapid change in the way educational policies are created (Moos, 2009b).

Decentralization

Traditionally the two educational systems are different: in Denmark much of the decisions were made at local levels, in schools and in municipalities, while in Sweden the tradition has favored centralization of decisions about the aims, syllabus, and national testing (Lundahl, 2008). Denmark has shifted over the past few decades toward more national discussions and decisions on frameworks, principles, purposes, and aims. In Sweden, in contrast, the last two decades of decentralization of funding and decisions about resource allocation have left national politicians with a narrower arena for policy action. In both countries, local governments and schools bear the greatest responsibility for charting their way toward better education. In sum, changes in the two countries have made them more alike in this respect.

Rationality

In both countries the vision of a Democratic Bildung, with its emphasis on a holistic view of developing the child, has shifted toward more emphasis on basic academic achievement. The explanations to this movement are to be found in the development of the state as a marketplace in the global competition and the fast tempo of the media-driven politics together with a strong influence on the political debate that comes in from international organizations like the IEA, the OECD, and the European Union. Nevertheless, in spite of these challenges, both countries have maintained a view of educational change that is premised on a slow evolution rather than fast reengineering.

The two countries have, however, somewhat different approaches to how changes are initiated. In Sweden, there have been two major policy initiatives (the grundskola and the decentralization to kommuns) that have taken years to formulate and years to work out. Most policy initiatives between these two events involve working out the details, with attendant consultation, experimentation, and adjustments. In Denmark, educational policymaking has never been sufficiently centralized to propose a long-term reform strategy with an attendant implementation of ten or more years. Rather, due to rapidly changing coalitions and a preference for setting policy through more direct democracy at the municipal level, policymaking appears more fragmented and less coherent.

Egalitarianism

Historically, Denmark has spent the last one hundred years promoting equality in and through education, while in Sweden, initiatives to restructure the system to be more egalitarian emerged just before World War II, and were not fully implemented until later. They are, nevertheless, deeply embedded in the Swedish way of looking at educational values.

Traditionally both countries have linked educational policy with the drive toward creating more equal opportunities and life chances for all citizens. In Denmark, this singular focus has become less visible in recent educational rhetoric, as the previous government took up the NPM language that tied education with the development of the state, and shifted the aims of education away from "pure Bildung" toward including education for competition and employability. This trend has resulted in some policy adjustments that permit streaming (if local municipalities decide to allow it), and more focus on outcomes than previously. Some free-standing schools are choosing to develop a profile to attract parents who see their children as especially talented. The fact that attention is being paid to small shifts suggests, however, that the norm of egalitarianism is being violated. In Sweden there are fewer signs that the state is backing away from an egalitarian stance. Efforts to introduce the possibility of streaming into national debate have fallen on deaf ears, and when the OECD raised the question about fees for Swedish universities, the suggestion was met by silence.

Efficiency

Concerns with efficiency have never been traditionally on the top of the educational policy agenda in either country. However, in recent years, economic arguments are made more openly in both countries. Politicians occasionally debate the efficiency of the schools, which would have been unheard of a couple of decades ago. One possible reason for this is the increased use of evaluation in both countries, which have led to more questions about the consequences of various initiatives that cost money. However, in spite of the change in rhetoric, few political initiatives have been taken to change resource allocation or to create incentives more efficiency.

Quality

Both countries have initiated more national testing and quality reports. The core of this concept of quality is student outcomes. Still it is rare in both countries that the quality of the work of the teachers are scrutinized and related to the learning of the students, and in spite of the singular publication of "league tables" by the outgoing minister of education in Denmark's previous government, there is little public demand for more information about quality. While Sweden and Denmark have not scored as highly on international tests as their Finnish neighbor, this has not caused permanent debates about quality as a serious problem, and in both countries the main responsibility for the provision of quality education lies with the local municipalities, where discussions of quality are still more influenced by parent and citizen preferences than international tests.

Choice

Denmark has had a tradition of private schools (publicly funded) for more than two centuries. At this point in time approximately 15 percent of a student-year cohort attends private schools. In inner cities this figure is rising rapidly, with some potential for deepening the social divide. Swedes followed the Danes, and on basis of freedom of choice arguments allowed establishment of schools that are funded by the kommun, but with an independent governance structure. It is important to emphasize that the arguments for free schools in Sweden were based on democratic choice theory, and not on the market-competition language that characterizes NPM. By 2009, almost 10 percent of the students of grundskola age went to so-called free-standing schools, and almost 20 percent of the 17- to 19-year-olds. In the larger cities these quickly rising figures have also contributed to growing segregation between social classes in both countries. The potential conflict between the principles of choice and of the long-standing commitment to comprehensive and egalitarian educational opportunities may become a challenge for both countries in the future.

Notes

1. Today there are 290 kommunes.
2. The expectation of differentiated instruction did not include all students: an increasing number of students received "special needs" education, both part- and fulltime.
3. Goal-oriented thinking in education parallels a shift away from the role of the state in ensuring citizen welfare toward educating to support a more competitive state (Pedersen, 2010).
4. This is particularly evident in the 1975/76:39 government bill addressing "the inner work of schools."
5. An exception is the Social Liberal Party, which does not have a strong position in negotiating educational policy.

13

North Carolina and Nebraska: Two States, Two Policy Cultures, Two Outcomes

Molly F. Gordon and Karen Seashore Louis

Introduction

As noted in chapter nine, when it comes to educational policy, the United States might be better thought of as 50 countries tied together with packing tape. Education in the United States has historically been a local affair, and as recently as the mid-1960s, change in schools from outside came indirectly from professional networks and textbook publishers (Miles, 1964). States and the federal government had little role in funding, policy, or oversight in many states; these were the province of more than one hundred thousand autonomous locally elected school boards scattered across a country that was still predominantly characterized by small towns and rural areas.[1] As the world has become flatter and more urbanized, the speed with which ideas travel across states has increased and, at the same time, the role of states in funding has expanded greatly. In addition, the federal government has also increased funding targeted to specific objectives, ranging from special education to the adoption of state curriculum standards.

One would expect, in this environment, that schools across the United States would become more alike, both within and between states. In this chapter we will explore that assumption by examining two states, North Carolina and Nebraska, that are largely nonurban, and that are rarely highlighted in the national news media. The focus of this chapter will be on their similarities and differences using the dimensions of political culture that were outlined in chapter one, with a particular focus on the legislative actions related to the accountability movement that has dominated much of the national conversations about education since the ominously titled 1983 report, "A Nation at Risk" (Gardner et al., 1983). We will begin with a description of the educational systems of the two states and review the evidence related to the political cultures and how educational policy is made. We will then examine how schools in each state have responded to increasing pressures for the development of accountability to state and federal expectations. Finally, we will develop some conclusions about the convergence in stated educational profiles and cultures.

Educational Systems in North Carolina and Nebraska

These two states were chosen based on several purposive criteria.[2] Both are moderately sized states that are still characterized by smaller urban areas and significant rural agricultural populations. Neither has a mega city: Omaha is the largest city in Nebraska with a population of slightly less than half a million and Charlotte is the largest in North Carolina, with a population of just over 730,000.[3] Despite the superficial demographic similarity, they have distinctive histories. North Carolina was one of the original 13 states, was part of the South during the Civil War, and has, until recently, been among the poorer states in the United States. Nebraska, in contrast, was not extensively settled until the 1860s, and did not become a state until after the Civil War (although the citizens volunteered for the North). In addition, Elazar's (1970) classic description of three distinct political subcultures within the United States places these two states in different categories. North Carolina is classified as having a "traditional" political culture, which is characterized by elite-dominated power structures, and a preference for the role of government as a custodian of social order. Nebraska, in contrast, is classified as an "individualistic" political culture, which Elazar defined as one in which the government's role should focus on maintaining the practical needs of the population and encouraging private initiative. Finally, the fact that neither is well known in educational policy analysis led us to believe that contrasting the two would be of interest both to US and non-US readers.

North Carolina: A Brief Overview

The history of North Carolina is intertwined with the region that was dominated by a plantation system with large agricultural holdings and slave labor along a thick coastal belt that wraps around the southeastern part of the early United States. The eastern part of the state was more mountainous and characterized by small farms that had little use for slavery. Early residents (before and during the eighteenth century) came willingly from all over Northern Europe and unwillingly from Africa. Later waves of southern and central European immigration largely passed the state by. After the Civil War, the economy evolved to focus on tobacco, but other crops are also important, as is the furniture and textile industry. Increasingly, however, the state's economy is focused on the development of the financial and high-tech industries. This once poor state is now one of the most economically vibrant in the southeastern part of the country (Fleer, 1994). In fact, North Carolina is one of the most rapidly growing states in the United States, largely through migration of citizens from other states rather than from immigration. The out-migration of blacks starting in the 1930s has left a population that is predominantly white (68 percent), but with a substantial and increasing black population (22 percent) and a very rapid increase in Hispanics (approximately 8.5 percent).[4] Urbanization represents a major shift for North Carolina, with many residents living in areas that are regarded as "rurban" (meaning that they have high population density but don't "feel" like a suburb).

However, for most of its history, both the economy and the educational system have been weak, and economic gains have not been accompanied by educational progress to the same degree. Many of those who move to North Carolina to work in the new industries are highly educated, but the graduation rates of North Carolina residents are still well below the national average for white students (64 percent compared to 76 percent) as well as Hispanics (44 percent compared to 55 percent), while blacks and Asians graduate at about the same rate as the national average, at 50 percent and 76 percent, respectively.[5] Those who graduate from high school are as likely to attend college as in other states, but those who do not make it through high school are left behind in the rapidly changing economy. Spending on primary and secondary education—$8,500 per student per year—is nearly $2,000 below the national average. Most funding for education comes from the state: only 38 percent is provided through local taxes. Educational governance is organized by the 212 counties, with the size of districts varying widely, but the state determines many budget options, including teacher salaries and textbook options.

The most apparent political characteristic of North Carolina is the fluid boundaries between political parties and the lack of a dominant perspective. Barak Obama carried the state in 2010; state elected officials come from both parties and represent both traditional and more progressive perspectives within each party. The state legislature is semiprofessional and meets for six months in one year, alternating with three months in the other. This means, of course, that most legislators have other jobs.

Nebraska: A Brief Overview

Nebraska's history cannot be separated from its engagement with Midwestern populist movements, which fostered a strong concern for the rights of farmers and other small business people operating under the harsh economic conditions of the American frontier (Ostler, 1992). The original settlers were predominantly German, Czech, and Scandinavian, and they maintained their distinctive social connections and religious affiliations until after World War II. Although there is diversity among the original immigrants, Nebraska remains one of the least diverse states, with over 85 percent of the population reported as white. The United States as a whole has encountered a surge in immigrant populations, but less than 6 percent of Nebraskans are foreign born (OLLAS, 2010).

Politics in Nebraska has always revolved around farming. While the Populist Party was a major force in the state, it faded in the late 1890s, replaced by a dominance of a strong conservative Republican party. Nebraska also retained a focus on progressive policies and was an early proponent of laws protecting children and ensuring food safety. Nebraskans have a long tendency to be fiercely independent, resisting intrusion of the state and federal government into local decision-making. It is the only state to have a nonpartisan unicameral legislature—which is also the smallest (49 representatives).[6] The legislature meets relatively briefly, for 90 days in odd-numbered years, and 60 days in even-numbered years, suggesting that its duties should be relatively constrained; some analysts have observed that the leadership structures of the legislature are also deliberately weak (Comer, 1980).

These features of Nebraska history are interwoven with the educational structures that have evolved. According to the most recent federal reports, the state spends an average of approximately $10,000 per student per year (just slightly below the national average) and 57 percent of that comes from local property taxes. There are 253 school districts (governance units) and most school districts are small or medium-sized—there are only 3 in the state that enroll more than 10,000 students.[7] Nebraska has traditionally placed a high value on education. Nebraska students tend to do relatively well on the National Assessment of State Progress tests: for example, only two states (Massachusetts and Connecticut) scored significantly higher in reading for fourth graders (9-year-olds), and they rank with other higher scoring states among eighth graders (13-year-olds). In addition, it has one of the highest high-school graduation rates (87 percent), and an above average proportion of college-age youths are enrolled in higher education (57 percent, as contrasted with 46 percent nationally).[8] The "gap" between the performance of white and black students in fourth and eighth grades was not significantly different than the national average, but students in poverty performed relatively better than for the country as a whole (NCES, 2002).

Comparing the Political Cultures of Two States

North Carolina

North Carolina is generally regarded as a traditional state (Elazar, 1970); more recent authors have noted that there are a few progressive strands. Overall, North Carolina is considered semiopen and centralized because the concentration of power and influence is primarily with the governor's office and the general assembly, but there are a few avenues for the public to get involved and exert their influence. Historically, the governor's office has been the dominant political player in the educational arena, with the general assembly/legislature a close second. North Carolina has a long history of rationalism, most notably in their gradual movement toward a comprehensive state accountability framework well before No Child Left Behind (NCLB). Efficiency and egalitarianism have taken a backseat to quality and choice in the state, although the state has been forced by the court system to address inequality and by fiscal restraints to be more efficient. Overall, North Carolina state policymakers have used mandates to implement educational policies, while building capacity and focusing on systems change as policy levers.

How Education Policy is Made in North Carolina
Power to create and influence education policy in North Carolina is concentrated in the governor's office and the governor's presence is felt in almost every educational policymaking arena. For example, the governor has the authority to appoint people to the state board of education, the state standards and accountability committee, and the education cabinet. The governor is also able to nominate or appoint four people to the only independent advocacy-oriented education group with influence, The Public Forum. The public elects a state superintendent to the North Carolina Board of Education, but this position generally has not held real statutory authority or power within educational policy circles.

The governor appoints other members of the state board of education, and the general assembly has great authority over educational policy decisions and has historically micromanaged the state board.

Education has been a top priority for governors of North Carolina for a long time. The current governor, who has been in office since 2008, was a schoolteacher and holds a doctorate in educational administration, so it is not surprising that she has made education one of her top three priorities. Besides the governor, the North Carolina Department of Public Instruction is the state agency that is charged with implementing state public school laws, policies, and procedures. Thus, educational policymaking in the state of North Carolina primarily is a top-down process, but with lot of influence exerted by prominent outside stakeholders, many of whom are appointed.

The main avenue for external stakeholder involvement in North Carolina is through the Public School Forum, an advocacy group for K-12 public education comprised of about 64 members. The forum was initiated by two members of the state legislature with a grant from a prominent local foundation. The two legislators were adamant supporters of the public school system in North Carolina, but were concerned about the lack of long-term strategic thinking. The purpose of the forum, then, was to bring together political and business figures as well as parents and community stakeholders interested in public education to advocate for their joint agendas and introduce bills into the legislature. Most of the people who serve on the forum are considered "high rollers" who are very influential in the state with about one-third business members, one-third elected or appointed officials, and one-third educators such as the head of the teacher's union, the state superintendent, and the president of the community colleges. The executive director of the forum observed that "the business representation really brings a bottom line business-like view when it comes to deliberating over ideas, the general assembly gives us reality therapy and the educators bring along their best hopes, and it's a nice combination as a board because there are checks and balances there." Every other year, the forum conducts a study on a major educational issue and then they go out into the community to build external support for their agenda. The legislature and the public look to the forum to provide the "real story" of what is happening in North Carolina schools. As a consequence, the forum's agenda is sometimes at odds with the governor's, especially when it comes to issues around funding. Overall, however, the various individuals and groups involved in policymaking in North Carolina tend to collaborate with one another and work together to focus on broad policy systems changes. Unions have relatively little influence in the "right to work" state, except through their representatives on the forum.[9]

Standards and Accountability Policies in North Carolina
North Carolina has a long history of accountability policies dating back to the late 1970s and early 1980s. In 1977 the governor's office required all high-school students to pass a competency test to graduate from high school, and by 1983 the Department of Public Instruction required students to take part in state accountability tests for reading, writing, and math. In 1985 the general assembly made the first move toward a statewide comprehensive and rational curriculum framework. Toward the end of that decade, the general assembly passed the School Improvement Accountability Act, which restructured leadership and responsibility for accountability in schools. In 1990 the state began providing the public with School Report Cards that showed how well students were doing on statewide assessments. The ABC's of Public Education, which was passed by the general assembly in 1996, established an accountability plan that included an individual school growth model that systematically measured students' yearly academic progress and a state curriculum that was linked to the goal of high student performance. The law made five strategic goals set by the state board of education and the Public School Forum concrete, including (i) high student performance; (ii) healthy students in safe, orderly, and caring schools; (iii) quality teachers, administrators, and staff; (iv) strong family, community, and business support; and (v) effective and efficient operations. By the time the federal NCLB was passed in 2001, efforts for testing and standards were already well under way in the state. The only difference it made in the North Carolina education system was that the test data had to be disaggregated to show performance of different student groups.[10]

Although the decision-making power in North Carolina is centralized and governor-driven, accountability policies have given school districts more control and flexibility over setting goals and how funds are used to help achieve those goals. The "School Improvement and Accountability Act" of 1989 increased the authority and capacity of school districts to address their local individual needs to improve student achievement. This act also decreased the size and power of the State Board of Education in order to provide more funding and infrastructure at the local levels. The ABC's policy also increased required each school to set achievement goals and targets for student improvement. Funds again were diverted from the Department of Public Instruction to local school districts for professional development use and other needs. Thus, while policymaking during the standards and accountability movement was centralized in North Carolina, the state gradually decentralized some of the responsibility to districts by encouraging them to create their own local school improvement practices that fit their contexts and situations.

By 2008, The North Carolina State Board of Education adopted a policy called the "Framework for Change: The Next Generation of Assessments and Accountability" in an attempt to modernize the state's previous standards and assessment system. Because of this, the state will begin adopting a new statewide curriculum, testing, and accountability model that will be fully implemented by the 2012–2013 school year. More recently, however, the state has rolled back some of its previous accountability laws because of fiscal concerns in the wake of the state's economic downturn. Funding problems have forced the government to focus on saving money where they can (e.g., by eliminating the end of high-school exams). In early 2011 the governor signed a bill ending statewide testing programs that were not required under the federal NCLB law.

Additional Elements of Political Culture in North Carolina
In addition to implementing a comprehensive and rational system of rigorous standards and testing, North Carolina state officials also prioritized quality through their efforts to recruit and retain high-quality teachers from inside and outside of the state and through various leadership development efforts. More specifically, the legislature passed "The Excellent Schools Act" in 1997, which increased teacher salaries to the national average while also increasing teacher accountability. At the same time, the state began providing incentives to strong teachers, while changing laws to make it easier to dismiss poor teachers. As early as 1979 North Carolina began a campaign to improve educational leadership, through the Educational Policy Fellows Program, which sponsored by the forum, and has graduated seven hundred mid-career school leaders. It also began recruiting and retaining quality administrators through a state leadership development program in collaboration with local university partners.

Although North Carolina emphasized teacher and leadership quality, the state historically did not focus on egalitarianism. In 1994, a group of parents, their children, and school districts in five of the low-wealth rural counties sued the state, alleging that the tax structure was unequal and that the inequality meant that they could not provide an equal education opportunity for their students (*Leandro v. State of North Carolina*). The state's supreme court ruled that the funding mechanisms were unconstitutional. In 2005, the state appealed the decision, but it was unsuccessful. Therefore, the state continues to work with these low-wealth school districts to try to help them provide quality education to their students and increase student performance.

North Carolina did not focus on eliminating the last vestiges of segregation until forced by court order, but has made some efforts to provide students and parents a variety of educational options. In 1996 legislation was passed to support the creation of charter schools, with a cap of one hundred schools, although periodically consideration is given to raising this cap. The National Alliance for Charter Schools ranks North Carolina 32/50 in terms of the effectiveness of its policies, noting that, in addition to the cap, "[i]t also needs to improve its requirements for charter application, review and decision-making processes, charter school oversight, and renewal, non-renewal, and revocation processes and provide facilities support to charter schools."[11]

In sum, North Carolina's response to the federal push for increased standards and accountability was to continue on the course that they had already set, with minor modifications. With a 35-year history of rational and comprehensive policies, state policymakers have encouraged continuous improvement at the local level, thus increasing the capacity to handle all of the system changes. While still relatively centralized, policymakers also recognized that they needed to decentralize some of the responsibility to school districts so that they could remain "customer-driven." The state continues to work on providing equitable funding to both rural and urban school districts, but because of fiscal restraints has had to roll back some of their statewide assessments.

Nebraska

Nebraska historically has exhibited a minimal state policy presence in education, maintaining a strong emphasis on local control and decentralized decision-making processes. The political culture of the state is "individualistic" (Elazar, 1970, 1984) in the sense that the state gives districts as much autonomy and local control as possible while still maintaining compliance with state and federal policies. The state has an open policymaking process, with multiple avenues for internal and external stakeholders to provide inputs on educational ideas, which result in state frameworks that are to be locally adapted.

The state of Nebraska had standards in place by 1997 and assessment regulations by 1999, but until very recently, allowed districts to create their own standards and assessments as long as they were aligned with the state standards. Nebraskan state policymakers have been reluctant to change their system until pressures from the federal government became too pervasive. In 2009, Nebraska finally set in motion an implementation plan for an accountability framework whose details were more fully articulated by the state, because their access to federal funding appeared to be in jeopardy. They were the last state to do so.

The low-profile approach to state educational policy has implications beyond accountability and testing, however. It also means that the state has not focused on egalitarianism, which would have challenged the principle of local funding. As a result, rural districts have filed lawsuits to force the state to take a closer look at equity and their public education funding formula, but none have been successful in the state's supreme court.[12] Efficiency and choice have also taken a backseat to discussions about quality, in which the state focused on maintaining separate, but rigorous, standards and assessments across multiple districts. Because of their commitment to local control, the state has not used inducements as a policy lever, but they do have a history of building capacity by training administrators and teachers in how to create and use locally designed assessments.

How Education Policy is Made in Nebraska
Education is listed as a top priority in the governor's office, but fiscal concerns over the cost of education usually take precedence over other educational issues. The legislature has also focused primarily on fiscal issues. However, the most prominent political players in Nebraska are not the governor or legislature, but the elected members of the State Board of Education and the commissioner of education, and nonfiscal educational initiatives and policies are usually addressed by them, but with broad public input. The State Board and the commissioner have regular "policy forums" where they elicit inputs and have discussions and open dialogues over education policy issues, which they take out into community conversations with administrators, school board members, teachers, and parents. The State Department of Education also has regular communication with the education community through workshops and by providing information to the public about current education initiatives. For example, the State Department of Education hired a group to conduct focus groups to gauge the public's reaction to one proposed education initiative and to build grassroots public support.

While the State Board of Education and the commissioner have a lot of influence in the policymaking arena, the Nebraska State Education Association (a teachers' union) and a group of superintendents around the state also exert significant influence on how educational policies become implemented into the local school contexts. In addition, Nebraska has a group of regional education service units across the state that provide resources and help individual school districts implement policies. The business community and the chamber of commerce exercise their influence regularly, but although they are supportive and proud of the education in the state, they tend to only look at efficiency and take a hard line when it comes to increased funding. Raising property taxes to pay for education is a major issue in the state and most oppose it. In sum, most educational decision-making is decentralized with power given to local school citizens and educators to make the best decisions for their communities.

Standards and Accountability Policies in Nebraska
The federal push for comprehensive statewide standards and accountability had a greater impact on a state like Nebraska than it did on states whose policy cultures favored centralization and uniformity. Prior to the federal NCLB Act, Nebraska had standards and testing in place, but these were presented as models for districts to work from and adapt to their local contexts. Districts were required to create standards that matched (or were higher than) rigorous state standards. This system allowed individual districts to determine what standards were important for their local population and community contexts and to design assessments that fit their standards.

Even though state leaders were reluctant to mandate one accountability system across all districts, the state recognized in 1997 that they needed to have a statewide effort to improve student achievement through the cooperation of all educational sectors. The Nebraska P-16 Initiative voluntarily coordinated educational efforts across Nebraskan systems through an alignment of curriculum documents in English and language arts, mathematics, and world languages. By 1999 Nebraska passed the Educational Quality Accountability Act, which required assessment of student learning and the regular reporting of student performance by each school district. With this act, the State Board adopted an assessment and reporting plan, which began with statewide writing assessments. For the other subject areas, however, districts could either adopt the state's assessments or create their own. District-created assessments had to be reviewed and rated by the State Department of Education and independent assessment experts to make sure that they met or exceeded the rigor of the state's assessments. The amount of time and effort districts put into creating their own standards and assessments varied, but for most, it involved significant work that was led by teachers and district curriculum staff.

The Education Quality and Accountability Act was amended in 2000 to establish general procedures for implementing standards and assessments and to require districts to report student achievement. The School-Based Teacher-Led Assessment and Reporting System (STARS) required districts to adopt measurable quality standards and to report the results of all local assessments on a building-level basis to the state. By the time the NCLB legislation was passed in 2001, Nebraska professionals were very invested in their system and, with leadership from the commissioner of education, fought hard to keep local control. The commissioner of education at the time was successful in getting the Nebraska model approved as a legitimate alternative.

In one Nebraskan district, assessments were created primarily by a team of experts prior to the NCLB Act, and then tweaked to fit NCLB requirements. For other districts, however, the change was difficult because it involved local effort. One consequence was that, from 2000 to 2009, the standards and accountability movement in Nebraska allowed district-level staff greater influence over what happened at the school level and gave districts a greater sense of responsibility and ownership in the process. The political culture of Nebraska is evident, also, in the inclination of districts to distinguish themselves by creating standards that went above and beyond state expectations, thus demonstrating their quality to their stakeholders.

The state continued to fight with the federal Department of Education over the Nebraska model. One sticking point with the federal legislation was that the state of Nebraska could not properly comply with the law's requirement to report comparable "annual yearly progress" measures for each school because they had multiple locally designed assessments rather than a single statewide assessment. In 2005, the commissioner of education proposed and the legislature adopted the Creating Essential Educational Opportunities for All Children Act, which besides funding some essential school components such as all-day kindergarten, also set aside funds for teacher-mentoring programs and for teacher time to work on local assessments. By 2009, however, the Nebraskan legislature caved in to federal demands and proposed the Nebraska State Accountability Framework, a statewide assessment system that outlined a plan to test students in reading, writing, math, and science using the same assessment across the state. The commissioner of education, who had fought hard to keep standards and assessments local, retired. State education leaders continue to struggle to make sense of these changes in the context of their commitment to local control.

Additional Elements of Political Culture in Nebraska
Besides fighting hard to keep the standards and accountability movement locally controlled, the most contentious issue in Nebraska is financing public education. The legislature in Nebraska has full responsibility over financing education in the state and provides state and local aid to schools, and provides 32.5 percent of the money available to local districts.[13] As mentioned earlier, the main area of concern for the legislature

is balancing the budget and being fiscally responsible while funding all schools so that they can run effectively. For many years, Nebraska has struggled with the high funding inequity that invariably results from the dependence on local revenue sources, which has called into question the state's ability to provide equal educational opportunity for all children in the state. Urban (wealthier) and rural (poorer) districts are at loggerheads over funding and this has resulted in unsuccessful lawsuits within changing the system. In the last decade, funding differences between districts have increased.

In an effort to create more equity and efficiency, especially in rural communities, state and business leaders have pushed to consolidate the large numbers of small rural districts into fewer larger districts. This process has been contentious because it too goes against the idea of local control of education. Both the governor's office and the groups of small rural districts oppose the move. The rural community in Nebraska does not buy into the argument that combining smaller districts into larger ones would save the state money or improve funding equity.

In sum, the state's reaction to the national standards and accountability policy discussions reveals a focus on collaboration that is combined with the dominant Nebraskan individualism. The unwillingness to give up local stakeholder control over quality was premised in the sense of mutual responsibility of the residents of small towns, and unwillingness to give governor or legislature any more control than was absolutely necessary. Nebraska has an open system with ample room for face-to-face participation at every level of policymaking. The state still struggles with issues of inequality and efficiency, which are discussed but not resolved. Neither is choice a state priority. It is one of a handful of states that has no law authorizing charter schools: although several efforts have been made to introduce legislation to permit them, they never made is out of the education committee. There is no state legislative support for other forms of choice.[14]

Comparing Political Culture, Policy Levers, and Their Consequences

The differences in the political cultures of North Carolina and Nebraska appear more evident than their similarities, especially when looking at how each state responded to federal legislation to create accountability systems. North Carolina, on the one hand, was one of the first states to develop a statewide accountability system that included state curriculum standards, testing, and rewards and sanctions years before NCLB was enacted. Consistent with a traditional political culture, the North Carolina system has been quite stable, and has been driven by centralized gubernatorial policies and groups that are appointed by the governor. Accountability policies in the state have been developed over a long period of time in a comprehensive and rational way, including regular adjustments over the years. Nebraska, in contrast, was the last state in the United States to agree to a statewide testing and standards model, two years after the implementation of NCLB. Even then, Nebraska fought with the federal government to retain district-level rights to create their own standards and assessments as long as they were as rigorous as (or more so than) the state's standards. Nebraskan state leaders eventually lost that fight and recently began to implement a statewide accountability model. Although this new development has forced the state to centralize their accountability framework, it has not changed the political culture of the state, which still favors local control and decentralized decision-making. While both states have used mandates to implement their accountability policies, the Nebraskan way of mandating is much less heavy-handed than North Carolina's. The one new thing that NCLB contributed to both states was the impetus to develop a statewide student information system and a push to disaggregate data by groups to look for and address achievement gaps.

Nebraska and North Carolina have resisted most trends to define educational policies in terms of cost effectiveness and efficiency. Business communities in both states have lobbied to keep taxes low, but there has been little effort devoted to systematically minimize inefficiencies in the state's educational structures. In North Carolina, the effort to put more money into teacher salaries has led to attempts to eliminate state-level jobs, but is viewed as eliminating "dead wood" rather than changing the structure or processes. In Nebraska, the only serious discussion of efficiency involved merging small districts—an unpopular proposition that died a quick death.

Nebraska's concerns about quality improvement and building capacity are as long-standing as North Carolina's, but the political culture of individualism in Nebraska is evident in the commissioner's push to maintain local self-determination with teachers and administrators defining and measuring educational quality. Maintaining local control and keeping quality standards and assessments in Nebraska was no easy feat (and certainly not efficient). State leaders implemented an elaborate process of checks and balances including a process of rating each districts' accountability systems on a quality scale. Nebraska state report cards included not only the results of local assessments, but also a rating of the quality of those assessments in comparison to each district in the state so that parents and community members could see how their local assessments measured against neighboring school districts. Resources in

Nebraska were diverted to help individual school districts train teachers and administrators in how to create and administer high-quality standards and assessments, since doing so was new for Nebraskan teachers. Quality in North Carolina took a more traditional form, with state leaders charged with maintaining a rigorous system of standards and testing, and mandating all districts implement them. Preserving quality in North Carolina also meant putting policies into place to help retain and recruit high-quality teachers and administrators.

Both states are considered open systems, but Nebraska is much more open to external stakeholder influences in the policymaking process than North Carolina. The state board of education in Nebraska and the commissioner of education have built regular contact with school personnel and the public into the policymaking process, with state leaders going out into the community to gather input during each phase of the policy development process. In comparison, there is only one real avenue for stakeholders to influence education policy in North Carolina, and that is through The Public Forum, which is stocked with business, government, and school-level elites, with fewer teacher, parent, or interested community member voices.

The two states are the most similar in how they have dealt with issues of funding and equity, with both states experiencing a rural and urban divide. Neither state prioritizes egalitarianism, and have faced lawsuits by districts and families because of it. The lawsuits in each state challenge the existing funding formulas by arguing that because the states do not distribute resources in an equitable fashion, districts, especially rural ones, are unable to provide quality educational opportunities for all students. Both lawsuits have resulted in attempts by state officials to redistribute funds more equitably, although with the current economic forecast, these issues are unlikely to go away.

In the beginning of this chapter, we set out to answer the question, are states becoming more alike because of the accountability movement? The answer to this question is both "yes" and "no." On the one hand, each state now has a statewide test and prepares public annual reports on school and district results. In addition, each state prepares and distributes annual student report cards so that parents and the larger public can see the results of the assessments and follow student progress. As a result of the accountability movement, each state has also had to discuss—if not resolve—achievement gaps between white students and students of color and between students in high- and low-income communities. Despite these similarities, the embedded political cultures of each have resulted in two very different approaches to accountability. While NCLB has created superficial similarity in some accountability structures, the basic process of setting and monitoring educational quality remains, underneath, more different than similar, and is largely consistent with the classification of these two states as "traditional" and "individualistic" (Elazar, 1970; Herzik, 1985). In the educational arena, this difference is nowhere more prominent than in the choices that the states have made—and continue to make—about promoting common standards for all schools, and monitoring outcomes based on those standards. Our findings are also consistent with the observations of political scientists that national trends may hide the prominence of local interest groups (Wolak et al., 2002). Nebraska and North Carolina have indeed become more alike where federal pressures has been most acute and specific. At the same time, however, local political culture adapts and subverts national trends and even national mandates to create unique educational solutions within each state.

These trends have not yet fully played out, but their consequences continue. A recent federal inducement program, Race to the Top, was intended to promote educational quality through coherent state policy. North Carolina's proposal for a grant was highly ranked in 2009 and funded in 2010. One observer noted that "[i]t's not surprising that North Carolina made the top in almost every section . . . North Carolina has been doing this (quality assessment) work a long time" (Bornfreund, 2012). Nebraska's initial proposal was ranked 37th of 40, largely because of questions about the degree to which all state "partners" were united behind state-level reforms. The commissioner of education noted that "'[w]e knew this was a tough effort at a time when we had many other issues under way, and in a state where local control is still abundant, and the role of the state in turnaround schools and teacher evaluations is pretty minimal." The state scored particularly low because of its apparent reluctance to intervene in weaker schools, and its lack of a charter school law (Dejka, 2010). The state also failed to become a finalist in subsequent rounds.

Notes

1. http://www.census.gov/population/www/censusdata/files/urpop0090.txt.
2. The states were chosen from a larger random sample of nine states that were part of the Leadership for Learning study. The sampling strategies are described elsewhere (Louis et al., 2010).
3. The 2010 census lists them as the 42nd and the 17th largest cities, respectively.
4. http://quickfacts.census.gov/qfd/states/37000.html. Retrieved July 24, 2011.
5. http://www.all4ed.org/files/NorthCarolina.pdf.
6. Unofficially, the Republican Party dominates among the elected senators.
7. Figures are derived from U.S. Census Bureau (2011).

8. http://trends.collegeboard.org/education_pays/report_findings/indicator/College_Enrollment_Rates_by_State;http://www.all4ed.org/files/Nebraska.pdf.
9. Laws governing teacher unions are state-based, and "right to work" states do not require union-eligible members to join or to pay union dues, which typically reduces their funding and influence.
10. The federal law mandated that states report achievement on state tests for a variety of subgroups: high poverty students, minority students, girls and boys, special education, limited English language, and migrant students.
11. http://charterlaws.publiccharters.org/charterlaws/state/NC.
12. http://www.schoolfunding.info/litigation/recent_decisions.php3.
13. http://www.lincolninst.edu/subcenters/managing-state-trust-lands/state/ed-funding-ne.pdf.
14. The other states with no charter law are Alabama, Kentucky, Maine, Montana, North Dakota, South Dakota, Vermont, and Washington. http://www.charterschoolsearch.com/schoolsbyState.cfm.

Part IV

Reflections

In this book we have used the lens of political culture to examine educational policymaking processes in six European countries and the United States. By choosing culture as our focus, we have necessarily been drawn into an examination of enduring collective values and normative behavior on the part of governments and key educational stakeholders (Elazar, 1970; Lieske, 1993). Interviewing stakeholders, reading books, papers, and other relevant country-specific information created a firm base for examining these values, both within and across the countries that we included. What have we learned from our efforts to delve in political structures and cultures so far?

Chapter one outlined our definition of the components of political culture as it pertains to education, but our interviews, along with our group discussions, allowed us to develop our initial thinking about political culture more fully. In particular, our respondents helped us to make ideas that emerged in the United States more robust in their application to other countries with different political traditions and systems. Some of this enriched understanding is presented in parts two and three, and we will discuss some additional observations later in chapter fourteen.

We placed our study of political cultures in the center of larger debates about global discussions about what educational systems and structures should look like, which have a normative basis that is typically captured by the term New Public Management (Tolofari, 2005). These debates are increasingly supported by the role of transnational agencies, like the OECD and European Union, which, by drawing attention to educational policy expectations, including outcomes, standards for what children should know and be able to do at various ages, both reflect discussions that are already ongoing among their member nations, and also stimulate further discussion. While we do not claim to an analysis that covers "global trends," by examining what is happening in seven countries we are able to illustrate both the formal and informal ways in which their influence is felt. Our study suggests that the epistemic community of educational scholars, policymakers, and practitioners are responding to the easy access they now have to both ideas and practices that have been developed elsewhere. However, access to the conversations does not determine the responses in any uniform way (other than generally short-lived media attention to international test results).

What we described in chapter two was the arena in which the global language meets the historical context of key national events that are part of the shared historical memory of the country respondents whose insights have provided the basis for our work. We started out with three assumptions that might provide a counterpoint to the globalization trends. First, new educational initiatives may filter through a political culture that is long-standing and unique to each country; second, policy initiatives shift over time and currently those initiatives call for local accountability to stakeholders as well as the demand to become more efficient and meet international standards; and third, local accountability demands are regarded as consistent with the development of international standards for cognitive student achievement. We believe that our study supports the relevance of all three.

The country case studies, presented in part two, summarize the way in which the general global conversations and the specific historical and cultural expectations in each country have worked themselves out over the last decades. These cases revealed that below the surface of current policy discussions that attract the ever-changing flow of media attention, there are many discussions and policy issues that result in action, at some level of the system, that are unrelated to the issues of quality and efficiency in the organization of schools as public agencies. The comparisons between pairs of countries that are discussed in part three begin an effort to use some of the dimensions in the framework. The chapters in this last part will begin to tie together some of the threads of what we believe we have learned on our journey (chapter fourteen).

This part of the book also offers some additional reflections from policy scholars who read our manuscript in a draft form and reacted to it. Chapters fifteen and sixteen both point to the value of the political culture framework, and also to its limitations. Gábor Halász from Hungary discusses the transitions that have occurred in Eastern Europe in the last two decades, and contrast their speed and force to the relatively sedate process of policymaking that we observed in this volume. He argues that while the concept of political culture as we use it in our studies is applicable to the press for "Europeanization," it is less helpful as an explanation of education policy and its development in countries that are economically developed, but are living with a very different set of externally imposed pressures. Ben Levin, an experienced policymaker and scholar from Canada, raises a different challenge. His comments suggest that the political culture, even when it reflects a sensitizing framework for politicians, is an insufficient guide for resolving the practical challenges of policymaking. These involve an even more intimate knowledge of the capacities and limitations of a particular government, but also the ability to support and monitor implementation of a given policy in any country. Both of these chapters serve as indicators of new directions for both research and more practical policy analysis.

14

"Wer Vorwärts Kommen Will, Muss Auch Mal Rückwarts Denken": Reflections on the Case Studies

Boudewijn van Velzen, Karen Seashore Louis, Geert Devos, Mats Ekholm, Kasper Kofod, Lejf Moos, and Michael Schratz

Revisiting the Political Culture Framework

We began our book by outlining a simple set of categories that can be used to describe a political culture, but we have concluded that the dimensions that we chose are, by themselves, too simple a tool to capture all of the challenges that await each of the governments we have examined. Nonetheless, we also discovered some intriguing confirmation that political culture is a useful lens for understanding how different governments have coped with 25 years of increasing pressure to modernize and reform their school systems. It is worth revisiting our categories to see how they held up in our critical application. What we offer are some conclusions, and also a variety of questions that deserve further investigation.

Openness

Our description of the policymaking process in eight different settings has led us to expand our thinking about the meaning of openness. We started with the idea that openness was largely a reflection of how easy or difficult it was for internal stakeholders to gain access to and influence in the policymaking process. All of the governments that we studied are representative democracies and are, therefore, characterized by commitments to transparency and governance structures that embody the will of the citizens. What we have seen, however, is that country and state systems differ widely in the degree to which decision-making processes are accessible to a wide variety of nonelected actors.

In most of our countries, the degree of openness that our respondents described was perceived as a stable characteristic. Whereas some coalitions or governments might encourage more participation than others and some groups have become more influential while the power of others has declined, the variations over the last several decades has been quite small. Some countries consistently encourage, or even require, extensive consultation with multiple formal groups at every stage of the policy-making process. The Netherlands and Sweden are very different in many ways, but on this dimension the norm of formal consultation is deeply embedded. Some, like Nebraska, use extensive consultation, but it tends to occur more informally rather than as part of a recognized process. Other countries are more limited in who is consulted and when. In England, for example, consultation typically occurs within the government, civil service, and trusted advisors; in Flanders and North Carolina, only a few recognized nongovernment groups are involved. Only in Denmark did respondents report that there was a trend toward less openness at the national level.

One of the best unobtrusive indicators of normative behavior is when people report being offended because something unusual has occurred. In most countries the expected level of openness was occasionally violated or inconsistent. For example, we noted that the minister of education in Denmark published league tables of test results although a majority of stakeholder representatives reported to us that they were against it: although Denmark sees itself as a very open and participatory country, openness does not, apparently, extend to transparency of all data. In Sweden the government provided targeted local funding to be used only for specific government priorities, while at the same time it verbally promised autonomy to the kommunes in budgetary matters—again, a controversial action. Both of these examples suggest that openness is not limited to a simple dimension of encouraging broad participation in policy formulation.

We also observed another aspect of openness in political culture that we did not take account of in our initial framework: government openness to new ideas from the global conversations. We have not explored this in detail in our data collection, but we can informally observe that some countries, such as the Netherlands, seem almost obsessed with gathering the latest ideas and research findings from around the globe, while others, such as Austria or Nebraska, tend to look at ideas from elsewhere with a considerable dash of skepticism. This is perhaps not surprising given the very different histories of these countries and states.

Decentralization

We can easily, on the basis of our case studies, classify North Carolina and England as more centralized because the policy process is vested with a small number of stakeholders who operate under executive auspices. Denmark and Nebraska, in contrast, are more decentralized, with a long tradition of limited role for the national/state government and a strong role for municipalities.

In other instances, the idea of decentralization is less straightforward than we expected, however. In some settings (Austria and Flanders) there is a deliberate mix of complex networks at multiple levels whose implicit purpose is to buffer policy changes that are inconsistent with historical preferences and norms. This results in a very stable structure, but nevertheless real and functional decentralization. In others cases, we may even question the meaning of decentralization. If the Dutch government delegates all financial, organizational, curriculum responsibility to school boards, but school boards voluntarily organize to become a stable national force, can we really speak about decentralization as it appears in Nebraska and Denmark? Or, building on our discussion in chapter one, can we say that the Dutch structure has devolved as part of an emerging system of checks and balances prevents any group, including the government, from gaining too much power? The degree to which the devolution has created a permanent tension between two *national* groups, one representing the government and the other a powerful association, suggests that our original notion of devolution also needs to be further interrogated.

The increasing power of midlevel actors who control the policy dialogue is relevant, largely because it presents a significant and unanticipated structural challenge to simple models of New Public Management (NPM), which are premised on the national or state government retaining control over the framing of goals, but delegating the responsibility for determining how to meet them to semiautonomous units. As we see in the cases of Flanders and Austria, powerful midlevel governance units preclude rapid action in system-wide educational policymaking.

Decentralization also challenges the routines of decision-making. Education, as a public service, is obligated to produce the public value authorized by a public authority (Moore, 1995). But what if a public authority has decided to functionally decentralize so drastically that its responsibility to ensure public value is eroded? In some countries, this is the argument against the rapid expansion of free schools (also known as academies or charter schools). In countries where this sector has recently expanded (Sweden and North Carolina), it appears to be contributing to racial or socioeconomic segregation (Gajendragadkar, 2006); countries where freedom of education is well established (such as the Netherlands and Flanders) have higher-than-average socioeconomic disparities between schools. Concerns over the tensions between decentralization and inequality are often muted, even in countries where the political culture emphasizes egalitarianism. However, decentralized and semiautonomous units must build trust about the ways that they contribute to public value if they are to retain current levels of flexibility.

Rationalism

We defined rationalism as the presence of educational policies based on comprehensive and/or coherent solutions to perceived needs for change. This approach is frequently promoted by educational analysts who espouse NPM approaches to school improvement (Elmore & Fuhrman, 1995). Like decentralization, it is fundamental to NPM's understanding of the role of the central government in formulating broad and enduring frameworks and standards (Christensen & Lægreid, 2001). This comprehensive policy approach may be contrasted with a muddling-through approach to policy that is characterized by multiple initiatives that are designed to address short-term issues.

Some of our countries seem to be a model of coherence—Sweden has had only two major educational reform "bundles" over more than 50 years, the first introducing comprehensiveness and the second working out a difference balance of policy relations between the central government and the kommuns. Its close neighbor Denmark has had many individual policies, but no white papers, omnibus education bills, or broad government frameworks. But wait! Danish policies, even those designed to promote a better prepared workforce, have not seriously disrupted the "spirit" of Bildung among the kommunes, where most policies that affect students and teachers are made. Nor have they seriously questioned the belief that those closest to the students should make their own choices.[1] Does the presence of a set of assumptions about the goals and structures of education create coherence that is more difficult to see because it is not articulated in a white paper or a specific law?

In addition, the idea of policy coherence or rationalism is frequently associated with government activism. But when the attachment to NPM principles is persistent, governments may choose to keep control centralized and increase activism (as has apparently been the case in England), or may choose to limit government coherence by delegating more and more responsibility to quasi-autonomous units over which they have limited control (the Netherlands and Nebraska).[2] It is also important not to overemphasize the influence of rationalism as a quality of national political cultures: Sweden and North Carolina, both of which are characterized by more rationalism, have tinkered many times with smaller components of their educational policies.

Egalitarianism

We were surprised at the limits on public discussions about egalitarianism that appeared in most countries in this study. Although education is, everywhere, seen as a vehicle for increasing the life chances of all citizens, the role of equality is more often debated at the level of high principle than at the ground level of how to ensure it. Even in systems such as Sweden and Denmark, which were designed to promulgate equal opportunity and access for all through a strictly comprehensive system, the degree to which the goals were achieved has been subject to limited questioning. We conclude that in most places there are significant taboos that prevent serious discussion of how to improve equitable outcomes—often because egalitarianism conflicts with and comes up short when compared to other values.

For instance, in the Nordic countries it looks as if new policies, like freedom of parental choice or permission to use soft streaming or specialized classes, may undermine the older commitment to achieving equality through a comprehensive school experience for all children. In Belgium and the Netherlands, the value of freedom of choice is embodied in the constitution, and it outweighs the nonconstitutional value placed on equal opportunities for all. In others, like England, equality was a hallmark of many of the policies of the recent Labour government, but by targeting projects to cities or areas where there was high poverty, the initiatives did not disturb the existing advantages of higher socioeconomic families.

Efficiency

We expected, based on the prevalence of financial restrictions that were increasingly apparent in all countries, that efficiency would be a significant component of our respondents' perspectives both on how educational policy was made in the past, and how it should be designed for the future. What we saw, however, is that only superficial attention is paid to increasing efficiency, and that respondents rarely interpreted the past through a lens that incorporated language giving significance to prior inefficiency.

In some of the governments that we studied, respondents reported that rhetoric emphasizing efficiency is more common and intense (England, the Netherlands, and Denmark), while in others, references to efficiency are largely the province of stakeholders representing employers and industry (Nebraska and Sweden). In others, however, the notion of efficiency barely arises when discussing educational policies and politics (Flanders, Sweden, Austria, and North Carolina).[3] In addition, the way in which efficiency arose in the interviews suggests that our respondents see little change over the past 20 years, during which the NPM language has become part of the global language of public sector reform. In countries where it was an issue in the 1980s, it remains an issue today. Where it was rarely a part of the discussion of how policy is made, it remains of limited concern.

Quality

The definition of what constitutes a quality school or a quality education is remarkably different between the countries in this study. Even within countries, definitions of quality that clearly link education to a public or private value are sometimes weak. However, in some countries, governments seem to turn more often to research to raise issues about quality or to inform politicians and policymakers that (a) it is time to clarify what definition of quality they are seeking and (b) they should think hard about the extent to which they are in position to make that call. In Sweden, for example, there is evidence from both this study and others that the role of scholarly expertise is deeply rooted (Neave, 1985), while in Belgium and England, many respondents noted that governments were increasingly eager to rely on research and data as part of formulating policy alternatives. The use of data is often linked to efforts to promote quality.

Still, it is critical to note that data-driven decision-making is not always an indicator of a broad effort to investigate quality. In fact, it can sometimes sidestep broader conversations about the meaning of quality that would invoke broader citizen participation. In governments that have been somewhat resistant to expanded testing (Nebraska, Denmark, Austria, and Flanders), one of the reasons is a concern that test results are easy to study, but do not reflect the political culture's emphasis on a broader definition of quality that is hard to measure. In all countries we studied, school quality—however it is defined—is and will continue to be a top priority in the foreseeable future. But for schools it will be necessary to know how to create quality once its implicit and explicit definitions are agreed to, closely followed by accepted ways of assessing it. Recent efforts in England to use the inspectorate as a vehicle for creating consensus around quality have promising effects (Matthews & Sammons, 2006).

Choice

Choice can be either a controversial or an uncontroversial aspect of political cultures. In none of the countries in this study are parents and children given only one option for education, although choosing an option other than the closest school in some countries might involve both expense and time. However, the value placed on choice is far more prominent, deeply embedded, and uncontroversial in the political culture of some countries than in others. In Flanders and the Netherlands, if most stakeholders were asked to choose which value they would be least likely to challenge in a public debate, we are convinced that it would be "freedom of education," and in Denmark the historical presence of free schools is an unremarkable but permanent feature of the educational landscape. In these countries choice is not linked with the premise that it will introduce market competition. Rather, it is seen as a fundamental right that is based on individual liberty and freedom from government oppression.

In Austria and Nebraska, in contrast, choices are more limited and the issue is hardly on the agenda. The notion that markets could improve the quality of education is not absent, but also not taken seriously, although Nebraska provides a favorable legal environment for homeschooling.[4] In some countries and states, choice is on the agenda, but has emerged more recently and in a variety of guises. In Sweden, it is a logical extension of the new emphasis on the school as a more autonomous, self-governing/self-evaluative unit. Only in England do we encounter strong evidence of the NPM-influenced language that associates choice with market pressures on schools to improve quality.

The Consequences of Political Culture for Policy Instruments

NPM, PISA data, and reauthorizations of No Child Left Behind are in the wind and affect the media and (temporarily at least) public opinion. However, no matter what issue is currently receiving intense policy attention, the preferred ways of formulating, shaping, and implementing policies seem to change slowly. In addition to stability in the political culture, we also observe some stability in the preferred mechanisms or instruments for achieving the goals articulated in an educational policy. In England, policy is typically introduced with mandates, which sometimes include capacity building; in the Netherlands and Nebraska the preferred route for the government to initiate change has been seduction (significant inducements, many of which involve customized professional development to fit the perceived needs of the school).[5] Sweden prefers a "soft" version of mandates, which involve periods of testing and experimentation until the desired implementation is achieved. Flanders and Austria rely heavily on formal and informal compacts, but Flanders relies more on inducements to implement change whereas Austria invests more in nationwide capacity building.

We anticipated seeing a connection between the types of policy instruments used and the language our respondents used to describe the political culture. Other than the simple conclusion that more centralized and less open governments can make better use of mandates than those that are less centralized and more open, we are limited in the conclusions that we can draw.

New Questions and Observations

Like all research that is not designed to test a single hypothesis, we saw much more emerging from our joint work than we initially anticipated. The remainder of this chapter presents some of the emergent ideas that we encountered.

Policy Responsiveness and International Trends

Albert Camus once opined that "[b]y definition, a government has no conscience. Sometimes it has a policy, but nothing more." Camus's dyspeptic observation is based on the notion that both the will of the rulers and the will of the people are based on temporary self-interest rather than principle. There are, however, other ways of thinking about the responsive role of government. As we laid out in chapter two, we interviewed policy actors and developed case studies to explore the question of whether the governments in question are more responsive to the broad currents of policy discourse about the reform of public agencies that have swept through much of the Western world, or local policy considerations, values, and preferred ways of doing things in their setting. This distinction is summarized as "rhetorical responsiveness" versus "effective responsiveness" (Hobolt & Klemmensen, 2008).

In order to make progress in improving education, it makes sense to think about what has occurred in the past and policymakers usually do so, at least reflexively. This is not because they are sentimental, but because they are products of their own space and time, and to the degree that these perceptions are shared among different key stakeholders, they will influence the arguments that inevitably arise around any policy decision. They are, however, invariably influenced by what they read and hear, both locally and globally.

Language travels fast, and it seems to impact thinking about the purpose of education policies in an ambivalent way. The discourse on national and supranational levels in general often seems to be far away from what pedagogues and teachers in schools feel to be their main concern: the development and well-being of students. We often got the impression that the discourse on education policy is sometimes a horizontal one—stakeholders in each level discuss what they think makes sense as an effective and efficient policy, but with no link to the other levels.

Rhetorical Responsiveness

One example of rhetorical responsiveness that is not part of our study illustrates this point. In 2002, the United Nations proclaimed the "Decade of Education for Sustainable Development" and designated UNESCO as the lead agency to promote and implement the initiative (UNESCO, 2002). The assumption driving the proclamation was that the present generation bears the responsibility for educating future generations about how the world needs to change to meet environmental and food security challenges. International conferences and consultations were organized and it turns out that this basic assumption was open to many interpretations. A broad international dialogue to chisel out the role of education was seen as necessary, but the meetings also concluded that there was a need to continue this dialogue within countries, linking local, regional, and national levels in education systems to create a more concrete program for change.

How well has this worked in practice? Many countries that signed on have done little or have continued the conversation almost exclusively at the highest and most symbolic levels. One example is the United States, where the federal Department of Education has been a strong proponent of improved education for sustainability across Republican and Democratic administrations. Meetings with professional associations were held, a website developed, and multiple speeches were given by the secretary of education. A national group of educators developed a set of standards for a sustainable development educational curriculum, and a website with Facebook and blogging is easily available.[6] However, evidence of any significant impact at the state and local level is absent, with only one state (Illinois) reporting a parallel cooperative effort to support the initiative. Another of the involved countries, Sweden, funded an evaluation to see how the "Decade for Sustainable Development" affected schools. The conclusion in 2004 was that schools would need to introduce new subjects to meet the initiative's ambitions, and that instruction should change to create more experiential opportunities and student responsibility for their own learning (Utbildningsdepartementet, 2004). Approaching the end of the decade the evaluation has established that nothing has happened that could enable Swedish schools to meet the challenges that were outlined in 2002.

Effective Responsiveness

The trajectory for NPM is different. Although never announced as a worldwide vision, this book, like others, has documented the way in which its language and practices have had an impact on schools and teachers in many countries. Its emergence is not illusory, but its policies and associated practices differ between countries or states. NPM promoted a radical change in public administration that relied on applying strategies and models. In our studies we have used NPM as an example to demonstrate the impact of political culture on the implementation of some of the powerful ideas.

In none of our countries has local political culture blocked the radical ideals associated with NPM, such as developing a standard of educational quality that can be measured internationally or holding schools accountable for students' tested results, from entering national conversations. In all countries, some aspects of these changes have been endorsed by parliaments or legislatures. From our cases, however, we can derive the following hypothesis: the political culture of a country has a profound influence on the way reforms are defined, integrated with existing or parallel policies, and implemented in practice. As a consequence, their results are variable.

A major reason emerging from our cases is the way in which educational stakeholders gain influence in policy discourse, which we have captured under the terms "openness" and "centralization." When policymakers respond to international dialogues, whether formally in the United Nations, or informally as in the case of NPM, they reach out to ideas that are circulating among the policy elite. They are open to new ideas that they then discuss and disseminate as internationally sourced policy initiatives in whatever forums are available within the country. This level of openness is clearly the norm among key stakeholders in all of the countries in this study.

There is, however, a great deal of variability among our cases in the access that *local* stakeholders or their representative organizations have to policy conversations, both at the national and more local levels, and this affects the degree to which policymakers consider the views from nonelite members of the society. In only a few countries are the unwritten rules governing responsiveness to stakeholders clear. In England, for example, everyone agrees that policies are, for the most part, centralized and made by a relatively small number of nonelected people or advisors inside the government. In at least one other study, England was categorized as having low effective responsiveness in health policy compared to the United States and Denmark (Hobolt & Klemmensen, 2008).

In Nebraska and Flanders, in contrast, the central government is designed to be a weak actor in educational policy, and although there are stakeholders who have influence at that level, their primary function is to ensure that the government passes as few and least restrictive policies as possible. The elite do not need to worry about being responsive, because they are not allowed to be in charge. For NPM to influence educational practice in these settings requires that the policy dialogues devolve to the networks of educators and local stakeholders who deliver policy messages and capacity building that may have a direct effect on teachers and classrooms. This systemic characteristic reduces the potency of the international dialogue about NPM-influenced ideas.

How influence works in these and other settings is even more convoluted. In the Netherlands, one of our respondents (a key civil servant) noted that if he were going to try to influence educational policymaking, he would need to telephone at least three hundred people. In Austria, with its checks and balances at national and regional levels, policymaking requires a different kind of negotiation, and a deep understanding of people, positions, and informal influence. In other words, effective responsiveness, which requires incorporating the desires and preferences of the nonelite, varies not only in degree but in how it occurs.

Change Processes are Highly Variable

Weick and Quinn (1999) define two different types of change:
- *episodic change* tends to be infrequent, intentional, and discontinuous, and often imposed from the top;
- *continuous change* that tends to be ongoing, evolving, and grows more bottom up.

They also point out that it is generally recognized that most quick, central, radical reforms are not as effective and are less likely to endure as slowly developed reforms (Weick & Quinn, 1999).

This conclusion helps us to interpret some of the findings that we observed both in individual cases and in the cross-case analysis. Episodic change often comes into the policy agenda too fast to take account of and accommodate the assumptions and values of all the actors in a system. Policies that are introduced rapidly and without attention to the perspectives of multiple stakeholders may also be easily discontinued if they remain "foreign" or incompatible with the assumptions and values underlying the political culture in educational systems. At the very least, they may result in surface adaptations on the part of those who are mandated to change, without significant changes in core behaviors. Policy analysts have long observed the "slippage" between policies and practice that occurs when the views of stakeholders who are expected to implement policies are not connected with the perceived realities of their world (Weatherly & Lipsky, 1977).

This seemed to occur in Denmark: an outgoing minister published national test results without the usual extensive consultation with stakeholders, but the new government does not intend to continue the practice. Similarly, in England, a rapidly introduced merger between educational and social service ministries was just as rapidly undone by the subsequent government.

A political culture favoring continuous change in systems as different as those of Sweden (highly stable coalitions), the Netherlands (rapidly changing coalitions), and North Carolina (traditional and centralized) has led, in contrast, to a far slower pace of policy implementation that gradually reshapes the system in ways that outlive the aspirations of an individual or particular political party. In all three settings, the systems have endured shifts in political power while maintaining the ability to make adjustments to changing external circumstances.

In addition to differences in the tempo of change processes, we observed types of change that are characterized in the organizational literature as *adaptation* of existing policies and practices (first-order change) or *radical change* (second-order change) (Argyris & Schön, 1978). Adaptation often is the natural response of human beings and social system when confronted with change propositions; radical change only occurs when there is an effort to disrupt existing assumptions and to induce significant changes in behavior.

In each of the countries in this study, there are a many more policy initiatives each year than those identified by our respondents as important. Most of these politically initiated reforms represent first-order changes that are not intended to up-end the existing system. Changing the Swedish Läroplan, for example, occurs on a regular basis and, while sometimes controversial, affects the life of teachers and students in minimal ways. In other cases, we see policies that are described in the country's media as radical assaults on the status quo that do not induce the similarly radical change in the governance and policies. An example of this is the minimal disruption to ongoing educational practices in North Carolina of the far-reaching NCLB intervention—arguably the most dramatic initiatives of the US federal government since the requirement that special education students be integrated into regular classrooms in the mid-1970s. Similarly, the deeply contested debate about making national test scores public in Denmark seems to have had, at least at this point, limited impacts on behavior of municipalities. In contrast, changes that are clearly radical in hindsight were not viewed that way when they were first introduced. The description of the shift of policy control from the national government to school boards in the Netherlands was unintentional and occurred so incrementally that it only recently that the change has been seen as fundamental.

Figure 14.1 illustrates our conclusion that the tempo of change and the mode of change are not associated, illustrated with examples from our country studies.

We conclude that political culture is an important determinant for the way in which larger visions develop and are implemented, but that these are worked out in different ways in different settings. No matter how often global gatherings convene, little will happen in schools if the outcomes are not translated in such a way that they fit in with the way decisions are made in countries or states. But our cases suggest that grand visions are often not apparent until after they have been implemented and their consequences are observable. Visions emerge as a consequence of learning from policy implementation, not the other way around.

Tempi		Mode	
		Adaptation (first order change)	Radical (second order change)
	Episodic	NCLB in South Carolina	Educational Reform Act 1988 in England; Decentralization in Sweden
	Continuous	Introduction of national tests in Flanders and Austria	Decentralization and devolution in The Netherlands

Figure 14.1 Types of change in political culture.

Political Cultures and Policy Learning: The Impact of NPM

Our analyses of the different countries have indicated that all are affected by forms of NPM in one way or another. One obvious way is the participation in international testing as part of a general assessment of the status of a country's educational system. A definition of quality as performance on a standardized or national test was, until quite recently, foreign to a number of the countries engaged in this study: Denmark, Flanders, Austria, and Nebraska were states that used other ways of assessing educational quality. By the time we conducted our interviews, policymakers were not only discussing performance on international tests, but had initiated some kind of national or statewide testing schemes of their own. However, one might argue that in these countries/states, the use of standardized tests has resulted in an adaptation to more local ways of assessing quality, which often relied heavily on professional judgments. Even in the United States, where tests are now mandated, the two states included in this study have made relatively modest accommodations to new federal mandates that were touted as "game changers."[7] In Denmark, Flanders, and Austria, tests are still regarded as a limited way of looking at schools, and test results are not viewed as a way of comparing or judging individual schools.

As standardized and international tests become more prevalent, an increasing number of actors may enter the public debate with different perspectives on what test results represent. Thus, there is the potential that introduction of national tests is not limited to an episodic mandate, but blends into a continuous change process. When this does happen it will have longer-term spillover effects in the schools and may influence the dimensions of openness and quality in our model of political culture. In the Netherlands, all tests except the school-leaving examination were voluntary until the late 1980s. The first public ranking of schools by newspapers in the early 1990s created an uproar in the school boards, but the same boards now use these rankings to promote the qualities of their schools. In Denmark media and nongovernmental action committees continued to produce comparative tables after a new minister had abandoned them. Limited policy adjustments, such as making examinations obligatory, may lead to radical change in the long run. What is more important, however, is whether the accumulation of small shifts in Danish education actually results in public debate, made visible in policy, that changes what they expect from their schools (better test results or Bildung). While this change in basic assumptions about the goals of education is feared by some of the people we interviewed, there is little evidence from any country that it has occurred as yet.

Political Cultures, Policies, and Learning

Our data motivated us to introduce an idea that was not an element of our original framework: policy as a learning process. Bennett and Howlett (1992, p. 289) distinguish between three different ways in which learning intersects with policymaking that are relevant to thinking about political culture and NPM.

Government learning occurs when official policymakers study their own and others' policies to generate adaptive change. Each government in our study has been absorbing NPM-influenced lessons. Absorption occurs directly through participation in transnational agencies, and indirectly through attending to media and stakeholder reactions to transnational conversations. We observe that there is explicit reference to the importance of comparative test results, but there are also changes in thinking about what constitutes quality. In the settings we have studied, this kind of learning is limited, and largely sensitizing: it creates new NPM-influenced ideas, which in turn creates new issues for a policy agenda. It does not, however, typically result in explicit policy-borrowing, where any one of our countries looks to a policy developed in another setting and attempts to replicate it. Every government in our study had engaged in some debates about issues such as choice or how to think about, promote, and assess quality.

Lesson-drawing occurs when internal policy networks and key stakeholders outside the government engage in a conversation about how specific policies might affect an intended area of improvement or change. This is where, in our countries and states, ideas that may have been stimulated from transnational conversations begin to be filtered through the preferences and constraints that are implied by their political culture. In Flanders and Austria, for example, this means that tests are developed, but are not used to "rank" schools because to do so would violate other fundamental values.

Social learning begins when larger policy communities—including the general population that has more limited access to the policymaking process—engages with the implications and meaning of a more enduring shift of basic assumptions. In Sweden, this is exemplified by the measured discussions that ultimately resulted in a fundamental change in the locus of policymaking from the national government to kommuns. In England there is consensus among all observers of a fundamental shift toward greater competition and market-driven models during the same time frame.

Complexity and the Demands for Change

As the earlier discussion suggests, the pace of educational policymaking has shifted in every setting that we have described. Even in places like Austria, Flanders, and Nebraska, whose systems are designed to limit government intrusion into local practices, we see increased activism due to the transnational pressures that we and others have described. There is little question that a simple view of the educational system (specific kinds of schools designed to carry out age-old transactions between teachers and students) has become more complex and problematic. Schools are not only places where children are taught well enough to allow them to become well-functioning adults; they are also expected to drive future economic development and to help compensate for social problems that were previously assumed to be someone else's responsibility.

Educational systems and institutions

> face three types of complexities: *dynamic complexity* (defined by cause and effect being distant in space and time), *social complexity* (defined by conflicting interests, cultures, and world-views among diverse stakeholders), and *emerging complexity* (defined by disruptive patterns of innovation and change in situations in which the future cannot be predicted and addressed by the patterns of the past. (Scharmer, 2007, pp. 242–243; emphasis added)

Most of the governments described in this volume have reacted to increasing pressure, at least initially, with an attempt to improve achievement within the existing framework. This "more of the same" often only leads to little improvement, since a typical learning curve within an existing system quickly plateaus. Current discussions are beginning to take for granted the need for a paradigm shift. Old patterns and forms of schooling are seen as limiting the ability of schools to solve problems like increasing inequality, rapid integration of the new waves of migration, and providing knowledge workers.

Sometimes special arrangements are made (e.g., through incentives) to create best practice models, which are, depending on how different they are from current practice, difficult to bring to scale. A number of authors (Hentig, 1993; Scharmer, 2007; Senge, Smith et al., 2008), therefore, argue that it is not enough to renew or improve schools; they call for rethinking policy, which demands a new mindset for how we envisage school. In other words, they call for deep *social learning* accompanied by a paradigm shift. The consequence, in the simple language of policy pundits, would be to see policy renewal as a shift of pattern from *best* practice to *next* practice (Kruse, 2004). However, as we have seen, a fundamental paradigm change through social learning is a long-term process that is rarely understood until it is virtually completed. That these larger shifts can occur in political cultures as varied as North Carolina, Sweden, and the Netherlands suggests that it is not a function of a vision-driven stable political system, or of a "muddling through" process, but can occur in systems with highly variable valences and preferences.

Local and Global Revisited

In chapter two we set out a tension between two distinctly different perspectives that have emerged within the sociological literature examining international trends. On the one hand, studies have documented the sweeping changes in structures that suggest that all national educational systems are beginning to resemble each other. On the other, scholars that have looked at institutional changes in more depth have emphasized the importance of "path dependence," which argues that every policy choice influenced by global policy conversations must be adapted to the historical paths that created a region's political culture.

The notion that history matters in educational policymaking is an important reminder when we are caught up in the latest media-inspired drama—but is also relatively trivial. What we have tried to elaborate in this volume is the notion that the historical decisions accumulate in each country in ways that may make them resistant to the direct import of globally circulating ideas. For example, when a decision is made to ignore education in a constitution, or to explicitly guarantee "freedom of education," subsequent decisions that are consistent with the constitution become embedded to the degree that some policy options are entirely off the table. This is exemplified in this study by the absence of any serious examination in most settings of internal inefficiencies and inequities in the educational system that are engendered as a result of the accumulated decisions made within an existing culture.

The idea of path dependency is not incompatible with the significance of global trends. As Karl Marx noted, simple measureable differences today may be reflected in significant qualitative changes in the future.[8] The time frame in which this truism can be observed is, however, not clear. It is easy to point to the fact that all of the settings that we studied now have testing systems, while few had those 20 years ago. However, it is equally important to acknowledge that although path dependency doesn't eliminate the testing structure, it may still limit, for the foreseeable future, the meaning of tests in formulating new policies, and that the differences that we observe could continue to impact on these policies for many years to come.

Conclusion

We have looked into educational policymaking in eight settings, including five Western European countries, one autonomous Western European province, and two states in the United States. We have illuminated the complexity of educational policies. At first sight there seems to be common understandings of many core concepts that education policies take into account, such as school, school board, school leader, accountability, inspection, national test, and curriculum. At a closer look there are many differences between different cultures that sometimes have made it difficult to communicate. In our international group we struggled to come to an agreement about what we mean when we speak about the concepts that we have used through the book. But we have not only been troubled with semantic definitions, but also become fascinated by the way we understand concepts that we share but interpret in different ways. We had, for instance, a prolonged debate in which the presenters of a case were certain that they had demonstrated dramatic change, while the others saw that all remained the same—but with a different label.

We found that there are many differences in the ways policymakers in different countries use terms like "efficiency," "decentralization," or "quality." Explanations of why variations are found can be traced in the differences in education history of the countries. We have investigated in what ways political culture has had an effect on educational policies, and have concluded that political culture in these settings has not constrained any government from entering an unknown and complex future—sometimes boldly, sometimes cautiously. We have also seen that political cultures not only affect the educational reforms and innovations that are proposed or enacted; they also help to explain what we see when we look at schools and school systems. The larger impact of the policy culture on local implementation processes represents one next step for research, but we also support the importance of interrogating the effects of political cultural assumptions, as embedded in policy, on the key stakeholders: teachers and school leaders, students, parents, and community agencies.[9]

In a way, we found the results that we present in these chapters reassuring. They reinforce the conclusion that political cultures have a persistent moderating effect on both national and international dialogues, and often result in small policy presents that are wrapped up in elaborate packages with large bows that obscure their less dramatic effects. The comparisons made clear to us that education reform policies may be inspired by macrolevel goals, but that in the end, in democratic settings, the people in the schools and communities must make sense of them.

Notes

"Wer Vorwärts Kommen Will, Muss Auch Mal Rückwarts Denken" in the chapter title translates as "Those who want to go forward should also think backward" (personal communication, Professor Uwe Hameyer, Bad Berka, October 24, 2011).

1. Some of the previous government's language seemed to many Danish respondents to challenge Bildung, but in the end the new language provides an overlay to existing Bildung-infused goals rather than a fundamental shift.
2. See also an early article comparing NPM in New Zealand and Norway, which made a similar point (Christensen & Lægreid, 2001).
3. It is important to emphasize that these observations do not generalize to higher education in a number of countries. For example, in both United States as well as Flanders, efficiency in higher education is a major policy issue.
4. http://www.homeschoolinginnebraska.com/. Note that in spite of all of the debates that have accompanied the introduction of charter schools in the United States, homeschooling is apparently growing more rapidly than charter school enrollments. It has been estimated that 1.3 million children are homeschooled and 2 million are enrolled in charter schools. Homeschooled children can enroll in online charter schools, and may therefore be double-counted.
5. In the Netherlands, inducements can be quite substantial. The government once again signed an open covenant with the national association of school boards in primary education with the aim of improving how boards make decisions about what to improve. Since they have no power to require changes, the government has promised a €150,000,000—not an insubstantial amount in times of recession.
6. http://www.uspartnership.org/main/view_archive/1.
7. And there are suggestions that the federal mandate may be limited by the generous granting of "waivers" to an increasing number of states who object to parts of the law.
8. "Merely quantitative differences, beyond a certain point, pass into qualitative changes" (Marx, *Das Kapital*, V.1).
9. One tantalizing ethnographic investigation of how political culture and policy affects teachers in an English and Flemish vocational school suggests that there are clear lines of influence (Stevens & Van Houtte, 2011).

15

Policy Cultures and Education Policy: A Central and Eastern European Perspective

Gábor Halász

This book is about the way national education systems are shaped by or show resistance to transnational influences. It is based on two key assumptions: one is that transnational influences have a major impact on the development of national systems; the second is that these influences are filtered by national political cultures. The first assumption was introduced, at the beginning of the book, with the metaphor of international airports; the second by that of the coastal rocks hit by the waves of the sea. The seven country cases illustrating the analysis have been selected from the most advanced regions of the world. This naturally raises the question of how far these cases are representative for other regions. Are transnational influences perceived, welcomed, absorbed, resisted, damped, and so on in a similar way in all educational systems or are there clearly distinctive patterns? Is the dynamic of the national and the transnational alike in the more developed and the less advanced parts of the world? The simple answer to these questions can only be "no," but we have to go beyond this.

Another Europe

One specific region that probably deserves special attention is Central and Eastern Europe (CEE), where countries regained their national sovereignty following the fall of the Soviet Union. They are now members of the North Atlantic Treaty Organization and the European Union (EU), that is, part of a community that shares the democratic values of the rule of the law, political pluralism, and market freedom. For the last two decades they have been going through a *double transition* (Birzea, 2008; Halász, 2007), both of which are strongly influenced by "external" factors. The first transition was from a command economy and one-party system to a market economy and political pluralism. The second was becoming members of the EU and being obliged to adapt the rules of their national public sector systems, including education and training, to community standards.

The dynamic of the "national" and the "transnational" or the "internal/domestic" and the "external/foreign" has been, in these countries, quite different from what has been presented in the previous chapters. As they moved, in a very short time, historically, from one world to another, their educational systems were exposed to extremely strong forces from their turbulent social and political environments. These systems spent the last two decades in a permanent state of turmoil, and we can never make a clear distinction between what originated from within and from outside the country. Internal and external influences have been confused: sometimes particular institutions, *imported* in earlier historical times from outside, were perceived as "national traditions"; sometimes genuine *internal* developments were thought to be the traces of "foreign influences" and were, because of this, seen with suspicion by those defending the integrity of the national culture.

Objectively, the educational systems of CEE countries that, prior to the 1990s, belonged to the Soviet Block have been exposed to powerful transnational influences since the collapse of communist regimes. This does not mean that such influences were weak before the great democratic transformation. On the contrary, they were stronger than in most other parts of the world. The members of the *Council for Mutual Economic Assistance* (Comecon) and the *Warsaw Pact* were linked together with particularly firm ties and the "community" they belonged to exercised a much tighter external control over them than any other similar regional or global alliances. Their internal policies, including education and training, were strongly coordinated from a clearly identifiable "coordination center," that is, Moscow. At the beginning of the 1960s, for example, most countries started similar reforms that aimed at making secondary education "general" (i.e., allowing the whole age group to have access) and, at the same time, "polytechnic (i.e., making the whole system vocationally oriented). Central planning was a fundamental feature in all of these reforms, which led, later on, to noticeable similarities in their enrolment structures: only a small fraction of students were allowed to enter academic secondary schools and the overwhelming majority were funneled into vocationally oriented tracks, tightly connected with the state enterprises of the favored industrial sectors, first of all, heavy industry. After 1990 these countries fell out of the safety system of "care and control" by the Soviet Empire and were left to themselves. Most of them inherited an ineffective industrial infrastructure producing technologically backward, unsalable products. In a formal sense they possessed relatively well-developed education systems (most of them were quite proud of its performance) with particularly high-level enrollment rates at both ends (preschool and upper secondary education), but the skills produced by these systems were desperately obsolete regarding the needs of the emerging knowledge and service economy. Modernization was seen by the elite groups leading the transition as a key goal also in the education sector (Radó, 2001, 2010). All countries had to face dramatic adaptation challenges: whole industrial sectors collapsed, millions lost their jobs and their resources for living, hundreds of thousands were forced to become self-employed "entrepreneurs," thousands of institutions lost their financial background due to galloping inflation, and "confusing" pluralism took the place of the former "reassuring" monolithic ideology.

Turmoil of this scope can be experienced only during and after wars. But the social and political vacuum was quickly filled in by new political parties: some were restored from forgotten historic remnants—after decades of Cinderella sleep, they were completely detached from the new realities of the modern world. Others emerged from the void, having no life experiences at all in how to operate in a democratic polity. The new democratic parliaments were populated by these new parties, which started making policies, including in the education sector, relying on references either from a long past national experience (sometimes going back as far as the prewar period or further) or on various beliefs about the world of advanced market economies, often regarded with admiration.

The World Bank, the EU, and the Transition

The most important external partner during this painful transformation and transition process, in the early 1990s, was the World Bank. In all countries of the region the costs of the transformation—such as the creation of a new financial infrastructure (e.g., bank systems) or that of labor services supporting the masses of the unemployed—were covered in a great part by loans provided by this organization. It played a key role not only in financing education reforms but also in designing them. In many countries systems like secondary school-leaving examinations, labor market oriented vocational training and retraining institutions, textbook markets, or professional development infrastructures for teachers were built or rebuilt in the framework of large World Bank loan programs, which brought in not only dollars but also ideas. In some countries the attentive observer could not see much difference between the content of national reform programs adopted by national parliaments and the planning documents of loan agreements.

It would be misleading to describe the dynamic of the interaction between the "donor organizations" and the "recipient countries" simply as foreign influence that directly shaped the emerging national systems. Some CEE countries became interesting and vibrant reform laboratories. Their new political and professional elite became eager to absorb the most up-to-date reform ideas. They quickly got familiar with the new borrowed terms like "normative financing," "output measurement," or "accountability." They were quick learners and they genuinely needed this international learning since the mental models they inherited from the past were simply not suitable for understanding and treating the problems they faced. In some other countries, time seemed to have stopped. The old "red" bureaucracies established curious alliances with the emerging new nationalist and populist political forces: together they repainted the colors of the existing institutional architecture, which allowed them to block every meaningful change. In some cases they tried to keep the access to the financial support of Western democracies open by using a kind of *double speak*, reconciling the reform discourse on the surface while stalling changes in the depth.

The new democracies of CEE have faced a double transformation challenge in all sectors, including education. On the one hand, they had to create the new social, economic, and political order, based on free market and pluralistic parliamentary democracy; on the other, they had to come to realize that their new community was also facing serious challenges. Most countries of the region submitted their accession requests to the EU at a time when the political leaders of the latter started to understand that Europe was no longer the center of global economic and technological development. The famous Delors report on growth, competitiveness, and employment in the European Union (EuropeanCommission, 1993), which presented an alarming new picture about the deepening gap between the dynamism of America and South Eastern Asia and Europe's sluggishness, was made public by the European Commission when countries in CEE started concluding accession agreements with the EU. Most of them had very little knowledge about the serious economic difficulties of Europe and they discovered only several years later that the admired community they wanted to join was, to use a deliberately impolite metaphor, not the lifeboat but the sinking ship. Another major shocking experience from the same period was the realization that the political and military weakness of Europe proved incapable of preventing the violent ethnic war on the Balkans.

In spite of the economic malaise and the political weakness of Europe, the EU remained the strongest modernization model for the CEE countries. In their efforts to adopt the "*acquis communautaire*"[1] they had to be completely open to the new European approaches in all sectors, including in education. Although in this sector there were only a few mandatory community regulations, the spirit of the time encouraged an adaptation behavior that went far beyond the mandatory aspects. The countries were eager to join the educational programs of the EU (first Tempus and later Comenius, Erasmus, Leonardo, and Grundtvig),[2] that is, they encouraged their institutions and their citizens (including teachers and students) to take part in mobility programs, to develop joint courses, or to launch transnational cooperative projects. They were particularly content to have access to the so-called pre-accession funds that they could use to start ambitious development programs aimed at better connecting education and industry or promoting social integration—guided, of course, by the educational policy priorities of the EU.

After accession, CEE countries became the recipients of the European "structural funds," which allowed them to launch even more ambitious programs. The resources they could channel into educational development exceeded anything that they had experienced in their history. In the case of Hungary, for example, the planned yearly budget of EU-funded programs in school education was around 4–5 percent of the total spending in this sector (Hermann & Varga, 2010). But, in order to become eligible, countries had to create cross-sector national development plans and to formulate development goals that were in accordance with the EU regulations for the use of the structural funds. One of the components of these regulations has been the principle of "additionality," which means that countries had to add their matching part to the EU money and, as a consequence, no resources at all were left to finance goals other than those included into the EU-supported national development programs.

But structural policy has not been the only instrument for Europe to shape educational development in the CEE countries. The latter also became involved in the new European policy coordination mechanisms, launched in Lisbon in the year of 2000, called the "open method of coordination" (OMC). There is now ample literature analyzing the impact of this new EU instrument on national education policies in the EU, including the CEE region (Gornitzka, 2005, 2006; Lange & Alexiadou, 2007; Štremfel & Lajh, 2010). The "soft" OMC instruments, such as common goal setting, reporting, peer evaluation, benchmarking, and peer learning, taken together have constituted a powerful tool that no national system could eschew. All in all, the development of the educational systems of the member states of the EU has been increasingly coordinated and the impact of this has been particularly strong in the CEE region where the Union has been not only providing direction but also financed, in a coordinated way, practically all development interventions.

It is important to stress that the adjustment of the education systems to the common European goals is a process full of tensions and adaptation difficulties. There are many actors in the CEE national education policy arenas that have negative attitudes toward the common European policy lines and the intended changes often cannot reach the grassroots. As their implementation capacities are weak, national governments, even if they support the common goals, are not always able to implement them. There are also cognitive barriers. The emerging and continuously evolving European paradigm of lifelong learning, always enriched by new and new elements—such as the recognition of competencies gained through nonformal and informal learning, or the use of learning outcomes and the connection of the subsectors of the education system in the new national qualification frameworks—is not easy to understand and to put into practice for many players of the national education policy game field.

Europeanization and its Consequences

Although this book is about transnational influences on national educational systems, it is surprising from a CEE perspective that the word "Europeanization" did not appear in its original manuscript. There is now abounding literature about "Europeanization," including its impact on the development of education (Alexiadou, 2007; Bache, 2006; Walkenhorst, 2005), and its special impact in the CEE region (Börzel & Buzogány, 2010; Štremfel & Lajh, 2010). Europeanization is a key notion for those studying the educational development of CEE since the beginning of the 1990s when the first developmental interventions supported by the EU started. This is important for at least two reasons in the context of this book. First, because what this book describes as the eight key dimensions of policy cultures can easily be connected in the CEE region with the notion or the idea of Europe. These dimensions, interpreted as specific public policy goals, norms, and values, may get different emphases in the various advanced democracies and market economies but none of them can be neglected. Openness, local autonomy (decentralization), rationalism, equity (egalitarianism), efficiency, quality, and freedom of choice are goals and values that most people in CEE would connect with

Europe. Many people would see the guarantee of the protection of these values, so often violated during the violent history of the twenty-first century in the EU. Perhaps the most important implication of becoming part of Europe (the EU) for the countries in the CEE region is that in this community they can feel: none of these values can be denied or neglected any more.

But the meaning of Europeanization covers an extremely complex phenomenon that cannot be described as a top-down process in which Europe is influencing, from above, the development of the educational systems of its member countries. There is no one-way, linear form of influence. Europeanization means a complex dynamic web of interactions between national and supranational actors who make the various education policy themes continuously "travel" between the national and the European level, sometimes even pushing them, provisionally, out of the EU—as it happened with the Bologna process (Corbett, 2011)—and then bringing them back, sometimes making them change the definitions of where they belong in social policy (e.g., transforming education policy issues into items on the agenda of employment policy and back). Europeanization means, in this context, the change of the dynamics of the internal education policy scene: some stakeholder groups getting "better winds" while others losing ground, some ideas being said louder, others becoming less and less heard. Europe has simply changed the winds that drift the things in the "garbage can" of education policy (Cohen & March, 1972) and the waves that carry the "surfs" of the "policy entrepreneurs" (Kingdon, 2003) in the education sector. Or it has simply added a new level of complexity to the process of "muddling through" (Lindblom, 1959) across the complicated field of education policy construction.

Europeanization cannot be described simply as "external influence" exercised by well-identifiable "European" actors on homogenous "national" educational communities. What we have in front of us are turbulent national education policy arenas with many different actors fighting or making alliances with each other both "internally" and "externally." It is not surprising that the dynamics of policymaking and the nature of policy outcomes become different when the borders of national education policy arenas become easily permeable and many of the national actors start having interactions not only in the domestic sphere but also outside. Often they do not want to do things differently because they have been "influenced" by external factors but simply become stronger as they are acquire stronger backing within the enlarged European policy scene. Membership in the problem-community called the European Union has created a particularly big challenge for education policy actors in the CEE countries because the culture of governance based on "soft" instruments (such as the open method of coordination) was entirely new for them. Policymaking, and particularly policy coordination, in the EU is conceived in great measure as learning (EuropeanCommission, 2000), which is not easy to reconcile with the legalistic traditions of CEE countries.

Public-Sector Management and the Limits of Rationality

Since this book devoted special attention to the impact of New Public Management (NPM), this has to be reconsidered also in connection with the education systems of the CEE region. In this respect the most important feature seems to be related with the paradox of inherited and new inefficiencies of public services (including education), on the one hand, and the efforts to overcome them through organizational or management solutions that are often increasingly formal and bureaucratic. The problem is not the importation of effective management procedures from the business sector, which characterizes the CEE region as much as other parts of the world, but the often weak capacity to make an effective adaptation of these to the particular needs and characteristics of the education sector. Measures aiming at improving quality, effectiveness, and efficiency become mechanistic and bureaucratized when they are not tempered with an understanding of complex organizational processes and when they do not reflect the need for a learning culture that focuses on the human side of the organization. And this happened particularly often in the education systems of CEE that were historically shaped by the "Prussian spirit" and, as its reflection, pedagogical Herbartianism,[3] which was later reinforced by the state bureaucracy of Soviet-type command economies. In this context, NPM might have appeared as a progressive approach bringing relevant responses to the most burning questions.

But, as this book suggests, there is no one single NPM. Current thinking about the organization of public services has many faces, which can be more or less well adapted to the education sector. In the case of Hungary, for example, the introduction of systematic processes of quality assurance into schools since the late 1990s has led not only to mechanistic solutions but also to hundreds or thousands of initiatives aiming at genuine organizational development (Révész & Szabó, 2008). Leadership development also emerges from NPM's focus on locally driven management systems, and is a good possible solution for school improvement. In most CEE countries there have been serious attempts to develop school leadership (Emese, 2009) and now probably all are running various leadership training programs. But leadership development is again one of those areas where transnational influences have been very strong. In most countries of the CEE region leadership development programs have been developed in close cooperation with English, Dutch, or Scandinavian partners, through joint projects, by developers who have been sharing a common culture of thinking about organizations and organizational behavior. When they try to reconcile leadership and management, they are, in fact, using international knowledge to "domesticate" NPM, stressing both effectiveness and efficiency, on the one hand, and the importance of the human side of the school organization, on the other. For them, NPM is typically not a threat, but an opportunity.

Testing is an important carrier of the NPM paradigm in the education sector. But in most countries of the region the key issue is not the risk of overstressing test scores or that of impoverishing pedagogy through making teachers "teaching to the test." On the contrary, the problem is the "*lack of a reliable internal assessment system that would provide information about the effectiveness of educational services beyond the traditional statistical or anecdotal ones*" (Radó, 2010; emphasis added). There seem to be too many actors in the education policy arena of these countries who disdain facts, who do not attribute much importance to evidence, and who are led less by knowledge than by beliefs. Evaluation and assessment is one of the most important channels in these countries through which relevant international knowledge can be accessed. Evaluation and assessment communities are typically much more internationalized than other professional circles, often through being connected to major international assessment exercises, such as PISA or TIMSS and PIRLS. In the case of Hungary, for example, educational scholars who connected to the IEA[4] beginning in the early 1970s were the most important builders of bridges between the rather closed traditional disciplinary cultures and modern curricular ideas fostering cross-disciplinary approaches.

Those committed to the paradigm of NPM are typically using rational governance models and are often exposed to the risks of bureaucratic distortions. But there is another paradigm that we should have in mind when thinking about education systems and education policymaking in the CEE region. This is the *nonrational* way of making policy when, instead of putting arguments against arguments, policy players are led by emotions and simplifying beliefs. The education policy scene is nowhere exempt from nonrational factors but this is probably stronger in the CEE countries where the legal system is typically unstable, where even low-level professional bureaucrats are often replaced after political elections, and where the knowledge bases that support education policy are often destroyed by frequent restructurings or the short lifecycles of expert organizations. It is important to stress, however, that the often chaotic institutional context does not prevent the emergence of rational solutions.

A good example is the gradual emergence of an effective curriculum regulation system in Hungary since the beginning of the 1990s: although some of its elements were destroyed, then rebuilt, and then redestroyed and rebuilt again, a relatively high-level coherence and institutionalization could be reached (Halász, 2003).

Conclusion

This chaotic or at least "limited rationality" development paradigm is close to what the "garbage can" model, mentioned earlier, symbolizes. The ideas of NPM—or, as it could also be said, this set of logical, rational, and simple reactions to the often roaring and scandalous inefficiencies of the public sector—constitute just one single, although important, factor among the many things swirling in the "garbage can" of education policy. To conclude: what we see in this particular CEE context is not only transnational influences filtered through national political cultures, but also national political cultures themselves being shaped by transnational influences. To put it in a simplified and ironic way: the filters we use to filter what we import might have also been imported.

Notes

1. This term refers to legislation and court decisions that the EU members have agreed upon.
2. These are the names of various educational programs of the EU targeting higher education, vocational education, and adult learning.
3. German philosopher/educator Johann Friedrich Herbart (1776–1841) advocated education that focused on developing citizens with a strong sense of social responsibility. His approach is often contrasted with progressive educational philosophies because of its emphasis on character development.
4. International Association for the Evaluation of Educational Achievement.

16

Reflections from Practice on Political Culture and Education Reform

Ben Levin

The temptation to compare education policy across countries is hard to resist, as shown by the many papers, conferences, and books devoted to doing so. These activities extend well beyond official comparative societies and associations; comparative work is done in many other forums as well. Nor is it limited to academics; in their constant quest for new approaches, policymakers are also quite interested in learning about the experiences of other countries.

The essays in this book show clearly both the potential and the limitations of this kind of comparative education policy analysis. Possibilities because looking at other countries is a way of understanding our own place more deeply; limitations because comparative work inevitably simplifies the very complicated ways in which ideas are taken up in different places.

In this chapter I have been asked to comment on the earlier chapters from the standpoint of someone who has been both a policy researcher and a policy actor. Much of my academic work looks at education policy (e.g., Levin 2008, 2010) and although I do not regard myself as a scholar in comparative education, I have had the opportunity to be involved in education policy discussions in quite a few different countries, and have written about it. The other half of my career has been as a senior official in ministries of education in two provinces of Canada, where I have been actively involved in developing and implementing policy, including considering how my jurisdiction could or should learn from efforts in other places. So I am both a purveyor and consumer of education policy, including its comparative aspects.

In this short commentary I want to advance four assertions about comparative policy work in general, drawing on other chapters in this book, on comparative policy work more generally, and on my own experience, and conclude with some suggestions about how we should think about comparative policy. I am speaking here primarily about policy comparisons broadly across jurisdictions, many of which are made based on far less careful analysis than is the case in this volume. Readers of this book will see that much of what follows is embedded in previous chapters.

These points are:

- Ideas about education policy are promoted internationally, but one should not assume that this means the organizations that promote these ideas or comparisons are necessarily powerful. The reasons why some ideas get more attention in international discussions are not self-evident; both politics and evidence matter in different ways.
- Whatever ideas may get discussed at a comparative level, the take-up of ideas in any setting is mediated by the specificities of each context; its history, politics, and institutional structures. However, these characteristics are themselves not fixed, either geographically or over time, so characterizing the political culture of a country is fraught with problems.
- Even where similar ideas are adopted, policymakers may have quite different intentions behind them. It is a common error in policy analysis to give too much importance to policy documents.
- Even where similar ideas are adopted with similar intentions, they typically look quite different in practice and exhibit a variability that may make the facts on the ground very different from the policy intent.

For all these reasons, there are serious limits to what one should claim as being the "internationalization" of education policy. Perhaps policy borrowing or international policy development gets more attention than it merits in terms of its real impact on education.

Let's consider each of these points more fully, using my own experience to elaborate on the messages of this book.

The Limits to the Influence of Transnational Agencies

Many policy analysts argue that we are living in a world in which international influences are increasingly important in shaping education policy.

There seems little doubt that there is more international discussion of education policy. Whatever one thinks about the idea of globalization, countries are paying more attention to each other's policies. PISA, the OECD assessment of students, is probably the most important single instance of this; it has now become a de facto standard of education for international comparisons and has had substantial impact on education policy in many places because the OECD has worked hard to draw out specific policy implications of the results. The growth in the number of participating countries is another sign of the importance ascribed to PISA, which has pretty clearly outstripped other international assessments such as TIMSS or PIRLS.

It also seems to be the case that international and multilateral organizations, such as the OECD, the World Bank, or UNESCO, are playing an important role in international policy discussions. As the place of education has been given increasing importance on the international economic and social policy agenda, these organizations have devoted more attention to education policy.

Regional groupings of countries are also involved. The stronger role of the European Union and its increasing attention to education has heightened comparative education work there, while the collective organizations in Asia, the Arabian Gulf, and Africa are also increasingly important.

So there are many organizations now creating comparative education policy activities of various kinds, gathering data, bringing people together across national boundaries, making comparisons, issuing reports, and not infrequently providing policy advice to governments.

Still, the existence of these organizations or the widespread citation of their materials does not necessarily mean they are all that influential. For one thing, these organizations often choose themes for their work that are already being widely discussed. The work of the OECD in education is largely financed by countries that are willing to participate in specific projects. This means that the organization must propose projects that will attract a significant number of countries to contribute funds. So in some ways the pattern of influence is not from international organizations to member countries, but the other way around. Unless international organizations have a big lever to support adoption of their policies, such as is the case with the World Bank, they must often take their cue from their members more than leading them. Several of the earlier chapters show just this pattern of limited impact of these policies on national education systems.

Further, much of the advice given by international organizations on education policy is not widely spread or adopted. Citing a few instances where an organization's work is influential and then claiming that these examples show the organization as a whole is influential is a dubious practice. One should rather consider the whole range of the organization's work and see how many of its activities actually have an impact across member countries. Otherwise one might be mistaking existing receptivity to an idea for the influence of the promoting organization.

To take the OECD as an example again, critics complain that the organization promotes a neoliberal education agenda; that claim is cited, though not necessarily defended, earlier in this book. However, over the last 10 years, the OECD has issued reports in many other areas of education policy that have quite different orientations. For example, a major theme of the organization's work has been around the need to improve equity in education systems and education outcomes (Field, Kuczera, & Pont, 2007; OECD, 2012). The recommendations on equity made by the OECD are not consistent with a neoliberal agenda. Similarly, although the World Bank certainly promotes ideas such as the privatization of education (Read, 2011), it also makes recommendations that speak to improving the equity of educational provision and outcomes. So the question is less whether these organizations have an agenda—though they may—and more about which of their messages are actually influential.

The question of which of these ideas get picked up by various countries is an interesting one on which we do not have good evidence. It may be that countries seize on ideas promoted by international agencies that align with their existing dispositions, in which case the international analyses have more to do with policy-based evidence than with evidence-based policy (Marmot, 2004). Alternatively, these choices may have to do more with the networks and personal connections among countries, and between countries and international organizations—for example, the adoption by Julia Gillard as national minister of education in Australia of ideas promoted by Joel Klein who was then chancellor of the New York City schools, or the influence of aspects of the British National Literacy Strategy on the Ontario Literacy Strategy due to the connection between Michael Barber and Michael Fullan.

Whatever the explanation, one should not confuse the attention to international issues and comparisons, or the work of these organizations, with real impact on policy around the world. As earlier chapters show, the ideas of NPM have been taken up in very different ways, if at all, in various countries. Although some argue—in work cited earlier in this book—that the work of the OECD or other similar organizations shapes policy around the world, this seems to me to be simplistic and usually based on the adoption in some places of some policies that the particular authors do not like. The empirical basis for most of these claims of influence remains, in my view, quite weak.

The Primacy of Location

The adoption of policy in any setting is almost always a result of internal factors, not external pressures. The researchers in this collection recognize that clearly. The exception, as noted, is when an international organization is in a position to dictate terms, as is the case with the World Bank. And even then, as World Bank staff have told me on many occasions, there is always some degree of negotiation with the receiving country as to how it will address the bank's overall policy desires.

In most cases, however, governments are motivated almost entirely by internal issues. Their interest in the international and comparative sphere is as a source of ideas or initiatives, which they can use to support their own agendas and predilections. Thus ministers can and do cite international evidence to support the development of greater competition among schools, or the reduction in it; the importance of school autonomy or the importance of greater networking among schools, and so on. It is not accurate to assume that because governments quote external bodies or sources in making their policy choices, their choices are influenced in important ways by those external sources. In some cases they may be; much more often they are not and the sources are cited primarily for show.

The authors in this book are well aware of these factors. Indeed, a central focus of the discussion is on understanding the political culture of different countries, and how that affects the choices made in various places. There is an explicit recognition in earlier chapters that policy is largely driven by the particular characteristics of a setting. This is why the book is organized around the issue of "culture," which is defined in the final chapter as "enduring collective values and normative behavior." Yet even this approach has its limits, as is evident when one looks at the summaries in each chapter of how each jurisdiction rates on the seven characteristics outlined in chapter one. First, reading the summary charts at the end of each chapter, it seems difficult to distinguish differences among countries on these dimensions. All have some degree of openness, or decentralization, or concern with efficiency, even if these values are expressed in quite different ways. I suspect it would be hard to guess which country was which just by reading the summary charts. So it's not evident that understanding the differences in national political cultures in terms of broad category levels really helps us understand the choices made in each setting. Indeed, at some points the authors seem to use the choices made by the countries as their evidence of political culture. There is nothing wrong with doing so, but it does make the argument about political culture circular—that is, a country has a culture that focuses on quality if it adopts policies concerned with quality—and vice versa.

Further, as earlier chapters also clearly show, national cultures are not homogeneous, either over time or from one region to another. A country may have a dominant orientation but that orientation may change, sometimes suddenly, and it may characterize some parts of a country but not others. Take the Scandinavian countries as an example. They are known for having open and tolerant cultures, yet each now has a significant political faction that is anti-immigrant and nationalist. The Danish chapter, as one example, clearly notes the contradictions in Danish political culture, but that is hardly unique; it applies to a greater or lesser degree—usually greater—in every country. As another instance, consider Sweden's high level of privatization in education in the last decade. That is a policy choice that would hardly have been predicted based on an analysis of the dominant patterns in Swedish culture previously, though there must have been important elements in the culture that supported it or it could not have taken place. In larger countries the variability is even greater, as the discussion of the United States points out. Indeed, as noted in earlier chapters, it's not evident that the United States currently has a dominant political culture at all, and is instead seemingly bifurcated into camps that have no interest in talking to each other, let alone building mutual understanding. Given this variability, how helpful is it to talk about "enduring collective values and normative behavior"? There is a risk here of a kind of ex-post-facto explanation, in which some aspect of national culture can be found to explain whatever policies get adopted.

Political cultures also change over time, sometimes through quite deliberate manipulation by particular interests within a country. The shift in English-speaking countries to more neoliberal economic and social policy was actively promoted by powerful interests, suggesting that political culture can be altered.

So, while the analysis of the seven categories is an interesting heuristic, one would not want to claim—nor do the authors claim in these pages—that these categories have some kind of independent status that can be used to predict policy activity. The final chapter reaches a similar conclusion, noting that the characteristics are both harder to pin down and less clear in their implications for policy choices.

Words are Imprecise Predictors of Actions

This leads me to another observation about much analysis of policy, including its international dimension, and that is the enormous interest in discourse analysis, or in combing through policy documents to see what they reveal about governments' thinking. Fortunately this volume is largely free of this kind of analysis, being grounded much more in the many years of direct experience that the authors have in their respective jurisdictions. As noted in several chapters, policy documents may embody a rhetoric that gets turned into something quite different through the political process, and even more when implemented.

Policy documents do matter, of course, but it would be a serious error to assume that any policy document either reveals a government's true intentions or is written to be consistent and coherent. Having participated in or witnessed the production of many of these documents in many places, I can testify that most of the time they are the work of many hands, reflect many compromises about content, and are primarily designed for rhetorical consumption rather than to reveal the actual intentions behind the policy. And I can say without hesitation that the views and ideas of researchers, especially those from other countries, have little or no effect on education policy choices unless those ideas are taken up by important actors within a country, such as key interest groups. It's nice to quote researchers, of course, to show one is "au courant," but as one of my political leaders once said to me when I was advocating a particular policy based on evidence, "That may be true, Ben, but it's sure not what anyone believes."

Policies rarely grow out of a single and unified view of what should be done. (I have written about these issues in more detail in Levin, 2005, 2009). Governments inevitably include disparate views and ideas, and most of the time policies are compromises, intended to satisfy as many of these different ideas as possible. Even in centralized systems, such as England in this book, various policy elements are contradictory and policies pull the system in multiple, sometimes inconsistent directions. In other words, rationalism or comprehensiveness in educational policy is always limited.

Moreover, the actual writing of policy documents in most governments is shared by the civil service and the political superstructure, and often by more than one part of each. This means that such documents go through many versions—dozens if it is an important policy—with many different people holding the pen at various times. In countries with coalition governments the bargaining over policy content and language can be quite ferocious, but even in Westminster-style systems there can be huge differences of opinion within a government that must be hammered out in some way before a policy is finally produced. Often the final product bears little resemblance to the starting point. Interpreting government intentions or dispositions from such documents is like trying to sort out culinary skills when ten chefs are all putting ingredients in the same pot of soup.

To some this may sound appalling or Machiavellian, with governments trying to conceal what they are really about under a barrage of nice words. That is sometimes true, to be sure. But in politics the goal of most policy documents is not only to guide what happens but to send signals to various sectors in an effort to build support for a government and its agenda. Sometimes this means soft-pedaling some parts of a policy to reduce opposition, while at other times it may mean exaggerating what is being done to satisfy a particular political group or demand. Language may be toned down to hide a stronger intention, or made stronger to hide a weaker real effort.

Rhetoric may be overrated in some comparative analysis, but it is not irrelevant either. A conservative government is less likely to appeal to issues of equity or inclusion—though some do. A socialist government is less likely to trumpet the virtues of the market—though again, some do. And policy documents do have real consequences. They allocate resources to some purposes rather than others. They valorize some ways of thinking over others. Even when not very potent themselves, they may fill the space that otherwise might have yielded very different ideas and options. The main point is that both the documents and the policies themselves should not be interrogated as if they represented the "true mind" of a government. As the last chapter in the book shows, policy also may differ between rhetorical commitments and actual practices; for example, countries that espouse equality in education do not necessarily practice it.

Implementation . . . Again

Whatever may be in the policy, every national or regional policy in education is put into place in many local settings. One of the clearest findings in all the policy literature is how important local adaptations or interpretations of policy are—something we have known for decades now (e.g., Ball, 1990; McLaughlin, 1987). To put it another way, creating good policy is hard, but it is far easier than ensuring real implementation. Moreover, in complex political systems, so much energy may go into getting some kind of policy agreement, or to getting legislation passed, that exhaustion sets in and no energy is left for the real work.

There is first of all the question of whether a system has the capacity to implement a new policy (Levin, 2008) in a serious way, even if everything else were ideal. For example, new curricula often require a depth of subject knowledge that is beyond that of many current teachers. If people do not know how to do something, they will not do it even if they support the policy. Moreover, very few ministries of education have the capacity to do much implementation beyond promulgating policies, providing a little bit of money for them, and trying to deal with the most egregious problems—even if the ministry sees implementation as its role, which is not always the case.

Then there are elements of the setting that may also constrain the effects of policies. Here political cultures and structures may matter. In countries such as the Netherlands or Denmark schools have a very different attitude to government policy than they do in a much more centralized system such as Austria. Then there are realities on the ground that constrain policy. For example, countries with many small rural schools cannot really implement a choice and competition policy. To take another example, countries that devolved authority to individual schools with the hope of generating much more community engagement have often found that there is very limited public appetite to sit on school-governing bodies, leading to their domination by small groups of people.

In every system, no matter how centralized, different schools or districts will reinterpret or adapt policies, in just the same way that countries reinterpret the recommendations of international agencies. Even within the same district there will be variations, sometimes large ones, in how schools adopt particular policies. The variance in implementation is proportionate to the degree to which a new policy challenges what currently exists; the bigger the change, the wider the variation in implementation will be. While the variation from school to school can be substantial, the variation at a regional or national level will inevitably be much greater. To complicate matters further, sometimes governments rely on this variation, since they are more concerned with being able to put themselves on the side of a particular approach than they are with whether the approach is carefully or fully implemented. As one of my bosses in government once said about a particular strategy we had adopted: "The minister said she was in favour of the policy; I do not recall ever hearing her talk about it leading to any results."

Of course some variation is good, even necessary. The mindless application of ideas to settings in which they do not work well cannot be in anyone's interests—though it does seem frequently to be the goal of senior leaders in all kinds of organizations. But some policy critics seem to celebrate variation when it suits their own agendas and bemoan it when that variation works against ideas they favor.

The challenge of implementation is made greater because at any one time schools are being asked to address multiple policies and priorities. No organization can give serious attention to more than a small number of priorities at any one time. Yet the policy world is one in which governments are compelled by public pressures to act when a problem is identified or seen as important by a significant part of the population. So inevitably there will be many more policy issues churning around any jurisdiction than can possibly be taken seriously.

These problems of policy formulation and implementation are familiar, so why raise them here yet again? The reason for doing so is the tendency in education to focus on analyzing policy as if it both explained what happened and accounted for results. Of course from a research perspective it is easier to study a few policy documents than it is to look at practice in hundreds or thousands of schools. And from a human perspective people are naturally curious about other people and other places, and how they do things.

None of this discussion should take away from the interesting analyses and insights to be found in the various chapters of this book. To be sure, policy has importance. It sets the frame within which practice can develop or is constrained. It matters a great deal whether a country promotes strict accountability rather than the building of a high-quality teaching force. The writers here are well aware of the limits of their analysis. And, as I said at the outset, we can learn about our own ideas and settings by comparing them with others. I am all for the kind of discussion that leads to products such as this book. But it is important to understand the limits, as well as the contributions, of comparative work.

Appendix

Interview Protocol: Educational Policy Cultures in Parliamentary Systems

I. Introduction

a. Purpose of study and scope of study (hand out)
b. Assure confidentiality
c. Handout current key parliamentary action/bills; handout of roles that we are interested in. Emphasize that we are aware of policy context . . . main purpose is to understand what they believe their state is doing to improve the capacity and motivation of district and school leaders to enhance student learning.

II. Policy Issues

a. What do you consider to be the most critical policy initiatives of the past decade or so, in other words, those actions that have shaped what is going on in educational policy now?
b. Which major educational policy issues or reforms have been most influential in [state] in the past few years? [Focus on current issues.]
   i. If they have changed recently, could you discuss what changes have occurred and why?
c. We are particularly interested in any recent changes in policies that directly affect people in educational leadership roles in districts and schools—are there any other policy initiatives that you think are important?
   i. Probe for:
      1. administrator preparation,
      2. curriculum standards and evaluation/accountability for schools, and
      3. professional development

d. We are also interested in policies that might have a significant effect on local educational agencies or boards, unions, or administrator groups... can you think of any others that you haven't mentioned that we should be aware of?

III. Policy Actors

a. In your experience, what groups or individuals in your country are currently most influential in determining the direction of educational issues? [If respondents are unsure what this means, mention policy stages like bringing issues to the table, moving issues through the parliament, making the public aware of issues, and helping with implementation.
   i. If only people in formal elected or appointed roles are mentioned, probe for other influential individuals or groups: e.g., business leaders, nonprofit groups, educational associations, lobbyists, academics, or people who have just been around for a long time and know everyone.
   ii. Have these groups or individuals always been influential in helping to determine what issues are on the top of the educational policy agenda in your country? Have there been any recent changes?
   iii. If there have been changes, what has caused the changes? Or if there have been no recent changes, how long has the system of influence remained stable?
b. Are their preferences/philosophies of what matters in educational policy well-known? What are their stakes in the current educational policy issues that you have identified?
c. Probe for whether the actors being discussed are equally important in
   i. drawing attention to new policy initiatives,
   ii. getting policy initiatives enacted by the legislature, and
   iii. making sure that their policy actually get implemented.

IV. Political Culture

a. When you learn about educational needs in [state], who are your most important informants?
b. We are interested in how individuals or groups work together to get educational policy initiatives enacted and implemented.
   i. How well do the individuals and groups that you have mentioned work together?

    ii. Are there any groups that consistently collaborate around educational policy issues? Consistently oppose each other?
    iii. How do key actors influence policy initiatives?
    iv. What metaphor, image, analogy, animal, or living organism comes to your mind when you think of the educational policy environment of [state]? Why?

V. Capacity Building

a. What do you view as the state role in helping to build the skills and knowledge of principals and teachers throughout the districts in your state?
    i. What strategies and policies exist to help carry out the role you just outlined?
    ii. Do principals have resources to be competent leaders?
    iii. Is there a procedure for assessing resources once they get into classrooms?
b. What are the greatest challenges you face in working to improve education in the state?
c. What are the major challenges to collaboration between state education officials and local stakeholder in efforts to promote effective teaching?
d. What are the trends in student achievement in [state] that are having the greatest effect on that achievement?
e. How would you characterize the relationship between the Ministry of Education and/or other national agencies and local educational agencies/school boards?

Bibliography

Alexiadou, N. (2007). The Europeanisation of education policy—changing governance and "new" modes of coordination. *Research in Comparative and International Education*, 2(2), 102–116.
Almond, G., & Verba, S. (1965). *The civic culture; political attitudes and democracy in five nations*. Princeton, NH: Princeton University Press.
Amrein, A. L., & Berliner, D. C. (2002). High-stakes testing, uncertainty, and student learning. *Education Policy Analysis Archives*, 10(18).
Andersen, S. C. (2008). Private schools and the parents that choose them: empirical evidence from the Danish school voucher system. *Scandinavian Political Studies*, 31(1), 44–68. doi: 10.1111/j.1467-9477.2008.00195.
Antunes, F. (2006). Globalisation and Europeification of education policies: routes, processes and metamorphoses. *European Educational Research Journal*, 5(1), 38–55.
ARDA. (2011). U.S. membership report (Data Base). Available from Association of Religious Data Archives Association of Religious Data Archives. Retrieved July 2011, from Association of Religious Data Archives: http://www.thearda.com/mapsreports/reports/US_2000.asp.
Argyris, C., & Schön, D. (1978). *Organizational learning: a theory of action perspective*. Reading, MA: Addison-Wesley.
Bache, I. (2006). The Europeanization of higher education: markets, politics or learning? *Journal of Common Market Studies*, 44(2), 231–248.
Bailey, I. (2007). Market environmentalism, new environmental policy instruments, and climate policy in the United Kingdom and Germany. *Annals of the Association of American Geographers*, 97(3), 530–550.
Baily, C. (2010). School choice and competition: a public-market in education revisited. *Oxford Review of Education*, 32(3), 347–362.
Baker, E. L. (2007). 2007 Presidential address—the end(s) of testing. *Educational Researcher*, 36(6), 309–317.
Baker, J. R. (1990). Exploring the "missing link": political culture as an explanation of the occupational status and diversity of state legislators in thirty states. *The Western Political Quarterly*, 43(3), 597–611.
Ball, S. (1990). *Politics and policy making in education*. London: Routledge.
Bangs, J., MacBeath, J., & Galton, M. (2010). *Reinventing schools, reforming teaching: from political visions to classroom realities*. London: Routledge.

Barbules, N., & Torres, C. (2000). *Globalization and education: critical perspectives*. New York and London: Routledge.
Beckett, F. (2005). On the comfort of the wilderness: the significance of Lord Andrew Adonis, de facto secretary of state for education. *Forum*, 47(2 & 3), 212–214.
Benavot, A. (1983). The rise and decline of vocational education. *Sociology of Education*, 56(2), 63–76.
Bennett, C. J., & Howlett, M. (1992). The lessons of learning: reconciling theories of policy learning and policy change. *Policy Sciences*, 25(3), 275–294. doi: 10.1007/bf00138786.
Berezin, M. (1997). Politics and culture: a less fissured terrain. *Annual Review of Sociology*, 23, 361–383.
Berman, P., & McLaughlin, M. (1978). Federal programs supporting educational change: Vol VII: implementing and sustaining innovation. Santa Monica, CA: Rand Corporation.
Biemans, H. (2010). New public management in het onderwijs—een bewandeld dwaalspoor MESO Magazine.
Birzea, C. (2008). Back to Europe and the second transition in Central Eastern Europe. *Orbis Scholae*, 2(2), 105–113.
Borman, G., & Kimball, S. (2005). Teacher quality and educational equality: do teachers with higher standards-based evaluation ratings close student achievement gaps? *The Elementary School Journal*, 106(1), 3–20.
Bornfreund, L. (2012). The "race to the top" winners: how states plan to use quality ratings systems. *Early Ed Watch*. Retrieved from http://earlyed.newamerica.net/blogposts/2012/the_race_to_the_top_winners_how_states_plan_to_use_quality_ratings_systems-63337.
Börzel, T. A., & Buzogány, A. (2010). Governing EU accession in transition countries: the role of non-state actors. *Acta Politica*, 45(1/2), 158–182.
Boston, J., Martin, J., Pallot, J., & Walsh, P. (1996). *Public management: the New Zealand model*. Auckland: Oxford University Press.
Bronneman-Helmers, H. (2011). Overheid en onderwijsbestel, beleidsvorming rond het Nederlandse onderwijsstelsel (Government and educational policy: policy formation in the Netherlands). The Hague, NL: Social Cultureel Planbureau (Social and Cultural Planning Agency).
Brown, P., & Lauder, H. (1996). Education, globalization and economic development. *Journal of Education Policy*, 11(1), 1–25. doi: 10.1080/0268093960110101.
Bryk, A., & Hermanson, K. (1993). Educational indicator dystems: observations on their structure, interpretation, and use. *Review of Educational Research*, 19(4), 451–484.
Carnoy, M. (1998). National voucher plans in Chile and Sweden: did privatization reforms make for better education? *Comparative Education Review*, 42(3), 309–337.
———. (2000). Globalization and educational reform. In N. Stromquist & K. Monkman (eds.), *Globalization and education: integration and contestation across cultures* (pp. 44–59). New York: Rowan and Littlefield.

Castle, F., & Evans, J. (2006). Specialist schools—what do we know? *Research and Information on State Education*. London: Institute of Education.

Cerny, P. G. (1994). The dynamics of financial globalization: technology, market structure, and policy response. *Policy Sciences*, 27(4), 319–342. doi: 10.1007/bf01000063.

Chavannes, M. (2009). *Niemand regeert. De privatisering van de Nederlandse politiek* (No one is governing: the privatization of Dutch politics). Amsterdam: NRC Boeken.

Checkley, K. (1997). Magnet schools: designed to provide equity and choice. *Education Update*, 39(2), 1, 3, 8.

Chilten, S. (1988). Defining political culture. *The Western Political Quarterly*, 41(3), 419–445.

Christensen, T., & Lægreid, P. (2001). New public management: the effects of contractualism and devolution on political control. *Public Management Review*, 3(1), 73–94. doi: 10.1080/14616670010009469.

Chubb, J., & Moe, T. (1990). *Politics, markets and America's schools*. Washington, DC: The Brookings Institute.

Clark, W. (1987). School desegregation and white flight: a reexamination and case study. *Social Science Research*, 16(3), 211–228.

Clemens, E. S., & Cook, J. M. (1999). Politics and institutionalism: explaining durability and change. *Annual Review of Sociology*, 25, 441–466.

Clune, W. H. (1993). The best path to systemic educational policy: standard/centralized or differentiated/decentralized? *Educational Evaluation and Policy Analysis*, 15(3), 233–254.

Cohen, M. D., & March, J. (1972). A garbage can model of organizational choice. *Administrative Science Quarterly*, 17(1), 1–25.

Collins, R. (1971). Functional and conflict theories of educational stratification. *American Sociological Review*, 36(6), 1002–1019.

Comer, J. C. (1980). The Nebraska nonpartisan legislature: an evaluation. *State & Local Government Review*, 12(3), 98–102.

CommissieParlementairOnderzoekOnderwijsvernieuwingen. (2008). *Tijd voor onderwijs* (Final report: Time for education). Den Haag: Tweede Kamer der Staten General.

CommonCore. (2011). National Governors Association and State Education Chiefs launch common state academic standards, from http://www.corestandards.org/articles/8-national-governors-association-and-state-education-chiefs-launch-common-state-academic-standards.

Consolidation Act No. 170 of 2. June 2006, Ministry of Education (Act on Folkeskole 2006).

Cools, K. (2005). *Controle is goed, vertrouwen is nog beter* (Control is good, trust is much better). Assen, NL: van Gorcum.

Corbett, A. (2011). Ping pong: competing leadership for reform in EU higher education 1998–2006. *European Journal of Education*, 45(1), 36–53.

Crepaz, M. M. L. (2002). Global, constitutional, and partisan determinants of redistribution in fifteen OECD countries. *Comparative Politics*, 34(2), 169–188.

Crosby, P. (1979). *Quality is free: the art of making quality certain*. New York: McGraw Hill.

Davenport, S., & Moore, D. (1988). *The new improved sorting machine*. Chicago: Designs for Change.

Dejka, J. (March 30, 2010). State near bottom in Race to Top, *Omaha World-Herald*. Retrieved from http://www.omaha.com/article/20100330/NEWS01/703309879.

Devos, G. (1995). *De flexibilisering van het secundair onderwijs in Vlaanderen. Een organisatie-sociologische analyse van macht en institutionalisering* (Flexibility in Flemish secondary education. A sociological analysis of power and institutionalization). Leuven: Acco.

———. (2008). Professionalisering van schoolbesturen: hefbomen voor een sterke bestuurskracht. *Schoolleiding en begeleiding 2. Personeel en organisatie*, 19, 1–21.

DfEE. (1997). *White Paper: excellence in schools*. London: HMSO, Department for Eduction and Employment Retrieved from http://www.educationengland.org.uk/documents/pdfs/1997-excellence-in-schools.pdf.

Dillon, S. (August 15, 2007). Imported from Britain: ideas to improve schools. *New York Times*. Retrieved from http://www.nytimes.com/2007/08/15/education/15face.html.

Dryzek, J. S., & List, C. (2003). Social choice theory and deliberative democracy: a reconciliation. *British Journal of Political Science*, 33(1), 1–28.

Duru-Bellat, M., & Suchaut, B. (2005). Organisation and context, efficiency and equity: what PISA tells us. *European Educational Research Journal*, 4(3), 181–194.

Earl, L., Watson, N., Levin, B., Leithwood, K., Fullan, M., Torrance, N., Jantzi, Doris, Mascall, Blair, and Volante, Louis. (2005). *Watching and learning 3*. Toronto, ON: Ontario Institute for Studies in Education.

Ekholm, M. (2007). *Institutionalised school leader education*. Paper presented at the European Educational Research Association, Ghent, BE.

Elazar, D. J. (1970). *Cities of the prairie*. New York: Basic.

———. (1984). *American federalism: a view from the States*. New York: Harper & Row.

Elmore, R. F., & Fuhrman, S. (1995). Opportunity-to-learn standards and the state role in education. *Teachers College Record*, 96(3), 432–457.

Emese, I. (2009). *The role of school leadership on the improvement of learning. Country reports and case studies of a Central-European project*. Budapest: Tempus Foundation.

EuropeanCommission. (1993). *Growth, competitiveness, employment. The challenges and ways forward into the 21st century*. Brussels: European Commission.

———. (2000). *Enhancing democracy in the European Union (Vol. 1547/7 final)*. Brussels: SEC.

Eurydice. (2007a). *School autonomy in Europe—policies and measures*. Brussel: Eurydice European Unit.

———. (2007b). *School autonomy in Europe—policies and measures*. Brussels: European Commission.
Ferner, A., Almond, P., & Colling, T. (2005). Institutional theory and the cross-national transfer of employment policy: the case of "workforce diversity" in US multinationals. *Journal of International Business Studies*, 36(3), 304–321.
Field, S., Kuczera, M., & Pont, B. (2007). *No more failures: ten steps to equity in education*. Paris: OECD.
Fielden, J. (2001). Markets for "borderless education." *Minerva*, 39(1), 49–62.
Fitzpatrick, J. L., & Hero, R. E. (1988). Political culture and political characteristics of the American states: A consideration of some old and new questions. *The Western Political Quarterly*, 41(1), 145–153.
Fleer, J. D. (1994). *North Carolina government and politics*. Lincoln, NE: University of Nebraska Press.
Folkeskole, T. F. S. o. t. (2010). *The Folkeskole of the future—one of the best in the world. Recommendations*. Cophenhagen: The Board for the Evaluation and Quality Development of the Folkeskole, the Danish National School Agency.
Fox-Piven, F., & Cloward, R. (1997). *The breaking of the American social compact*. New York: The New Press.
Gajendragadkar, S. G. (2006). The constitutionality of racial balancing in charter schools. *Columbia Law Review*, 106, 144–174.
Gandin, L. A., & Apple, M. W. (2002). Can education challenge neoliberalism? The citizen school and the struggle for democracy in porto alegre, Brazil. *Social Justice*, 29(4), 26–40.
Garvin, D. A. (1984). What does "product quality" really mean? *Sloan Management Review* (Fall), 25–45.
Gillard, D. (Ed.). (2011). *Education in England: a brief history*. www.educationengland.org.uk/history/.
Goodman, S., & Turner, L. (2010). *Teacher incentive pay and educational outcomes: evidence from the NYC bonus program*. New York: Columbia University.
Gornitzka, A. (2005). *Emerging practices of the open method of coordination on education and research*. Oslo: ARENA Working Paper.
———. (2006). *The open method of coordination as practice: a watershed in European Education policy?* Oslo: ARENA.
Gramberger, M. (2001). *Citizens as partners: OECD handbook on citizen participation, consultation and public participation in policy making*. Paris: OECD.
Green, A. (2002). The many faces of lifelong learning: recent education policy trends in Europe. *Journal of Educational Policy*, 17(6), 611–626.
Gregg, B. (2002). Proceduralism reconceived: political conflict resolution under conditions of moral pluralism. *Theory and Society*, 31(6), 741–776.
Gritsch, M. (2005). The nation-state and economic globalization: Soft geo-politics and increased state autonomy? *Review of International Political Economy*, 12(1), 1–25.
Haider, G., & Schreiner, C. (2006). *Die PISA-Studie. Österreichs Schulsystem im Internationalen Wettbewerb*. Vienna: Böhlau.

Halász, G. (2003). Educational change and social transition in Hungary. In J. P. Anchen, M. Fullan, & E. Polyzoi (eds.), *Change forces in post-communist Eastern Europe* (pp. 55-73). London and New York: RoutledgeFalmer.

Halász, G. (2007). From deconstruction to systemic reform: educational transformation in Hungary. *Orbis Scholae*, 1(2), 45-79.

Hämäläinen, K., & Jakku-Sihvonen, R. (1999). More quality to the quality policy of education. Background paper for the meeting of the ministers of education. Helsinki: National Board of Education.

Henry, M., Lindgard, B., Rizvi, F., & Raylor, S. (2001). *The OECD, Globalisation and Education Policy.* Amsterdam: Pergamon.

Hentig, H. v. (1993). *Die Schule Neu Denken: Eine Übung in Praktischer Vernunft; Eine zornige, aber nicht eifernde, eine radikale, aber nicht utopische Antwort auf Hoyerswerda und Mölln, Rostock und Solingen (2., erw. Aufl.).* Munich: Hanser.

Hermann, Z., & Varga, J. (2010). A közoktatás finanszírozása (The funding of school education). In É. Balázs, M. Kocsis, & I. Vágó (eds.), *Jelentés a magyar közoktatásról—2010 (Report on Education in Hungary—2010)* (pp. 109-132). Budapest: Országos Közoktatási Intézet.

Heron, T. (2008). Globalization, neoliberalism and the exercise of human agency. *International Journal of Politics, Culture, and Society*, 20(1/4), 85-101.

Herzik, E. B. (1985). The legal-formal structuring of state politics: A cultural explanation. *The Western Political Quarterly*, 38(3), 413-423.

Hobolt, S. B., & Klemmensen, R. (2008). Government responsiveness and political competition in comparative perspective. *Comparative Political Studies*, 41(3), 309-337.

Hofstede, G. (1991). *Culture and organizations: software of the mind. London: McGraw-Hill, Inc.* London: McGraw Hill.

Hood, C. (1991). A public management for all seasons. *Public Administration*, 69(Spring), 3-19.

Husén, T. (1984). Research and policymaking in education: an international perspective. *Minerva*, 21(1) 81-100.

Huyse, L. (1970). *Passiviteit, pacificatie en verzuiling in de Belgische politiek. Een sociologische studie* (Passivity, pacification and "pillarization" in Belgian politics: a sociological study). Antwerpen/Utrecht: Standaard Wetenschappelijke uitgeverij.

Ingenkamp, K. (1995). *Die Fragwürdigkeit der Zensurengebung.* Weinheim, Austria: Beltz Verlag.

Johnston, W. M. (1984). *The Austrian mind. An intellectual and social history 1848-1938.* Berkeley/Los Angeles, CA: University of California Press.

Juran, J. (1992). *Quality by design.* New York: The Free Press.

Kemenade, J. v. (1975). *Contouren van een toekomstig onderwijsbeleid.* The Hague: Ministerie van Onderwijs en Wetenschappen.

Kingdon, J. W. (2003). *Agendas, alternatives and public policies.* New York: Longman.

Koster, G. (2007). The effects of social and political openness on the welfare state in 18 OECD countries, 1970-2000. *Working paper 2007-47.* Amsterdam: University of Amsterdam.

Kristen, C. (2008). Primary school choice and ethnic school segregation in German elementary schools. *European Sociological Review*, 24(4), 495-510. doi: 10.1093/esr/jcn015.

Kruse, K. (2005). *White flight: Atlanta and the making of modern conservatism.* Princeton, NJ: Princeton University Press.

Kruse, P. (2004). *Next practice. Erfolgreiches Management von Instabilität.* Offenbach: Gabal.

Kuzmanic, T. A. (2007). *Challenges and critique of efficiency—autonomy, responsibilty and efficiency.* Paper presented at the International Congress for School Effectiveness and School Improvement, Portorož, Slovenia.

Kwok, C. C. Y., & Solomon, T. (2006). National culture and financial systems. *Journal of International Business Studies*, 37(2), 227-247.

Lange, B., & Alexiadou, N. (2007). New forms of European governance in the education sector? A preliminary analysis of the open method of coordination. *European Educationa Research Journal*, 6(4), 321-335.

Lawn, M., & Lingard, B. (2002). Constructing a European policy space in educational governance: the role of transnational policy actors. *European Educational Research Journal*, 1(2), 290-307.

Lee, J. (1997). State activism in education reform: applying the Rasch model to measure trends and examine policy coherence. *Educational Evaluation and Policy Analysis*, 19(1), 29-43.

Leijendekker, M. (January 19, 2011). Niet alle Europese landen kozen voor scherpe splitsing. *NRC Handelsblad.*

Leune, J. M. G. (1999). *Onderwijs in beweging; enige opmerkingen over veranderingen in het Nederlandse Onderwijs gedurende het laatste kwart van de twintigste eeuw.* The Hague: Social en Cultureel Planbureau.

Levin, B. (2005). *Governing education.* Toronto: University of Toronto Press.

———. (2008). *How to change 5000 schools.* Cambridge, MA: Harvard Education Press.

———. (2009). How governments decide: the role of research. In R. Desjardins & K. Rubenson (eds.), *Research of vs research for education policy in an era of transnational policy-making* (pp. 44-57). Saarbucken: VDM Dr. Müller.

———. (2010). The challenge of large-scale literacy improvement. *School Effectiveness and School Improvement*, 21(4), 359-376.

Lewis, T. (2007). What not to wear: religious rights, the European court, and the margin of appreciation. *The International and Comparative Law Quarterly*, 56(2), 395-414.

Lidegaard, B. (2005). *Kampen om Danmark 1933-1945* (The struggle for Denmark 1933-1945). København: Gyldendals Bogklubber.

Lieber, R. J., & Weisberg, R. E. (2002). Globalization, culture, and identities in crisis. *International Journal of Politics, Culture, and Society*, 16(2), 273-296.

Lieske, J. (1993). Regional subcultures of the United States. *The Journal of Politics*, 55(4), 888-913.

Lindblom, C. (1959). The science of middling through. *Public Administration Review*, 19(1), 79-88.

Lindgard, B. (2000). It is and it isn't: vernacular globalization, educationa. Policy, and restructuring. In N. C. Burbules & C. A. Torres (eds.), *Globalization and education. Critical perspetives* (79–108). New York: Routledge.

Lindvall, J., & Rothstein, B. (2006). Sweden: The fall of the strong state. *Scandinavian Political Studies*, 29(1), 47–63.

Linn, R. L., Baker, E. L., & Dunbar, S. B. (1991). Complex, performance-based assessment: Expectations and validation criteria. *Educational Researcher*, 20(8), 15–21.

Louis, K. S., Febey, K., Gordon, M., Meath, J., & Thomas, E. (2006). Educational leadership in the states: A cultural analysis. Retrieved January 18, 2007, from http://education.umn.edu/CAREI/Leadership/Reports.html.

Louis, K. S., Febey, K., Gordon, M., & Thomas, E. (2008). Does state leadership matter? An analysis of three states. *Educational Administration Quarterly*, 44(4), 562–592.

Louis, K. S., Leithwood, K., Wahlstrom, K., Anderson, S. A., & Michlin, M. (2010). *Learning from leadership: Investigating the links to improved student learning: Final report of research findings*. New York: Wallace Foundation.

Louis, K. S., Teichler, U., & Bodstrom, L. (1991). *Review of the educational system: The Netherlands*. Paris: Organization for Economic Cooperation and Development.

Louis, K. S., & van Velzen, B. A. M. (1991). A look at choice in the Netherlands. *Educational Leadership*, 48(4), 66–72.

Lov om folkeskolen. (June 26, 1975).

———. (1993 Consolidation Act No. 730 of June 21, 2000).

Lundahl, C. (2008). Inter/national assessment as national curriculum: the case of Sweden. An Atlantic Crossing? In M. Lawn (ed.), *An Atlantic crossing? The work of the international examination inquiry, its researchers, methods and influence* (pp. 157–180). Oxford: Symposium Books.

March, J. G., & Olsen, J. P. (1984). The new institutionalism: Organizational factors in political life. *The American Political Science Review*, 78(3), 734–749.

Marmot, M. (2004). Evidence based policy or policy based evidence? *British Medical Journal*, 328(7445), 906–907.

Marquart-Pyatt, S., & Paxton, P. (2007). In principle and in practice: Learning political tolerance in eastern and western europe. *Political Behavior*, 29(1), 89–113.

Martin, H.-P., & Schumann, H. (1997). *Globaliseringsfælden. Angrebet på demokrati og velstand* [The Globalizational Trap. The attack on democracy and welfare]. København: Borgen.

Matthews, P., & Sammons, P. (2006). *Improvement through inspection*. London: HMI (Inspectorate).

Mazzoni, T. L. (1993). The changing politics of state eduation policy making: A 20-year Minnesota perspective. *Educational Evaluation and Policy Analysis*, 15(4), 357–379.

McKevitt, D. (1998). *Managing core public services*. Oxford, UK: Blackwell.

McLaughlin, M. (1987). Learning from experience: Lessons from policy implementation. *Educational Evaluation and Policy Analysis*, 9(2), 171–178.

Mead, S. (2008). Educational reform lessons from England: an interview with Michael Barbor. Retrieved April 2011, from http://www.educationsector.org/publications/education-reform-lessons-england.
Meyer, O. W., Boli, J., Thomas, G. M., & Ramirez, F. O. (1997). World society and the nation state. *American Journal of Sociology*, 103(1), 144–181.
Miles, M. B. (1964). *Innovation in education*. New York: Teachers College Press.
Miller, R. (n.d.). *Education and economic growth: from the 19th to the 21st century* (p. 19). San Jose, CA: Cisco Systems.
Mintzberg, H. (1990). *Structures in five*. Englewood Cliffs, NJ: Prentice Hall.
Moore, M. H. (1995). *Creating public value, strategic management in government*. Cambridge, MA: Harvard University Press.
Moos, L. (2006a). A real change or a change in rhetoric?—comments to two OECD reviews on Educational research: England in 2002 and Denmark in 2004. *European Educational Research Journal*, 5(1), 63–67.
———. (2006b). What kinds of democracy in education are facilitated by supra- and transnational agencies? *European Educational Research Journal*, 5(3 & 4), 160–168.
———Moos, L. (2009a). A general context for new social technologies. *Nordic Educational Research*, 29(1), 79–92.
———. (2009b). Hard and soft governance: the journey from transnational agencies to school leadership. *European Educational Journal*, 8(3), 397–406.
Mortimore, P. (Tuesday, July 7, 2009). Missed opportunities and mad ideas: the government's legacy. *The Guardian*. Retrieved from http://www.guardian.co.uk/education/2009/jul/07/peter-mortimore-education-schools.
Nathan, J. (1996). *Charter schools: creating hope and opportunity for American education*. San Francisco: Jossey Bass.
The National Commission on Excellence in Education. (1983). A Nation At Risk: The Imperative For Educational Reform. An Open Letter to the American People. A Report to the Nation and the Secretary of Education (p. 72). District of Columbia: National Commission on Excellence in Education (ED), Washington, DC.
NCES. (2002). *State reading 2002: Nebraska*. Washington, DC: National Center for Educational Statistics. Retrieved from http://nces.ed.gov/nationsreportcard/pdf/stt2002/2003526NE.pdf.
———. (2008). *1.5 million homeschooled students in the United States in 2007*. Washington, DC: National Center for Educational Statistics.
NEA. (2009). *Rankings and estimates*. Washington, DC: National Educational Association.
Neave, G. (1985). Gentlemen, scholars, and administrators: the rise of the higher education research community in Sweden. *The Journal of Higher Education*, 56(1), 1–25.
NKSR. (1979). *Bouwen aan de relatief autonome school*. The Hague: NKSR.
Norrander, B. (2000). The multi-layered impact of public opinion on capital punishment implementation in the American states. *Political Research Quarterly*, 53(4), 771–793.
O'Neill, T. (1087). *Man of the house*. New York: Random House.

O'Toole, L. J., & Meier, K. J. (2004). Parkinson's law and the new public management? Contracting determinants and service-quality consequences in public education. *Public Administration Review*, 64(3), 342–352.

OECD. (1998). *Education catalogue*. Paris: OECD.

———. (2005). School factors related to quality and equity: results from PISA 2000. Paris: Organization for Economic Cooperation and Development.

———. (2008). Ten steps to equity in education. Paris: Organization for Economic Cooperation and Development.

———. (2009). PISA in Flanders. Retrieved January 25, 2012, from http://www.pisa.ugent.be/en/pisa-in-flanders.

———. (2010a). *Education at a Glance*. Paris: Organization for Economic Cooperation and Development.

———. (2010b). A family affair: intergenerational social mobility across OECD countries. Paris: Organization for Economic Cooperation and Development.

———. (2012). Equity and quality in education: supporting disadvantaged students and schools. Paris: Organization for Economic Cooperation and Development.

OLLAS. (2010). Nebraska's foreign-born and Hispanic/Latino population: demographic trends, 1990–2008. Lincoln, NE: Office of Latino/Latin American Studies (OLLAS), University of Nebraska.

Olssen, M. M. (2005). Neoliberalism, higher education and the knowledge economy: from the free market to knowledge capitalism *Journal of Educational Policy*, 20(3), 313–345.

Onderwijsraad. (2002). *Dereguleren met beleid. Studie naar de effecten van deregulering en autonomievergroting* (Deregulating with policies: a study of the effects of deregulation and the growth of autonomy). Den Haag, Netherlands: Onderwijsraad (Educational Council).

Ong, A. (2006). *Neoliberalism as exception: mutations in citizenship and sovereignty*. Durham, NC: Duke University Press.

Ostler, J. (1992). Why the populist party was strong in Kansas and Nebraska but weak in Iowa. *The Western Historical Quarterly*, 23(4), 451–474.

Palme, O. (1984). *Employment and welfare*. Paper presented at the The Jerry Wurf Memorial Lecture, Cambridge, MA.

Pareto, V. (1991). *The rise and fall of elites*. Rutgers, NJ: Transaction Press.

Parliament, N. (2008). *Tijd voor onderwijs* (Final report: time for education). Den Haag: Commissie Parlementair Onderzoek Onderwijsvernieuwingen.

Pedersen, O. K. (2010). *Konkurrencestaten* (The competitive state). København: Hans Reitzel.

Pierson, C. (1998). The new governance of education: the Conservatives and education 1988–1997. *Oxford Review of Education*, 24(1), 131–142.

Pierson, P., & Skocpol, T. (2002). Historical institutionalism in contemporary political xcience. In I. Katznelson & H. V. Milner (eds.), *Political science: state of the discipline* (pp. 693–721). New York: W.W. Norton.

Pollack, M. A. (1997). Delegation, agency, and agenda setting in the European Community. *International Organization*, 51(1), 99–134.

Radice, H. (2000). Globalization and national capitalisms: theorizing convergence and differentiation. *Review of International Political Economy*, 7(4), 719–742.

Radó, P. (2001). *Transition in education: policy making and the key educational policy areas in the Central-European and Baltic Countries*. Budapest: Open Society Institute.

———. (2010). *Governing decentralized education systems: systemic change in South Eastern Europe; Local government and public service reform initiative*. Budapest: Open Society Foundations.

Ramirez, F. O., & Boli, J. (1987). The political construction of mass schooling: european origins and worldwide institutionalization. *Sociology of Education*, 60(1), 2–17.

Ramirez, F. O., & Meyer, J. W. (1980). Comparative education: the social construction of the modern world system. *Annual Review of Sociology*, 6(1), 369–397.

Read, R. (2011). *Knowledge mobilization at the World Bank: a bibliometric analysis of World Bank publications on public-private partnerships in education*. MA: University of Toronto.

Révész, É., & Szabó, M. (2008). The role of school leadership in creating a learning environment that is conducive to effective learning with special regard to the improvement of the quality of teacher activity. Country Report, Hungary.

Rossell, C. (1975). School desegregation and white flight. *Political Science Quarterly*, 90(4), 675–695.

Sacken, D. M., & Medina, M., Jr. (1990). Investigating the context of state-level policy formation: a case study of Arizona's bilingual education legislation. *Educational Evaluation and Policy Analysis*, 12(4), 389–402.

Salcher, A. (2009). *Der talentierte schüler und seine feinde*. Salzburg: Ecowin.

Saporito, S. (2003). Private choices, public consequences: magnet school choice and segregation by race and poverty. *Social Problems*, 50(2), 81–203.

Scharmer, C. O. (2007). *Theory U: leading from the future as it emerges*. Cambridge, MA: SOL (Society for Organizational Learning).

Scheerens, J., Luyten, H., & Ravens, J. (2011). *Perspectieven op onderwijskwalitiet*. Den Haag: NWO.

Schefers, O. (2012). *How dual-credit programs can affect the relationship between secondary and postsecondary institutions*. Paper presented at the International Congress for School Effectiveness and School Improvement, Malmo, Sweden.

Schleicher, A. (2009). Securing quality and equity in education: results from PISA. *Prospects*, 39(NA), 251–263.

Schley, W., & Schratz, M. (2011). Developing leaders, building networks, changing schools through system leadership. In J. MacBeath & T. Townsend (eds.), *International handbook on leadership for learning* (pp. 267–296). New York: Springer.

Schmid, K., Hafner, H., & Pirolt, R. (2007). Reform von Schulgovernance-Systemen. Vergleichende Analyse der Reformprozesse in Österreich und bei einigen PISA-Teilnehmerländern (IBW- Forschungsbericht, 135). Vienna: IBW.

Schratz, M. (2003). From administering to leading a achool: challenges in German-speaking countries. *Cambridge Journal of Education*, 33(3), 395–416.

Schratz, M., & Hartmann, M. (2009). *Schulautonomie in Österreich: Bilanz und Perspektiven für eine Eigenverantwortliche Schule*. Graz: Leykam.
Schuller, T. (2006). Reviewing OECD's Educational research Reviews. *European Educational Research Journal*, 5(1), 57–61.
Seel, H. (2010). *Einführung in die Schulgeschichte Österreichs*. Innsbruck, Austria: Studienverlag.
Senge, P. (1990). *The fifth discipline: the art and practice of the learning organization*. New York: Doubleday.
Senge, P., Smith, B., Kruschwitz, N., Laur, J., & Schley, S. (2008). *The necessary revolution: how individuals and organizations are working together to create a sustainable world*. London, Boston: Nicholas Brealey Publishing.
Sharkansky, I. (1969). The utility of Elazar's political culture: A research note. *Polity*, 2, 66–83.
Shepard, J. (March 13, 2009). Slow education policy juggernaut, urges Lords report. *The Guardian*. Retrieved from http://www.guardian.co.uk/education/2009/mar/13/lords-report-dcsf.
Shewbridge, C., Jang, E., Matthews, P., & Santiago, P. (2011). OECD reviews of evaluation and assessment in education: Denmark. Retrieved from http://www.oecd.org/dataoecd/59/39/47696732.pdf.
Spring, J. (2008). Research on globalization and education. *Review of Educational Research*, 78(2), 330–363.
Springer, M., Hamilton, L., McCaffrey, D., Ballou, D., Le., V.N., Pepper, M., Stecher, B. M., and Lockwood, J. R. (2010). *Teacher pay for performance: experimental evidence from the project on incentives in teaching*. Nashville, TN: Peabody College, Vanderbilt University.
Stevens, P. A. J., & Van Houtte, M. (2011). Adapting to the system or the student? Exploring teacher adaptations to disadvantaged students in an English and a Belgian secondary school. *Educational Evaluation and Policy Analysis*, 33(1), 59–75. doi: 10.3102/0162373710377112.
Stoll, L., Moorman, H., & Rahm, S. (2008). Building leadership capacity for system improvement in Austria. In B. Pont, D. Nusche, & D. Hopkins (eds.), *Improving school leadership: Vol. 2. improving school leadership. Case studies on system leadership*. Paris: OECD.
Strange, S. (1997). The future of global capitalism: or, will divergence persist for ever? In C. Crouch & W. Streeck (eds.), *Political economy of modern capitalism: mapping convergence and diversity* (pp. 182–191). London: Sage.
Štremfel, U., & Lajh, D. (2010). Implementing EU lifelong learning policy through open method of coordination in new member states: comparative analysis of the Czech Republic, Slovakia and Slovenia. *Journal of Comparative Politics*, 3(2), 64–84.
Ten Have, J., Hiemstra, K., & van Velzen, B. A. M. (2009). *Het stelsel in de war, de mensen in verwarring*. Utrecht: APS.
Timar, T. B., & Kirp, D. L. (1988). State efforts to reform schools: treading between a regulatory swamp and an English garden. *Educational Evaluation and Policy Analysis*, 10(2), 75–88.

Tolofari, S. (2005). New public management and education. *Policy Futures in Education*, 3(1). Retrieved from Policy Futures in Education website: http://www.wwwords.co.uk/pdf/validate.asp?j=pfie&vol=3&issue=1&year=2005&article=8_Tolofari_PFIE_3_1_web.

Tooley, J. (1993). *A market-led alternative for the curriculum: breaking the code*. London: The Tufnell Press.

.Torfing, J. (2004). *Det stille sporskifte i velfærdstaten* (The silent switch in the welfarestate). Aarhus: Aarhus; Arhus University Press

Torres, C. A. (2002). Globalization, education, and citizenship: solidarity versus markets? *American Educational Research Journal*, 39(2), 363–378.

U.S.CensusBureau. (2011). *Public education finances: 2009* (G09-ASPEF). Washington, DC: U.S. Government Printing Office. Retrieved from http://www2.census.gov/govs/school/09f33pub.pdf.

UndervisningMinisteriet. (2008). Private schools in Denmark. Retrieved from https:\www.uvm.dk.

UNESCO. (2002). Education for sustainable development.

Utbildningsdepartementet. (2004). Learning to change our world: International consultation on education for sustainable development. Report of the Kommittén för utbildning fö rhållbar utveckling. Stockholm: Utbildningsdepartementet.

Van den Berghe, W. (1995). *Achieving quality in training. European guide for collaborative training projects*. UNESCO/International Institute for Educational Planning: Belgium.

van Velzen, W., Miles, M. B., Ekholm, M., Hameyer, U., & Robin, D. (1985). *Making school improvement work*. Leuven, BE: ACCO.

Wald, K. D., & Calhoun-Brown, A. (2009). *Religion and politics in the United States*. Lanham, MD: Rowman and Littlefield.

Walkenhorst, H. (2005). Europeanisation of the German education system. *German Politics*, 14(4), 470–486.

Warwick, D., & Williams, J. (1980). History and the sociology of education. *British Journal of Sociology of Education*, 1(3), 333–346.

Wassmer, R. W., & Fisher, R. C. (2002). Interstate variation in the use of fees to fund K-12 public education. *Economics of Education Review*, 21(1), 87–100.

Weatherly, R., & Lipsky, M. (1977). Street level bureaucrats and institutional innovation: implementing special education reform. *Harvard Educational Review*, 47(2), 171–197.

Weick, K. E. (1976). Educational organizations as loosely coupled systems. *Administrative Quarterly*, 21(1) 1–19.

———. (2001). *Making Sense of the Organization* (pp. 380–403). Malden, MA: Blackwell Publishers Inc.

Weick, K. E., & Quinn, R. E. (1999). Organizational change and development. *Annual Review of Psychology*, 50(1), 361–386. doi: doi:10.1146/annurev.psych.50.1.361.

West, A., & Penning, H. (2002). How new is New Labour? The quasi-market and English schools 1977–2001. *British Journal of Educational Studies*, 50(2), 206–224.

Whitty, G. (1997). Creating quasi-markets in education: a review of recent research on parental choice and school autonomy in three countries. *Review of Research in Education*, 22, 3–47.

Whitty, G., & Edwards, T. (1998). School choice policies in England and the United States: An exploration of their origins and significance. *Comparative Education*, 34(2), 211–227.

Whitty, G., & Power, S. (2000). Marketization and privatization in mass education systems. *International Journal of Educational Development*, 20(2), 93–107.

Winch, C. (1996). *Quality and education*. Oxford/Cambridge: Wiley-Blackwell.

Wirt, F., Mitchell, D., & Marshall, C. (1988). Culture and education policy: analyzing values in state policy systems. *Educational Evaluation and Policy Analysis*, 10(4), 271–284.

Wolak, J., Newmark, A. J., McNoldy, T., Lowery, D., & Gray, V. (2002). Much of politics is still local: multi-state lobbying in state interest communities. *Legislative Studies Quarterly*, 27(4), 527–555.

Wong, K. K. (1989). Fiscal support for education in American states: the "parity-to-dominance" view examined. *American Journal of Education*, 97(4), 329–357.

Wood, B. D., & Theobald, N. A. (2003). Political responsiveness and equity in public education finance. *Journal of Politics*, 65(3), 718–738.

Woodward, W. (March 24, 2008). The legacy of blue Ken. *The Guardian*. Retrieved from http://www.guardian.co.uk/politics/2008/mar/25/education.schools.

Yashar, D. J. (2007). Resistance and identity politics in an age of globalization. *Annals of the American Academy of Political and Social Science*, 610, 160–181.

Index

Absorption concept, 207
Academic achievement, 25, 167
Accountability: in Austrian educational system, 135; Catholic school and, 90–91; effects of, in Nebraska and North Carolina, 185–186; in England educational system, 108–109; local, 2, 150, 190; policies, in North Carolina, 177–178; and privatization, 149, legislative actions related to, 171–172; professional approaches to, 103; and voucher programs, 25
Adaptation concept, 204
Adonis, A., 108
Agenda setting, 12–13
Agrarian cooperative movement, 63
Agrarian cultures, 22
Austrian-wide Leadership Academy, 100, 133, 137, 138n3
Autonomous Council of the Education Community, 87
Autonomy: local, 18, 128, 132, 136, 218; need to increase, in Austria, 98–99; in The Netherlands, 74–75; and NPM, 74–75; of school board The Netherlands, 77–79, 83,148; of school boards in Belgium/Flanders, 86–87; of school in Austria, 136–138; of schools in Belgium/Flanders 39, 85–87, 91; of schools in England, 108,142–143; semi-autonomous schools in The Netherlands, 146; and standardized tests, 134, 136
Autonomy and decentralization. *See* Decentralization

Autonomy and school boards. *See* Autonomy

Baker, K., 107
Bennett, C. J, 207
BIFIE (Federal Institute for Educational Research, Innovation and Development of the Austrian School System), 100–101, 135
Bildung concept: associated with Wilhelm von Humboldt, 71n2; in contrast with more output centered policy, in Denmark, 67, 158, 206; definition of 37, 44–45; democratic, 68–70, 167; and NPM, 168
Bologna process, 5, 219
Braudel, F., 34
Bureaucracy, in Austria, 39, 96–97, 99

Capitalism, 7, 24
Catholic education in Flanders, 130–131
Catholic School Board Association (NKSR), 146–147
Catholic schools: in Austria, 134; in Flanders, 91–92, 130–131; in The Netherlands, 74; and non-Catholic educational systems in Flanders-Belgium, 39; in United States, 121
Centralization: of monitoring, 43; of school reform in Austria, 100
Centralized consultative process the, in Austria, 99
CERI (the Centre for Educational Research and Innovation), 32
Charter schools: definition of, 25;

and homeschooling, 211n4; in
Nebraska, 183; in North Carolina,
179; in Sweden, 55; in United States,
25, 121
Choice: cultural assumptions that
affect rational, 33; definition of, 2,
10-11; different values for, 25, 199;
and educational agenda, 199; and
efficiency, 69, 81; and equity, 24, 26;
freedom of, in Denmark, 63, 71n3;
freedom of, in The Netherlands,
79; history of educational, 24;
as instrument of competition in
public school systems, 24-25; local
and individual responsibility, in
Denmark, 69, 71; and market-
competition, 199; in The
Netherlands, 24, 38; in North
Carolina and Nebraska, 183; and
parental needs, 24; and quality,
20-21, 24; rethinking, 199; of
school subjects, in Sweden, 59;
as social value, 23-24; in United
States, 9, 24, and decentralist
political cultures and, 25; value
of individual, in Denmark, 63, 69,
71; as a value of pluralism, 24; and
voucher programs, 25
Citizen participation: and definition
of quality, 198; formal form to,
11-12
Coalitions: and informal networks,
12-13; in Denmark, 158-159, 168;
government, 68, 80; political, 147;
in power, 67; in Sweden, 162-163
Collective memories. See Mental
models concept
Competition: and charter schools,
25; and choice, 24, 231; global,
64, 164, 167; improve outcomes
and equity through, 109; and
individualistic political culture,
17; and market, 199; and NPM, 31,
168, 169-170; between providers of
transportation services, 149; and

quality, 141; among school board,
in The Netherlands, 82-83; between
schools, in United States, 24, in
The Netherlands, 81; within public
school sector,139
Comprehensive educational
system: and Catholic educational
network in Flanders, 91; and
decentralization, 14; in Denmark,
37, 63-64, 68-69, 70, 71n7, 158;
and Egalitarianism, 18, 197; in The
Netherlands, 38, 84n3; in Sweden,
6, 36, 45, 54, 56, 164; in United
States, 25-26
Continuous change: definition of, 203;
and national tests, 206; a political
culture of, 204
Council for Mutual Economic
Assistance (Comecon), 214
Counties: in Denmark, 66; in North
Carolina, 173, 178
Creating Essential Educational
Opportunities for All Children Act,
182
Cultural: competing values, 18;
definition of, 227; national and
local, 7; political values, 18;
preferences, 9; value of freedom of
choice in Denmark, 63, 69; value of
pluralism, 24-25; values, 6, 10

Dearing, Ron, 110
Decentralism. See Decentralization
Decentralist. See Decentralization
Decentralization: advantages of, 13; in
Austria, 101; and autonomy, 13, 14;
and choice, 25; and decision making,
196; definitions of, 9; de-regulation
de-concentration and professional
autonomy, 15; differences between
de-concentration and, 14; differences
between de-regulation and, 15;
and efficiency in local government
in Denmark, 66, 68; in European
countries, 43-44; in Flanders, 87;

functional, 14, 195; and neoliberal trends, 31; in The Netherlands, 76; and organizational theory, 13, 43–44; patterns of regional and functional, 50–51; and quality, 14; rationalism and, 196; rethinking, 195–196; and school-inequity in New Zealand, 14; in Sweden, 55–58, 165, 167; of the system, 38; territorial decentralization concept, 14; visions of, 13–14
De-concentration, definition of, 14–15, *See* also Decentralization
De-regulation, re-regulation, concept of, 15, *See* also Decentralization
Devolution: concept of, 14; constitutional, 39; and decentralization, 195
Dimond, J., 34
Discourse and policy analysis, 228–230
Dual credit programs concept, 25
Dynamic complexity concept, 208

Economic liberalism concept, 22
Educational policies: and choice, 25–26; comparison of patters of, 166–170; and culture values, 65; and efficiency, 10, 197–198; and equity, 16–18; in Herzik's components, 9; making, 12–13, 195, 203, 207–209; and measurements, 43; and OECD, 32; and policy instruments, 199–200; and rationalism, 229
Educational policy. *See* Educational policies
Educational Quality Accountability Act, 181–182
Educational reform: in Denmark and Sweden, 155, 196; in Flanders and Austria, 136; and globalizing forces, 35; and political culture, 46, 54, 126, 210
Effective responsiveness concept, 200, 202–203

Efficiency: and choice in Nebraska, 180; the concept of, 27n5; and cost-benefit models, 10; definitions of, 10; in educational policy discussions, 69; and local government in Denmark, 66; neoliberal emphasis on, 22; in The Netherlands, 81; and NPM in Dutch governmental policies, 76, 78; as political concept, 22–23; rethinking, 197–198; value of, 22
Egalitarianism: definition of, 15–18
Elazar, D., 8, 83, 116–118, 172
Emerging complexity concept, 208
Episodic change concept, 203–204
Epistemic communities concept: and globalizing forces, 35; and the role of localized cultural interpretations of events 30, 34
Equalitarian. *See* Egalitarianism
Equality: achievement and, 18; and choice in Flanders, 94, 137; and comprehensive programs, 18; definition of, 16–17; in educational policy, 17–18; and emergence of competitive state in Denmark, 69; in modern societies, 17; perspectives on, 17; rethinking, 197; and standards, 135–136
Equal opportunity policy, in Flemish education, 91–92, 132
Equity policy: in Austria, 103–104; in Flanders, 132
European commission: and Delors report, 216; influence of, in Denmark, 160; view of globalization, 6
Europeanization concept, 218–219
Excellence in Schools report the, 142–143

Federal government: in Nebraska, 174, 179, 184; responsibilities of, in Austria, 40, 101; in United States,

115–116, 118–119, 123n1, expanding the role of the, in United States, 171
Federal system of education in Austria, 101
Freedom: of choice, in Austria, 102–103, 128; of choice, in Denmark, 37, 63, 83; of education, 24, 84n3, in Flanders (Belgium), 39, 86,-87, 90–91, 130, 134, in The Netherlands, 38, 73–74, 79–80, 83, 151; and egalitarianism, 197; exercising, 123n2; and NPM, 147; value of individual, 26n3
Free school movement in Denmark, 63, 71n1
Freestanding schools: in 20th century, 63–64; and individual or parents' choice, 69, 71; introduction of, 63; for talented students, 168; within the municipal system, 68
Functional decentralization definition, 14; and decentralization, 195; unique patters of regional and, 50

Garbage can concept, 219, 222
GATS (the General Agreement on Trade in Services), 31
Global and local: lenses, 46; perspective, 30, 42; tensions between, 34
Global cultural thinking, 31
Global economic forces, 31
Globalization: alternative view of, 26n1; counterpoint to, 190–191; definition of, 30–31; in education, 19; forces of, 35, 49, 51; and international influences, 224–227; and neoliberal rhetoric, 6; and policy making, 6–7; processes of, 45; and resistance movements, 6
Global language and historical context, 190
Global marketplace, 64, 69
Global trends: explanations for the coexistence of 6; the impact of, in policy, 49; and national politics, 31; and path dependency, 209
Government learning concept, 207
Grundskola: policy initiative on professional development in Sweden, 165; and student assessment system, 159, 161; in Sweden, 36, 55–56, 58, 79
Gymnasium: concept of, 104; in Denmark, 157–158

Herzik, E.B., 9, 10, 11
Historical causation concept of, 33
Historical perspectives in the new institutionalism, 33
Horizontal equity policy concept, 17–18
Howlett, M., 207

Ideological domination, fear of, 129
Ideologies, and history, 29
IMF (International Monetary Fund), 31, 64
Informal agenda: concept, 12–13; and parliamentary or legislative discussions, 11–12
Inspectorate, role of, in Belgium, 90
International Mathematics and Science Study (TIMMS), 32, 43, 65, 67, 80, 134, 135
International testing, movement, 20; activities and international standards, 43–44; and efficiency, 22; in Austria and Belgium (Flanders), 127–129; and impact of NPM, 206
International trends: in England and the Netherlands, 45; in Flanders, 94; focus of, 136; and path dependency, 209; and policy responsiveness, 200–201; process influenced by, 136–137

Kommuns: and central government in Sweden, 196, 207; changes in, in Sweden, 54–57; concept of, 53;

current role of in Sweden, 59, 165; definition of, 61n1; in Denmark, 157-160; and local responsibilities in Sweden, 58; national Association of, in Sweden, 53, 160-161; origins of, 56

Läroplans: concept of, 159; for preschool, 62n4, 165; use of in Sweden, 159-160
Legislation: and accountability movement in North Carolina and Nebraska, 177-178, 181-183; and citizen participation, 12; connection, 11; construction of premises and framework of, 11; decision making, 11; for monitoring the quality of schools in United States, 44; and openness, 53, 166-167; parliament, 11; process of, 11; and teachers' union, 66
Lesson-drawing concept, 207
Lindgard, B., 32
Local (contexts) and globalization, 6, 30-31, 34-35; and decentralization in the governance, 43-44
Local (education) authorities: in Denmark, 68-69; in England, 23, 40, 105-109, 139, 141; in Flemish, 130-131; and governance, 144, 149
Local accountability. *See* Accountability
Local autonomy: in Austria, 128, 136-137; in Flemish culture, 132; in United States, 18; as value in CEE countries, 218
Local control: and Bildung, 37; and Folkeskole in Denmark, 63-65; in Nebraska, 179-180, 182-183
Local decision-making in Nebraska, 174
Local Education Authorities (LEAs) in England, 40, 105-107, 139, 141, 144, 149
Local education network: in Flanders, 94n2, 130; or local professional associations in Sweden, 61

Local governance: and efficiency, 66; and Kommuns, 55, 56, 58; and school boards, 76, 78, 80
Local history, 35, 47n3, 127
Local perspective, 30
Local school improvement practices in North Caroline, 177, 179
Local stakeholders: in Austria, 137; and NPM influence, 203; and policy conversations, 203
Local system of education, in England, 40-41
LOs (National Union of Unions), 163

Magnet schools, 24-25
Matura examination concept, 100-101, 135-136
Mckevitt, D., 15, 23, 77
Mental models concept, 29, 34, 216
Minorities' parties, and legislative processes, 12
Modernization: impact of, in educational sector, 215; model, 217
Mortimore, P., 145

National Agency for School Improvement, 53
National Association of Municipalities (NAM), 67
National Educational Association. *See* Teachers' union
National governments, role of as policy leaders, 105-106, 218
National identity (ies): in European countries, 44-46; and modernization processes, 45-46; and resistance movements, 6; role leaders in shape, 105
Nation-states: and history, 7; and neoliberal language, 26n2; role of in a modern economy, 45; and worldwide forces, 31
Nebraska State Accountability Framework, 182
Nebraska State Education Association, 180

Neoliberal: economic structures and NPM, 33–34; education agenda of OECD, 226, 228; emphasis on efficiency, 22; language, 26n2; market logics, 31; movement concept of, 22; rhetoric, 6; trends, 31
Neoliberal rhetoric. *See* Globalization
New institutionalism concept, 33–34
New Public Management (NPM): definition of, 30–31; in Denmark, 164; in England, 140–141, 143; in Flanders, 92; impact of, in Austria, 138; impact of, in Denmark, 69–70; impact of, in political culture, 140, 189, 202, 206–207; impact of, in Sweden, 61; impacts in England, 108–110; impacts in Flemish education, 89–90; impacts in The Netherlands, 74, 76–77, 78–79, 81, 83; and leadership, 220–221; and neo liberal economic structure, 33–34; in The Netherlands, 146–147; origins of the term, 47n2; outcomes of in public services, 23; paradox of, 220–221; and rationalism, 196; and standardization, 136; and testing, 221; and transnational agencies, 189
No Child Left Behind Act, 42, 123, 199; in North Carolina, 175
North Atlantic Treaty Organization, 213–214

Office for Standards in Education (OFSTED), 40, definition of, 106; and accountability, 106,108; external quality control, 141
Open coordination initiatives, 43
Open method of coordination (OMC): in CEE countries, 217, 220; definition, 32; in Sweden, 167
Openness: definitions of, 9; government openness, 195; impact of NPM in, 203; and legislation, 11–13; rethinking, 193–195; in Swedish policy making, 53–54, 61
Output centered policy in Denmark, 67

Parallel tests concept, 90–91
Parental school choice: in British system, 107, 141; in Denmark, 69, 71; and equity, 26, 197; in Flanders, 92, 94, 130–131; and inefficiencies in the system, 107; in the Netherlands, 38, 80–81; in United States, 24
Parental social status and student achievement relationship, 80
Parliamentary: agenda, 12; legislative process, 13, history in England, 109–110; modern process in Denmark and Sweden, 156–157, 216
Path dependency: and global trends, 209; importance of, 33
Polder model concept, definition, 79–80
Policy implementation: differences in, 204–205; and professional development in Sweden, 161
Policy instruments, 199–200
Policy making processes: in Belgium, 88–89, 131–132; in Denmark, 68–74; in England, 111; and Europeanization, 219; factors that affect, 2; history role in, 209; influence of international agencies in, 166–167, 226; in Nebraska, 183; non-rational, 221; and openness, 11, 13, 193–194; patterns of policy development in the United States, 9; and significant events, 35–42; in the state of North Carolina, 175–176, 177; in Sweden, 53–54, 56
Political: action(s), 18, 32, in Austria 100; alternatives. *See* Path dependency; behavior, 9; design decisions, 17; initiatives in Sweden, 56–57, 165–167; and institutional perspectives, 26n3, 33; language of efficiency, 23; pluralism, 214; processes and political culture, 11, 150, 166
Political culture: components of, 8–11; definition of, 8; dimensions, 2; in

England, 108; Europeanization and, 215; fundamental elements of, in Flanders, 92; individualist, in Nebraska, 172-173, 179-180, 184-185; shaping impact of NPM in The Netherlands, 76-78; shaping impact of NPM in Sweden, 61; traditional, in North Carolina, 172; types of: individualistic, 8, moralistic, 8, 11, traditional, 8; in United States, 116-117

Populist movements, in Nebraska, 174

Principals: changes in the role of, in The Netherlands, 77-78; in Leadership Academy participation of, 138n3; participation of, in Austria, 137; and school board, 147-148; school heads in Austria, 101; school heads in England, 109, 144

Principles: basic, in Belgium education system, 86; of choice, 170; in educational policy in United States, 115-116; financial, 80; of local and individual responsibilities in Denmark, 69; market, in England, 140-141; of NPM, 164, 196-197; of personalized education, 135-136; in Sweden, 59-60

Private schools: and choice, 23-24; and consultative processes in The Netherlands, 83n1; in Denmark, 169-170; inducements for, in The Netherlands, 75-76, 145-147; and public school in Flanders, 86-88; and public schools in The Netherlands, 38; into the public sector, in The Netherlands, 74; and religious controversy, 120-121; in Sweden, 156; in United States, 119; in voucher programs, 25

Probing test concept, 90

Professional development, teacher, 23; accountability for, in The Netherlands, 147; and changes in educational policy in Flanders, 131, 137; funds in North Carolina, 177; in The Netherlands, 75-76; by prescriptive approach in England, 107, 151; in Sweden, 137, 161

Public education: in Austria, 39; in Flanders, 88, 91, 94n2, 130-131; in Nebraska, 182; in The Netherlands, 145-146, 148; in North Carolina, 176, 177, 180; in United States, 115

Public forum the, 175, 185

Public school forum the, 176-177

Public schools: and charter schools, 25; and magnet schools, 24-25; organize in networks in Flanders, 94n2; and private (Catholic) schools in Flanders, 86-88; and private schools The Netherlands, 38; and religious controversies in United States, 121, 124n12; and role of the government in The Netherlands, 145-148; in Sweden, 55; systems and choice 24-25

Quality: alternative views of, 19-21; in Austria, 99-100, 102-103; changes in the meaning of, in Denmark, 70; choice and, 20-21, 24-25; control, 14; control in England, 141, 144-145, 199; control in Flanders, 81-91; control in Flemish, 90; control in Nebraska, 184; control in North Caroline, 186; control in Sweden, 59, 159, 161; and data driven-decision making, 199; and decentralization, 14; definitions of, 10, 19; different definitions of quality across countries, 198-199; educational question about, 19; of education in England, 139; and efficiency, 22; and external control, 134-135; in Flanders, 87; and globalization, 6; leadership, 133; monitoring the quality of schools, 44; in The Netherlands, 82-83, 147; and NPM, 206; public indicators of in education, 10; quality education

and economy, 19; reports, 67–69; rethinking, 198–199
Quinn, R.E, 203

Race to the Top program, 186
Radical change: concept, 204; in public administration and NPM, 202; in Sweden 55; in United States, 118
Radice, H., 7, 8, 9
Rationalism: definitions of, 9; and government activism, 196; rethinking, 196–197; tendencies in United States, 18, 25
Rhetorical responsiveness concept, 200–201
Rurban concept, 173

School-and-Society, Danish parents' organization, 163
School-based Teacher-led Assessment and Reporting System (STARS), 181–182
School board(s): and autonomy in Flemish education, 86–87; and autonomy in The Netherlands, 81–82; and charter schools, 25; in Denmark, 68, 158; de-regulation in The Netherlands, 14–15, 211n5; and The Inspectorate in, 81; in The Netherlands, 38, 74–75, 82–83; and NPM in The Netherlands, 78–79, 147–149, 151; in United States, 158, 171
School governance, public debates about, in The Netherlands, 74–75
School pact, in Belgium/Flanders: in Belgium history, 86–88; definition of, 39; in Flanders, 130–131, 134
School war concept, in Belgium, 39, 86, 89
Segregation: in Austria, 104; choice and equity, 24; in Denmark and Sweden, 169–170; in Flemish education, 91–92, 138; increase of, 196; and Islamic schools in The Netherlands, 80; in North Carolina, 178–179; and school autonomy, 138; in United States, 119, 123n8
Social complexity concept, 208
Social inclusion and equality, 18
Social integration, 25, 217
Social justice: in Austria, 102, tendencies in educational policy and, 157; in Denmark, 70; interpretation of and egalitarianism, 16–17; in Sweden, 54–55
Social learning concept, 207–208
Social policy: and efficiency, 10; and equality, 16; and Europeanization, 219; international economy and, 225, 228
Social responsibility, 222n3
Social service(s) and efficiency, 22–23
Sociological-historical approach, 30
Squad, in Denmark, 164
Standards: admissions, 113n1; in Austria, 100, 103, 135–136; curriculum in Denmark, 68; in Flanders, 94; in Flemish system, 87, 134; international, 43, 48; measures in USA, 42, 116, 123; in Nebraska, 179–182; in North Carolina, 177–179; and NPM, 206, 225; and NPM in England, 140–142; Policy and Standards unit, 113n3; and Rationalism, 196; in Sweden, 59; system in England, 40; for teaching, 20
State Board of Education: influence of, in educational policy in Nebraska, 180–181, 185; influence of, in educational policy in North Carolina, 175; and strategic goals, 177–178
Stinchcombe, A., 33
Street Level Public Organizations (SLPO), 23
Student achievement: efforts for improve, 177, 181–182; and local accountability demands, 2; parental

social status and, 80; and quality, 20; standards measure of, 41–42, 137; and voucher programs, 25

Teachers' Union: lost influence of, in Denmark, 162; in Nebraska, 180; role in Flemish education, 89; and testing in Austria, 135; and testing in Denmark, 66–67; in United States, 124n10

Testing: control through, in England, 143; in Denmark, 67, 68–70, 160; international and NPM, 206, 221; introduction of, 43; national regimen, 134, 135–136; national system in Sweden, 58, 160, 165, 200; in Nebraska, 181, 184; in North Carolina, 177–178; opposition to, 137; promote quality through testing in The Netherlands, 81; soft versions of, 166; and stigmatization of schools in Belgium, 91; systems, 209; in United States, 47n8

Thatcher Revolution the, 106

Tracking system: in Austria, 102, 104, 138n4; in The Netherlands, 38, 84n3

Transnational agencies: and absorption processes, 207; in Denmark, 64–65; examples of, 31–32; influence of, 224–226; and NPM in Flemish, 92; role of, 189–190

Vertical equity policy concept, 17–18

Vocational education: decline of, 46; in The Netherlands, 84n3, 147–148; political culture and policy in, 211n9; and provincial governments in Austria, 101; in Sweden, 36

Voluntary transfer programs, 25

Von Humboldt, W. *See* Bildung

Voucher programs, 25

Weick, K.E, 203

World Bank, the: and education policy, 225–227; role of, 215–216

World-wide: economic crisis, 147; forces, 34

WTO (World Trade Organization), 31, 64

Yashar, D.J., 6

GPSR Compliance
The European Union's (EU) General Product Safety Regulation (GPSR) is a set of rules that requires consumer products to be safe and our obligations to ensure this.

If you have any concerns about our products, you can contact us on

ProductSafety@springernature.com

In case Publisher is established outside the EU, the EU authorized representative is:

Springer Nature Customer Service Center GmbH
Europaplatz 3
69115 Heidelberg, Germany

www.ingramcontent.com/pod-product-compliance
Lightning Source LLC
LaVergne TN
LVHW011810060526
838200LV00053B/3723